Asian American Connective Action
in the Age of Social Media

James S. Lai

Asian American Connective Action in the Age of Social Media

Civic Engagement, Contested Issues,
and Emerging Identities

TEMPLE UNIVERSITY PRESS
Philadelphia • *Rome* • *Tokyo*

TEMPLE UNIVERSITY PRESS
Philadelphia, Pennsylvania 19122
tupress.temple.edu

Library of Congress Cataloging-in-Publication Data

Names: Lai, James S. (James Siu-Fong), 1968– author.
Title: Asian American connective action in the age of social media : civic
 engagement, contested issues, and emerging identities / James S. Lai.
Description: Philadelphia : Temple University Press, 2022. | Includes
 bibliographical references and index. | Summary: "Develops a 'connective
 action' model for Asian Americans to examine the relationship between
 social media platforms and civic engagement"—Provided by publisher.
Identifiers: LCCN 2021023013 (print) | LCCN 2021023014 (ebook) | ISBN
 9781439919088 (cloth) | ISBN 9781439919095 (paperback) | ISBN
 9781439919101 (pdf)
Subjects: LCSH: Political participation—Technological innovations—United
 States. | Asian Americans—Political activity. | Asian
 Americans—Political activity—Case studies. | Internet and
 activism—United States. | Internet and activism—United States—Case
 studies. | Civil society—United States. | Communication in
 politics—Technological innovations—United States. | Asian Americans
 and mass media. | Case studies. lcgft
Classification: LCC JF799.5 .L35 2022 (print) | LCC JF799.5 (ebook) | DDC
 323/.0420973—dc23
LC record available at https://lccn.loc.gov/2021023013
LC ebook record available at https://lccn.loc.gov/2021023014

Printed in the United States of America

9 8 7 6 5 4 3 2 1

In memory of my beloved mentors and friends

Rámon D. Chácon, Eric O. Hanson, Don T. Nakanishi,

and Michael B. Preston

Contents

Preface

The impetus for this book began after reading the news coverage of the February 20, 2016 national day of protests when several thousand first-generation or immigrant Chinese Americans organized public demonstrations in forty-one U.S. and Canadian cities through the popular social media smartphone app known as WeChat. They marched collectively in support of former NYPD officer Peter Liang, a Chinese American, who was undergoing a criminal trial for an all too common scenario—for negligently shooting and killing Akai Gurley, an unarmed African American male, while on duty. Prior to that day, many of these protestors had never participated in any prior forms of civic engagement such as attending a political rally.

These mass coordinated demonstrations could not have happened without the process of digitalized networked action known as connective action. As a political behavioralist who studies U.S. race and ethnicity, I was enthralled by the coordinated mobilization efforts that took shape but at the same time conflicted about its larger race relation context, given the Black Lives Matter movement, which I personally support. However, while in the process of researching this topic, it became clearly evident that Asian American connective action encompasses the entire gamut of ideologies from conservative to progressive political action.

The salience of Asian American connective action comes at a time of two current, divergent trends that shape the larger Asian American community: on one hand, they have one of the relatively lowest voter turnout rates for any racial group due to its majority foreign-born population; on the other hand, they are the most digitally connected racial group in the United States.[1] This book seeks to illuminate how connective action may facilitate and amplify traditional forms of political action as well as serve as an adaptive, political empowerment strategy for Asian Americans.

One of the virtues of online Asian American connective action is that it connects geographically separated Asian ethnic communities into a larger, unified voice at the local, state, and/or national levels, shaped by factors such as emerging political identities. Asian Americans, including youth, the elderly, and the unnaturalized, who have historically been muted in American politics, may find new political affordances during connective action that amplify their neglected voices in the civic arena regardless of ideology or issue stances. The diverse case studies featured throughout this book tell this larger story among Asian American groups seeking to express and establish their racial, ethnic, and transnational identities through ethnic networks in the age of social media.

Acknowledgments

Just as with every achievement in life, there are many people who played critical roles behind these book's pages that must be credited, as I am deeply indebted for their encouragement, time, and support. To Florence, Francis, and Desmond, thank you for your steadfast presence and love; to Mom and Dad for always leading by example; to Mark, Cecilia, Abigail, Audrey and her family, and Bachan for being sources of support through this journey.

I would also like to acknowledge my appreciation for the initial two reviewers for their substantial feedback and constructive suggestions.

My sincere gratitude to Aaron Javsicas, Editor in Chief at Temple University Press, for his patience and support of this book since the first time we discussed it at the 2014 Association for Asian American Studies Conference in San Francisco. In addition, I am deeply indebted to the entire production team at Temple University Press for their professional support with every aspect of this book.

Thank you to my three undergraduate research assistants, Kaylyn Arima, Javier Ortega, and Georgie Garner, for their diligent and precise work in helping code several hashtags and their background research, which is featured in several of the case studies.

Appreciation to those who shared their personal insights on connective action and how it works in the Asian American community: OiYan Poon, Diane Wong, Cayden Mak, Laura Li, Evan Low, Paul Fong, Darcy Paul, Gilbert Wong, Shannon Peng, Jason Xu, and Chris Zhang.

I wish to thank all of my colleagues in the Asian Pacific American Caucus, especially Andy Aoki, Oki Takeda, Loan Le, Pei-te Lien, and Janelle Wong, who provided help with data or feedback on early chapter drafts. Heartfelt gratitude to my colleagues in my Ethnic Studies Department for their support, encouragement, and collegiality.

And finally, my sincere appreciation for my students at Santa Clara University, who over the past twenty years have continued to motivate and inspire me both in and out of the classroom.

Asian American Connective Action
in the Age of Social Media

Logging On and Getting Civically Connected

Just as in offline politics, the well off and well-educated are especially likely to participate in online activities that mirror offline forms of engagement. But there are hints that social media may alter this pattern.

—Aaron Smith, Kay Lehman Schlozman, Sidney Verba, and Henry Brady, "The Internet and Civic Engagement" (2009, p. 1).

In other words, it's not true that the rich are getting richer online, as some have suggested. We find, rather, that those with more limited resources use digital media to learn, to speak out, and to amplify their voices.

—Matthew D. Luttig and Cathy J. Cohen, "How Social Media Helps Young People" (2016, par. 15).

Closing the Civic Engagement Gap through Connective Action

On March 23, 2018, amid the green, manicured lawns in Irvine, California, approximately 250 Chinese American immigrants gathered, carrying signs in front of Irvine's city hall that read "NO TENT CITY. OUR CHILDREN NEED SAFETY"; "NO HOMELESS IN IRVINE"; and "SCHOOLS ARE IN DANGER." Liqing Lee Sung, a former Irvine city council candidate and one of the public speakers at the protest, declared, "Can you imagine your child running on the lawn and step [*sic*] on a needle which could be contaminated by HIV? We cannot let that happen" (Shimura 2018, par. 3). The suburb of Irvine, located in Orange County, has become a popular destination over the past decade for many affluent first-generation Chinese Americans and their families. The Asian American population in Irvine is estimated at between 35 and 40 percent of the city's total population (Wheeler 2016).

The Chinese American immigrant demonstrators had gathered to protest the Orange County Board of Supervisors' proposal for the establishment of a homeless camp in the city (Shimura 2018). The online and offline civic engagement was led primarily by WeIrvine, an online start-up business with its own website of nearly forty thousand members run by four Chinese Americans that helps recent immigrants from Mainland China settle in Irvine because of the city's reputation for safety and outstanding public schools (Shimura 2016). The homeless camp was proposed on one hundred acres of county-owned land.

WeIrvine's role in the city's homeless camp protests is a conservative example of primarily organization-led connective action facilitated by its website portal, social media apps such as WeChat, and local Chinese American community-based organization networks. According to WeIrvine founder Xiaoxiang Lu, "It is going to destroy their belief in Irvine" (Shimura 2018, par. 6). The founders of WeIrvine would charter twenty-four buses from throughout Southern California to bring concerned Chinese American families to attend an Irvine Board of Supervisors meeting on March 27, 2018. According to one organizer who created a Facebook page called "Irvine Tent City Protest," which had more than five thousand members, "People who I never knew were calling me night and day and asking to do whatever they could to help. It's really proof that we are a community dedicated to a mission like never before" (Do 2018, par. 18). Like many of the Chinese American immigrants in this book's other case studies, this was one of the first political protests they had ever attended in the United States (Do 2018).

While there were other local protests of the Orange County Board of Supervisors' plan to create emergency homeless shelters in the affluent suburbs of Laguna Niguel and Huntington Beach, none of the protests in these cities compared to the swift mobilization and loud protests of the Chinese American immigrants in Irvine. The protests led the Board of Supervisors to overturn the homeless shelter proposal without providing an alternative solution, and the Orange County homeless population continues to grow.

The Irvine example of immigrant Chinese American connective action illustrates some of the potentials and challenges of the power of social media and civic engagement. On the one hand, social media provides ethno-racial immigrant groups, especially those who cannot participate through traditional means such as voting due to factors including citizenship and limited English proficiency, the ability to mobilize around collective concerns. On the other hand, some argue that these mobilization efforts are misguided by racial fears and based solely on group self-interests. These are two competing tensions that are at the crux of Asian American connective action. Asian-influenced suburbs, such as Irvine, will likely become the main battleground sites of future connective action efforts in local, state, and national contexts (Lai 2011).

The term *social media* became part of the United States' national lexicon in 2004 and is defined as "forms of electronic communications through which users create online communities to share information, ideas, personal messages, and other content" (*Merriam-Webster* 2017). Social media represents an emerging part of most Americans' lives regardless of their race, class, gender, age, and religious backgrounds. Perhaps no other platform has been more influential in the rise of social media networks than the smartphone, which has made a profound impact on our daily habits and consumption of information since Apple Computers released the iPhone in 2007. Since that time, the smartphone and social media networks have become synonymous and ubiquitous. In 2015, an estimated two-thirds of Americans owned a smartphone, with nearly one-fifth relying on them to access the internet (Smith 2015). For example, Twitter was predominantly accessed through the internet via a computer but now is overwhelmingly utilized on smartphones or other mobile devices (Murthy et al. 2015). As a result, more Americans are getting their news from mobile devices through social media.

With the prominence of smartphones and social media in our lives, scholars have begun to examine social media and its linkages with civic engagement in the form of international and domestic movements in what has been termed "connective action" (Bennett and Segerberg 2013). Other recent studies have examined how social media can provide new affordances with regard to the civic engagement of the youth in U.S. politics (Cohen and Kahne 2012; Jenkins et al. 2016; Luttig and Cohen 2016; Kahne and Bowyer 2016; Elliott and Earl 2018).

The impact of social media on civic engagement is apparent today with the sharing of political news and information on various platforms. According to the findings from a 2016 Pew Research Center national poll of 1,520 adults, more than half of Americans stated that they get their political news from social media sites such as Facebook and Twitter (Greenwood, Perrin, and Duggan 2016). Another Pew Research Center national poll of 3,760 adult respondents during the 2016 presidential election found that 14 percent (tied for second highest) got their news from a social media site and 13 percent (third highest) from a news website app compared to 24 percent from cable TV news (highest) (Gottfried et al. 2016). On Twitter, opinions, information, and news are shared among the global network of those who are "Following" or "Followers" through "tweets" or "retweets" that include hashtags, which are a string of words following a hash (#), the main method for organizing information on Twitter. In 2018, Twitter averaged nearly five hundred million tweets a day (80 percent from smartphones) for an average of six thousand tweets per second ("Twitter Usage Statistics" 2017).

The rise of social media has concomitantly resulted in a decline of the digital divide as the racial gap regarding social media usage and Internet access has completely disappeared. Vice President Al Gore's speech at the Digital Divide Conference on April 28, 1998, identified the Information Age as the "key to ensuring a lifetime of success" and asserted that it is necessary to ensure that all young people from every background have equal access to the internet (The White House, Office of the Vice President 1998, par. 1). The digital divide argument was bolstered by reputable sources such as a 1998 Pew Research Center poll that found White people were twice as likely as African Americans to use the internet. Today, nearly twenty years later, the Pew Research Center estimates that 40 percent of African Americans between the ages of eighteen and twenty-nine, compared to White people at 28 percent, were using Twitter in 2013. Twitter usage was nearly identical between White people and African Americans for those between the ages of thirty and forty-nine and fifty and sixty-four. On the internet usage and broadband access issue that Vice President Gore lamented about, African Americans across these age groups were either at the same percentages or better than White people (Guo 2015).

Empirical evidence of the emergence of a "Black Twitter" among the young adult African American online community can be seen clearly today with the rise of hashtag movements such as Black Lives Matter (Murthy, Gross, and Pensavalle 2016). The ability of African Americans to close the digital divide within nearly two decades, combined with their effective use of social media platforms like Twitter to communicate with each other, to share information, and to mobilize racial projects like Black Lives Matter to address social injustices, provides insights into the potential of social media as a mechanism for mobilization. Moreover, the affordances provided by connective action can also be uplifting to other racial minorities such as Asian Americans and Latinx, two groups containing large numbers of foreign-born and limited English proficient (LEP) members.

Text messaging apps have become critical in connecting people anywhere in the world in a myriad of ways, from discussing social issues to sharing photos. WeChat, which was created by the Chinese company Tencent in 2011, embodies a powerful mobilization tool used exclusively in Mainland China and its diasporic communities (Chen, Mao, and Qui 2018). By 2018, WeChat purportedly reached one billion monthly active users worldwide, which was a 12 percent growth compared to 889 million users at the end of 2016 (Hollander 2018). WeChat groups, which can consist of 500 members, are created around common interests, political issues, hobbies, alumni connections, and social events (Chen, Mao, and Qui 2018). In comparison, WhatsApp, a messaging rival of WeChat that is the most used instant messaging app in India, allows for 256 members per group. Owners manage each group on WeChat and determine the tone of the group. WeChat allows owners to spread the word of an upcoming event to their group's members, which encourages other people to sign up to a group (Chen 2018).

Former president Donald Trump attempted to ban WeChat and TikTok, a popular Chinese-owned video sharing app, through an executive order on August 6, 2020. According to the executive order, WeChat "automatically captures vast swaths of information from its users. This data collection threatens to allow the Chinese Communist Party access to Americans' personal and proprietary information" (Choudhury 2020, par. 6). On June 9, 2021, President Joe Biden signed a new executive order that would replace Trump's ban by calling for the Commerce Department to launch national security reviews of all social media apps that have links to foreign adversaries including Mainland China (Allyn 2021).

The focus of this book is not on these online mobile technological platforms per se but on how connective action can facilitate offline political mobilization among Asian Americans by providing them access to and communication of vital political information through online spaces and discussion forums, helping them to participate in public policy debates and social justice issues. Communication in one's native language is particularly vital for the Asian American community, which contains the largest foreign-born population at nearly 70 percent and one of the largest LEP populations at nearly 35 percent (Ramakrishnan and Ahmad 2014). In addition to these demographic challenges, one prominent scholar declared in 2016 that Asian Americans "still do not have the institutional means to communicate, to moderate, to resolve, and to anticipate future areas of tension" (Kwong 2016, p. 88). Connective action may allow large foreign-born racial groups such as Asian Americans the ability to communicate and moderate their voices and concerns at the local, state, and national levels. Indeed, if connective action has the ability to provide an online means of communication and moderation, historically disenfranchised groups should be able to participate in ways never seen before in the civic arena. This belief is arguably most visible among Asian Americans, a group historically stereotyped as quiet, docile, and apolitical in U.S. politics.

Social Media Effects on Participatory Democracy

While connective action through social media platforms may be seen as a potential panacea for politically disenfranchised minority groups, some argue that the rise of social media has also coincided with the decline of U.S. political parties and thus at the expense of participatory democracy (Edsall

2017). In a provocative *New York Times* editorial, Thomas Edsall (2017, pars. 1 and 31) wrote:

> It's clear that the Internet and social media have succeeded in doing what many feared and some hoped they would. They have disrupted and destroyed institutional constraints on what can be said, when and where it can be said and who can say it. . . . There is good reason to think that the disruptive forces at work in the United States—as they expand the universe of the politically engaged and open the debate to millions who previously paid little or no attention—may do more to damage the left than strengthen it. In other words, just as the use of negative campaign ads and campaign finance loopholes to channel suspect contributions eventually became routine, so too will be the use of social media to confuse and mislead the electorate.

The 2016 presidential election offers a salient example and a cautionary tale of how social media platforms such as Facebook and Twitter can be used on smartphones to spread misinformation or "fake news" on the internet to persuade voters toward or against a particular candidate. For example, one 2017 study on the impact of fake news on the 2016 U.S. presidential election found that during the election, thirty million fabricated stories that favored Donald Trump were shared through social media, nearly quadruple the total number of fabricated stories that favored Hillary Clinton (Allcott and Gentzkow 2017).

At the root of the political argument is the belief that individuals are not able to tell the difference between real news and fake news on social media. A 2016 Stanford University study found that among 7,804 middle school students to college students, many could not discern fake news from real news. Among the middle school students in this study's sample, many were unable to distinguish an advertisement story from a news story. Among the college student sample, many accepted, without any critical thinking, findings from a bogus study from a fabricated organization (Wineburg and Mc-Grew 2016). These findings from the study indicate that while the millennial generation may be more familiar with social media technologies than older generations, they are just as likely to have trouble judging the credibility of online information.

Because of this political misinformation from all ends of the political spectrum and the electorate being unable to distinguish between fake and real news, the question then becomes what the facts being debated are. According to an October 2016 Pew Research Center study finding, 81 percent of American registered voters of both parties stated that "basic facts," not just public policies, are in dispute (Pew Research Center 2016). The tradition of finding out the truth by seeking alternative sources and points of view has currently taken a back seat to ideological predispositions that shape where and with whom Americans communicate through social media platforms, whether it be on their computers or smartphones.

Finally, another democratic concern of social media is that it has made electoral politics more vitriolic and polarizing and less trustworthy in the minds of its users. With regard to news trustworthiness, one Pew Research Center survey found that nearly 62 percent of American adults get their news from social media but only 32 percent find that news somewhat trustworthy (Gottfried and Shearer 2016).

Despite the compelling arguments about the negative effects of social media, numerous positive influences exist in the relationship between social media and democracy. Social media has filled a necessary vacuum that has allowed millions of Americans to participate and voice their concerns in ways that they could not have done only a decade ago, before the invention of the smartphone and popular social media platforms such as Twitter and Facebook. As Edsall opined, this vacuum is the result of the gradual decline of local political party organizations in addition to other social and civic organizations, all necessary aspects of collective action in American politics. However, connective action might provide the bridge that allows online collective action to happen despite the decline in these local political party organizations. One connective action study found that not only were social media technologies during connective action a manner to spread the message but they also became a prominent part of the organizational structure itself (Bennett and Segerberg 2013).

Social media technologies may also provide a larger and more accessible infrastructure via the internet that social and civic organizations no longer have the capacity to provide. Social networking sites (SNS) such as Facebook, Twitter, LinkedIn, Instagram, and YouTube have also made political information more accessible to their users rather than requiring users to join a formal organization to gain access to such information. For example, SNS users grew from 33 percent of the total online community in 2008 to 69 percent in 2012 (Smith 2013). In addition, SNS can have a democratizing effect in that they provide a lower entry point into American politics for historically disenfranchised Americans from every demographic group, particularly youth and racial minorities (Kahne and Middaugh 2012; Zimmerman 2012; Mizuko et al. 2015). While social media networks can provide for increased leverage, social groups must be careful not to grow too fast without formal organization structures and social ties that bind them. In fact, one study found that online social networks possess both power and fragility in that they can be undermined by government institutions to maintain power through delaying, distracting, and spreading disinformation (Tufekci 2018).

The Significance of Connective Action
Literature for Asian Americans

With the prominence of social media in our lives, scholars have begun to examine it and its linkages with civic engagement in the form of international and domestic movements in what has been termed "connective action" where groups can voice and organize their concerns in different ways (e.g., posting, creating a chat group) via social media platforms (Bennett and Segerberg 2013). Connective action may allow activist groups, as seen with the Black Lives Matter, Arab Spring, and Occupy Wall Street movements, the ability to articulate, amplify, and coordinate their group interests around a particular policy or political outcome through either self-organizing (requiring no organizational coordination) or organizationally led (loose organization coordination) networks (Bennett and Segerberg 2013; Castells 2015; Papacharissi 2015).

Social media networks can also allow activist groups to band together online in a process known as "peer production" to shape political discourse around social justice movements (Benkler 2007). A vivid example of digital organized action among activists and organizations was seen on January 18, 2012, against the Stop Online Piracy Act (SOPA) and the Protect IP Act (PIPA), in which an estimated three million people emailed congressional representatives expressing their opposition to both bills (Wortham 2012). Both SOPA and PIPA would eventually be shelved in Congress as a result of the online protests (Weisman 2012). Coordinated physical protests would soon follow in New York, Seattle, and San Francisco, where protesters held signs reading "Don't Tread on the Internet" (Wortham 2012).

Political motivation is essential for connective action to allow minorities to close the participation gap in both traditional and nontraditional ways. Studies have found that increased social media and internet usage alone does not result in increased political knowledge and voter participation but may actually widen political gaps due to the presence of news and entertainment online sources (Chan 2020; Prior 2005). For example, an Asian American who spends hours engaging on social media platforms for gaming internet communities is not likely to engage in connective action around a particular policy, candidate, or social justice issue. Thus, the presence of political motivation among individuals or groups is critical for connective action to provide individuals with new opportunities to shape political discourse around public policies and political candidates (Chan 2020; Dalton 2017). This is particularly salient for outsiders in U.S. politics, as recent studies have examined how social media networks can provide youth and minorities with new affordances with regard to civic engagement (Jenkins et al. 2016; Luttig and Cohen 2016; Kahne and Bowyer 2016). In a 2016 *Wash-*

ington Post opinion editorial by Matthew Luttig and Cathy Cohen entitled "How Social Media Helps Young People, Especially Minorities and the Poor, Get Politically Engaged," the authors argue, "Social media has transformed the relationship among citizens, news and politics. . . . Our findings suggest that new media can encourage Millennials—the most enthusiastic users— to get actively involved in politics, albeit in different ways from previous generations. . . . That's because the Internet has opened up virtual spaces that bypass traditional gatekeepers" (Luttig and Cohen 2016, pars. 2, 3, 5).

Despite the above recent connective action studies in international and U.S. contexts, there has been very little specific focus on the processes and how connective action shapes Asian American political engagement, particularly given that it contains the largest foreign-born population among all racial groups. This is especially salient for Asian Americans for two reasons. The first reason is that Asian Americans currently have one of the lowest voter turnout rates among its adult voting-age population in comparison with other racial groups. In the 2010 elections, Asian American voter turnout was 31 percent nationally compared to White people at 49 percent, African Americans at 44 percent, and Latinx at 31 percent. Four years later, during the 2014 elections, Asian Americans accounted for an estimated nine million eligible voters but made up only 4 percent of all eligible voters (Krogstad 2014). The second reason is that Asian Americans are one of the most digitally connected racial groups in the United States. According to a series of 2015 national survey findings on digital media usage conducted by the Pew Research Center, 91 percent of English-speaking Asian Americans used the internet compared to White people at 87 percent, Latinx at 82 percent, and African Americans at 81 percent. In addition, 84 percent of English-speaking Asian Americans, 72 percent of White people, 54 percent of African Americans, and 50 percent of Latinx have broadband at home. With regard to owning a smartphone, English-speaking Asian Americans once again led the way with 91 percent compared to White people at 66 percent, Latinx at 65 percent, and African Americans at 62 percent (Perrin 2016).

Asian American Connective Action Rising: Evidence from Large-Scale Surveys

As social media becomes an integral part of most Americans' lives, one would be remiss to assume that the practice and extent of usage of social media as a mechanism for civic engagement is homogenous among all racial groups. This point is certainly true with regard to Asian Americans, the nation's fastest growing racial group from 2000 to 2010 with a 46 percent growth rate gain.

On the surface level, the statistics at the end of the previous section comparatively demonstrate that Asian Americans are one of the most digitally connected racial groups in the nation. Given their transnational characteristics, various platforms of digital media serve as a way of connecting individuals and communities across a larger transnational community that transcends traditional nation state borders (Laguerre 2010). Below the surface level, other salient questions also arise, such as what the social media usage for Asian Americans who are primarily LEP is, what the interethnic group differences among them are, and whether being digitally connected can lead to higher levels of civic engagement. These questions are necessary because they embody the three most crucial aspects of the national Asian American population: foreign-born, LEP, and diverse.

In addition to social media, ethnic media has become ubiquitous and critical for Asian Americans during political action efforts at the city level by providing political information and connecting ethnic candidates to both old and new Asian American voters (Lai 2011). According to the 2016 National Asian American Survey (NAAS) findings on sources for political information, as illustrated in Figure 1.1, in addition to being the most digitally connected racial group in the United States, Asian Americans are also more likely to get their political information from various ethnic media in the forms of newspapers, television, radio, and the internet than mainstream media (Ramakrishnan et al. 2016). Approximately 47 percent of Asian American registered voters identified getting "a lot and a great deal" of their political information from the internet and social media, which is the largest segment among all political information sources, followed by Same Generation (31 percent), Television (26 percent), and Family/Friends (24 percent).

While interethnic group differences exist among Asian Americans with regard to ethnic media and social media consumption of political information in general, the 2016 National Asian American Survey also found that 66 percent of Asian American registered voters receive "a moderate amount" of their political information through the internet and social media. Nearly 61 percent of foreign-born Asian Americans stated that they relied on the internet and social media for their political information. This percentage is even greater for U.S.-born Asian Americans between eighteen and thirty-four years of age, 77 percent of whom said they relied on the internet for political information and 89 percent of whom said they relied on social media for political information (Ramakrishnan et al. 2016, p. 41).

One common criticism of social media users on Twitter who tweet political hashtags is that such "hashtag activism" results in all talk, no action (Anschuetz 2015; Berlatsky 2015). Despite this criticism, recent national public opinion survey findings indicate that indeed, Asian Americans are

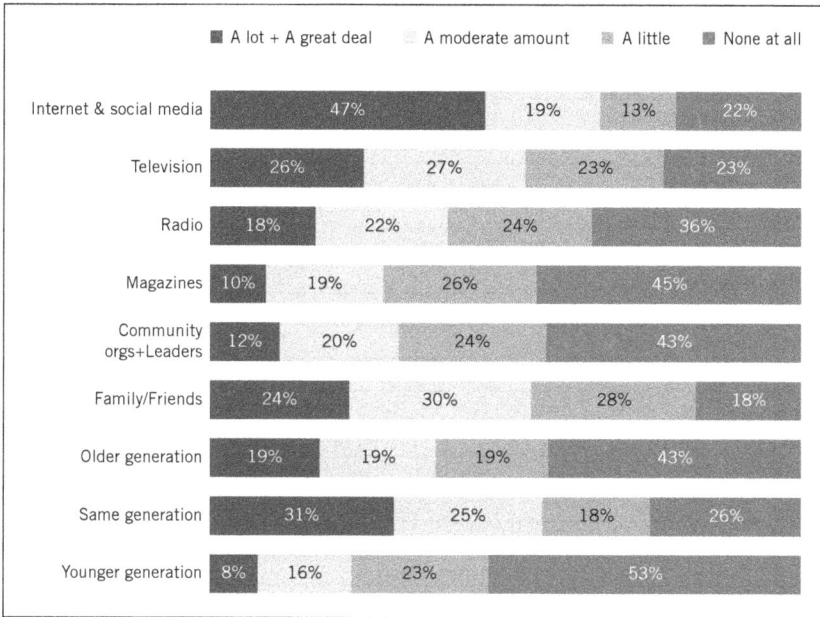

Figure 1.1 Sources of Political Information, Asian American Voters, 2016
(Source: Ramakrishnan, Wong, Lee, and Lee 2016, p. 43.)

utilizing social media to address social injustice issues through public demonstrations and other political activities. One question in the 2016 National Asian American Survey asked, "In the last 12 months, have you posted or commented about politics on social media, like Facebook, Twitter, WeChat (for Chinese American respondents) or KakaoTalk (for Korean American respondents)?" and 26 percent or a quarter of registered Asian American voters responded that they had engaged with a political issue on social media (Ramakrishnan et al., p. 38). Native-born Asian Americans and young Asian Americans (eighteen to thirty-four) responded to the same question at 44 percent and 50 percent, respectively.

According to Table 1.1, differences exist along ethnicity, nativity, gender, and age groups for Asian American registered voters with regard to civic engagement and social media. Filipino Americans (34 percent) and Asian Indians (33 percent) were the two Asian American ethnic groups most likely to use social media for civic engagement over the last twelve months during the time of the survey, compared to Chinese Americans (23 percent), Vietnamese Americans (22 percent), and Korean Americans (18 percent). Asian American male registered voters were slightly more likely to use social media for civic engagement at 23 percent, compared to 18 percent for Asian American female registered voters. Foreign-born Asian Americans

TABLE 1.1 CIVIC ENGAGEMENT ON SOCIAL MEDIA AMONG ASIAN AMERICAN VOTERS, 2016	
Total Asian American	26%
Asian Indian American	33%
Cambodian American	23%
Chinese American	23%
Filipino American	34%
Hmong American	29%
Japanese American	13%
Korean American	18%
Vietnamese American	22%
Male	18%
Female	23%
Native Born	5%
Foreign Born	29%
Age 18 to 34	7%
35 or older	26%
Source: Ramakrishnan, Wong, Lee, and Lee 2016, p. 38.	

(29 percent) were more likely than native-born Asian Americans (5 percent) to use social media for civic engagement. Older-generation (thirty-five and above) Asian American voters were likely to do so at 26 percent, compared to 7 percent for younger-generation (eighteen to thirty-four) Asian American voters. In summary, Asian American connective action is rising among all demographic segments and will likely continue in the future.

Given these findings of the 2016 National Asian American Survey, Asian American connective action can also challenge traditional models of political participation that argue that high socioeconomic levels and formal organizations are necessary to facilitate traditional forms of political participation such as voting, issue awareness, attending political rallies, and contacting elected officials. Past studies have shown that Asian Americans have one of the lowest voter turnouts among adult citizens, with only 47 percent voting compared to African Americans at 66 percent, White people at 64 percent, Latinx at 48 percent, American Indians at 51 percent, and Native Hawaiian/Pacific Islanders at 49 percent (Chen et al. 2016). Social media provides Asian Americans and other outsider groups the online infrastructure to interact with their specific and larger ethno-racial communities around pertinent issues taking place within the public and political spheres that transcend geographic boundaries without having to rely on formal organizations to mobilize them. In lieu of such organizations, online affinity groups have the potential, with caveats, to consolidate individual, diffused voices and information into organized and self-sustaining power. These online affinity groups differ sharply from traditional brick-and-mortar organizations in that they do not need office fronts and large staffs but can be created in a centralized, online location that can be visited and updated remotely from anywhere in the world.

The affordances connective action provides to Asian Americans may vary, as found in other studies. For example, among working-class Asian immigrants, social media gives them the ability to connect instantaneously in their respective native languages with others in the diaspora at relatively little cost. For wealthier Asian immigrants, the affordances of social media may provide them with communication channels to express their motivations in effective, rapid, and powerful ways to elected representatives in a state legislature. Thus, Asian American connective action may provide a lower entry to the traditional pathways of American political incorporation that require U.S. naturalization, registering to vote, and voting as cornerstones of political participation. While these traditional pathways are still critical, scholars would be remiss not to examine other pathways that are coming to fruition in an increasingly digital and transnational world.

The 2016 Collaborative Multiracial Post-Election Survey (CMPS), which over sixty social scientists collaborated on, also surveyed a multiracial sample on forms of social media and civic engagement from November 2016 to February 2017.[1] The CMPS included 3,006 Asian American respondents from national origin groups who were surveyed with civic engagement and social media questions.[2]

When asked, "*During the past twelve months, have you discussed a candidate or political issue on social media like Facebook or Twitter?,*" 74 percent (2,219 respondents) stated "no," compared to 26 percent (787 respondents) who stated "yes." A majority of all Asian national origin groups, with the exception of Bangladeshi, responded "no." Similar to the news source finding, this suggests that while Asian Americans still predominantly get their news from traditional sources such as mainstream television, the minority who get their news from social media sites such as Facebook and Twitter are likely to continue to grow.

For the question "*During the past twelve months, have you discussed a candidate on (smartphone) social media?,*" the Asian ethnic breakdown was the following: Chinese, 11.3 percent "yes" and 88.7 percent "no"; Taiwanese, 19.5 percent "yes" and 80.5 percent "no"; Indian, 30.9 percent "yes" and 69 percent "no"; Korean, 20 percent "yes" and 80 percent "no"; Filipino, 5.4 percent "yes" and 94.6 percent "no"; Vietnamese, 4.4 percent "yes" and 95.6 percent "no"; and Japanese, 6.9 percent "yes" and 93.1 percent "no."

When asked, *"Have you signed a petition regarding an issue or problem that concerns you in the past twelve months?,"* a majority of Asian American respondents (2,147, or 71.42 percent) stated "no," compared to 859 (28.58 percent), who stated "yes." The latter were asked a follow-up question: *"Was that an online petition or a hard-copy signed petition?"* A majority (687, or 79.98 percent) stated it was an online petition compared to 172, or 20.02 percent, who signed a hard-copy petition. This finding suggests that interest groups are using the internet (e.g., email and social media sites) as the primary method of disseminating their petitions versus the traditional hard-copy method. This finding also is supported by each of the case studies that are discussed later in this book. As Asian Americans continue to be one of the racial groups most connected to the Internet, this connective action finding is likely to continue among all age ranges of Asian Americans, as it will for other racial minorities as well.

Both the 2016 NAAS and the 2016 CMPS demonstrate the growing link between social media and civic engagement or connective action among Asian Americans. At the same time, the findings of both surveys illustrate intergroup differences among the diverse Asian American populations in regard to social media usage for political information and activities. Nevertheless, one thing is certain: Asian Americans are likely to continue utilizing social media platforms, as previous studies have shown that this racial group is one of the most digitally connected despite relatively low voter turnout rates.

Research Questions

Given the two opposing trends of low voter participation and high digital connectivity within the Asian American community, three primary research questions must be addressed. First, how can online connective action facilitate offline civic engagement besides voting, such as political protest, contacting their local and state elected leaders, and attending public forums? This is particularly important given the large and diverse foreign-born, LEP population that currently makes up the majority of the Chinese American and the larger Asian American community. Second, to what extent was the panethnic identity between Chinese Americans and other Asian Americans emerging during online connective action campaigns on social media platforms such as Twitter? For example, in Chapter 4's Peter Liang case study, did non-Chinese Asian American groups support Liang to the same extent as Chinese Americans based on their race, or did they diverge based on ideological differences? And third, given the ideological, ethnic, and class diversity within the national Asian American community, how can they fit in with future progressive, multiracial political coalitions around contentious public policy issues such as racial profiling and affirmative action? This topic is one of increasing political importance given the multiracial characteristics of the public policies and U.S. cities that Asian Americans are an essential part of, as well as their racial group position within the traditional U.S. racial hierarchy that has historically pitted them against other racial minorities (Kim 1999; Masuoka and Junn 2013).

Connective action has provided the largely foreign-born population of Asian Americans who are politically motivated with affordances to influence policy and political outcomes that defy traditional political science models of political participation in several important ways. First, social media such as instant messaging apps, Twitter town halls, and web-based discussion boards can have the profound effect of leveling the playing field by removing the traditional gatekeepers, such as political parties, to gain access to political information and to mobilize voters. Asian American communities are increasingly mobile and digital due to global social formation and emigration patterns. Social media, smartphones, and satellite television connect and provide continuity for Asian immigrants across their respective diasporic communities (Laguerre 2010).

Second, social media has provided new virtual spaces that allow individuals, regardless of race, class, and citizenship, to share and gain access to important information on policies, issues, and candidates that are relevant to their respective communities. For Asian Americans, this is particularly salient given their large foreign-born, LEP populations and low voting rates in U.S. politics. Language barriers that were once associated with formal organizations can now be overcome through social media. Third, as a result of the previous two factors, connective action may allow Asian Americans to challenge the traditional U.S. racial hierarchies that have limited them in two contradictory ways as both political outsiders in the form of the "forever foreigner" and as racially superior in relation to other minorities in the form of the "model minority"—two sociopolitical planes that have historically limited the public perception of Asian Americans from the 1960s to the present. Thus, connective action may provide Asian Americans, both U.S.-born and immigrants, the ability to challenge these two stereotypes by altering and shaping policy and political outcomes related to social justice and transnational identities in their favor in ways never before seen in American politics.

Overview of the Remaining Chapters

The primary focus of this book is to provide a detailed and nuanced glimpse into the multiple ways that connective action, the nexus of social media and civic engagement, takes shape within the Asian American community. As is argued, social media can provide greater access to and communication among all Americans so they may participate in American politics in ways they never have, but with caveats, including the danger of echo chambers that prevent a balanced discourse on various contentious issues that often drive nonvoters to mobilize. For Asian Americans, this is particularly important, given their long-standing outsider status in American politics as voters and elected representatives, in addition to their large foreign-born and LEP populations.

Chapter 2, "The Racial Paradox and Emerging Political Contours of Asian Americans: How Connective Action Challenges and Amplifies Them," examines the unique positionalities of Asian Americans within the traditional U.S. racial hierarchy and discusses the emerging political contours developing within Asian America as well as how connective action might alter what I define as the racial paradox that faces Asian Americans today and amplify ideological and intersectional identities. The coexisting stereotypes of Asian Americans as political outsiders/forever foreigners and a model minority are discussed in light of how connective action can challenge both. Previous social science models have illuminated both stereotypes but have failed to understand and incorporate how social media can shift and alter race relations and power differentials when it comes to political incorporation and the traditional racial hierarchies that often place racial minorities, including Asian Americans, beneath White people.

The book's focus then turns to establishing its theoretical model in Chapter 3, "Conceptualizing a Model for Asian American Connective Action," which examines how Asian American connective action occurs within three dimensions: the Medium Dimension (Mainstream and Ethnic Social Media), the Goals Dimension (Asian American Civic Engagement), and the Site Dimension (Asian American Immigrant Influenced Cities). Each of these dimensions is discussed with examples to give greater insights into both crowd- and organization-led typologies of Asian American connective action.

Chapters 4 through 9 continue to build on the book's theoretical model through six diverse empirical case studies to develop Asian American connective action through crowd- and organization-led networks. In these instances, crowds and organizations create personal action frames around an issue that they share information and thoughts on through social media platforms, which facilitate political action beyond the screen. These six case studies also highlight the emergence of political identities around contentious contemporary issues such as affirmative action, racial profiling, and transnational politics. In multiple ways, these case studies illustrate the complexities, limitations, and challenges of Asian American connective action that are relevant to all racial groups. At the same time, they also demonstrate how connective action can empower Asian immigrant groups by giving them a political voice that they would never have had prior to social media, and how social media platforms served as a vehicle for Asian American connective action (local, state, national, and international) in the context of challenging predetermined decisions and influencing political outcomes. In effect, connective action challenges traditional models of political participation such as collective action.

Chapter 4, "Case Study 1: The 2016 Trial of New York Police Department Officer Peter Liang and the Connective Action Mobilization by First-Generation Chinese Americans," examines the November 20, 2014, shooting tragedy that involved New York City Police Department (NYPD) officer Peter Liang and Akai Gurley, an unarmed African American man, during a vertical patrol in the Louis Heaton Pink Houses in Brooklyn, New York. Liang was the first NYPD police officer to be prosecuted by the city's attorney in over a decade, which created perceptions among first-generation Chinese American protesters that Liang was a racial scapegoat. Many of them began to discuss the topic on forums run by the Chinese-created social media app WeChat and subsequently mobilized through public protests both locally and nationally in forty-one cities (thirty-eight U.S. and three Canadian). Ideological divisions arose within the Asian American community between first-generation Chinese American protesters, who focused on predominantly Liang's civil rights, and progressive Asian American activists, who were part of the Black Lives Matter movement, on the issue of White supremacy and Asian American privilege.

Chapter 5, "Case Study 2: The Asian American Community's Online and Offline Affirmative Action Battle over the 2012 California Senate Constitutional Amendment 5 Bill," focuses on Asian American connective action around California's affirmative action policy in higher education admissions. WeChat was again instrumental in disseminating information to first-generation Chinese Americans statewide. As the case study reveals, social media was also critical in mobilizing this disenfranchised community and forcing the California State Legislature to table the Senate Constitutional Amendment (SCA) 5 bill that sought to reintroduce affirmative action into the University of California admissions process after a majority of voters supported Proposition 209 in a 1996 statewide election. For those outside of this conservative minority segment of the larger Asian American community, this movement appeared to be motivated by group self-interest. Contrary to this belief, public opinion polls indicate that a majority of the Asian American community actually favors affirmative action policies. As seen with the Liang case study, the ability of progressive Asian Americans to form multiracial coalitions with other pro-affirmative action groups was potentially endangered by such swift, conservative mobilization efforts of an anti-affirmative-action minority segment that did not reflect the larger community's perspectives. This chapter reveals that echo chambers that were formed in WeChat prevented balanced discussions about the effect of SCA 5 on Asian American admissions in the University of California system.

Chapter 6, "Case Study 3: Data Disaggregation and the 2016 California Assembly Bill 1726—How Connective Action Helped Determine the Narrative and Outcome," examines the online battle around Assembly Bill (AB) 1726, which sought to require state agencies to disaggregate data on Asian Americans given their ethnic and socioeconomic diversity. Many of the same Mainland Chinese activists who mobilized against SCA 5 were empowered and viewed AB 1726 as another attempt by the California State Legislature to target their children for unfair treatment with regard to admissions to the University of California campuses. Similar to the SCA 5 case study, echo chambers largely dictated the direction and parameters of the discussion on WeChat, which prevented a balanced discussion within the Chinese American community as well as the larger Asian American community with regard to the benefits and costs of data disaggregation. However, unlike SCA 5, the panethnic coalition of progressive Asian American activists was effective in getting AB 1726 passed in both houses of the California State Legislature and signed by Governor Brown, by getting and remaining in front of AB 1726's main narrative on social media platforms such as Twitter.

Chapter 7, "Case Study 4: The 18 Million Rising Website and Its Role as an Online Conduit for Progressive Asian America Activism," provides this book's sole example of Asian American connective action through an organization-led network. The 18 Million Rising (18MR) website illustrates how exclusively online progressive Asian American organizations and activists are using social media vis-à-vis the process of organization-led connective action in unique ways to influence and achieve political outcomes around various social issues. Two 18MR online campaigns (#ReleaseMN8 and #BlackAAPIAction) are discussed and analyzed to provide examples of how organization-led connective action takes shape around two critical public policy issues: the deportation of Cambodian Americans who are former felons and the creation of a biracial coalition between African Americans and Asian Americans for the passage of a clean Development, Relief, and Education for Alien Minors (DREAM) Act in the U.S. Congress.

Chapter 8, "Case Study 5: The 2016 California Textbook Controversy—South Asian Americans and the #DontEraseIndia Campaign," examines how political identities tied to regional culture and politics of South Asian countries can shape political action on the issue of how they are portrayed in required California middle-school textbooks. In 2005 and 2016, this issue became front and center among Asian Indians and other South Asian Americans. The two rival camps that would eventually emerge in the South Asian American communities during the 2005 and 2016 controversies were symbolized by #DontEraseIndia, which sought to prevent *India* from being replaced by *South Asia* in California textbooks.

Chapter 9, "Case Study 6: Establishing World War II Korean Comfort Women Memorials in U.S. Cities and the Online Mobilization against Them," demonstrates how social injustices during World War II among Japan, China, and Korea can shape Asian American connective action on the issue of comfort women and their symbolism many years after. In the United States, a panethnic coalition composed primarily of Korean Americans, Chinese Americans, and Japanese Americans took on the Japanese government and its ally nationalist organizations to commemorate the atrocity of Korean, Chinese, and Filipino comfort women forced to serve as sex slaves for the Japanese military during World War II in the form of remembrance statues. A common interest—achieving social justice for the remainder of the living comfort women—allowed this panethnic coalition to form in cities throughout the continental United States. The Japanese nationalist detractors from the remembrance statues the groups proposed raised concerns about national sovereignty and whether it was appropriate for another nation that was far removed from the historical events to erect such monuments.

Chapter 10, "On the Virtues and Perils of Asian American Connective Action," earnestly takes on key opportunities and challenges using this book's case studies' findings to address topics such as the echo chamber effect and how to mitigate it, emerging online pan-Asian identities building online multiracial coalitions, and the importance of controlling the online narrative for shaping political outcomes.

Ethno-Racial Group Terminologies

Due to the process of racial formation, the meanings of ethno-racial categories in the United States have been prescribed and challenged by both government institutions and the ethno-racial groups themselves. This book uses the term *Asian Americans* to describe the larger Asian American community, both foreign-born and U.S.-born, that specifically encompasses East Asian (i.e., Chinese, Japanese, Korean, and Filipina/o Americans), Southeast Asian (i.e., Cambodian and Vietnamese Americans), and South Asian (i.e., Asian Indian, Pakistani, and Bangladeshi Americans) national origin groups in the United States—the groups whose connective actions are primarily examined and discussed in this book's case studies. *Asian American Pacific Islander* will be used when discussing both Asian Americans and Pacific Islanders such as Hawaiians, Guamanians, Tongans, and

Micronesians. In specific instances when ethnic groups are discussed, terms such as *Asian Indians, Korean Americans,* and *Cambodian Americans* are utilized.

The term *African Americans* is used to discuss those with African descent in the United States. *Latinx* (singular) and *Latinxs* (plural) are used for those in national origin groups from Central America, Cuba, and South America.

Immigrant and *first generation* are used interchangeably to denote generational differences from the U.S.-born generations among ethno-racial groups. For example, *Chinese American immigrants* is used to describe those who are the first generation from Mainland China and does not include Taiwanese Americans.

Methodologies

This book primarily utilizes three methodological approaches to examine Asian American connective action: survey data findings, case studies, and social media content analysis. In part, each approach gets at the various aspects of Asian American connective action. As a whole, by utilizing these methods, a broader, clearer holistic picture of Asian American connective action is provided that captures the diversity among Asian Americans and their emerging political identities.

1. Case Studies and Interviews

To further develop the social media and civic engagement findings from the 2016 NAAS and the November 2016 CMPS, six case studies were examined to provide comparative insights on Asian American connective action and the many dimensions of participation through social media networks and online affinity groups. Qualitative interviews were also conducted primarily among individuals who participated in the four case studies, including community-based organization leaders and elected officials.

2. Twitter Hashtag Analyses

Each case study focuses exclusively on Twitter hashtag analyses. It is important to note that this book is not arguing that Twitter was the only form of social media utilized in all case studies, as that would be a fallacy. Instead, Twitter is exclusively focused on in this book for three primary reasons. First, it represents one of the most used forms of social media in the world. According to one source, on average, nearly 6,000 tweets are tweeted each second, which totals approximately 350,000 tweets per minute, 500 million tweets per day, and nearly 200 billion tweets per year ("Twitter Usage Statistics" 2017). Asian Americans of all backgrounds are utilizing this powerful social media platform to share information and ideas during connective action. Second, Twitter represents a critical way of gauging mass online public attitudes on various contested issues and policies at the heart of the case studies at the moment they are occurring. Such mass public attitudes are critical steps, along with political motivation, that facilitate an online consensus for offline civic engagement, which completes the process of connective action. Third, tweets around an issue will often use hashtags with the subject matter embedded, allowing them to be cataloged and connected to other tweets using the same hashtags, which can provide longitudinal context to a particular issue. This was very important since all of the book's case studies were examined retrospectively.

Locating and coding each of the Twitter hashtags examined in this book's case studies required a three-step process. One, each hashtag was located through the advanced search option available on the Twitter website. Two, the user option of the advanced search allowed for searching of any tweets a person or organization tweeted with a particular hashtag. This second step allowed me to find threads of hidden tweets that organizations and individuals may have sent out including the hashtag. Third, a general search of the term without the hashtag was conducted to get more tweet results.

The most common Twitter hashtags used by the Asian American community, not necessarily by other racial groups, during the six case studies are the following:

- #PeterLiang and #FreePeterLiang (Chapter 4, 2016 trial of New York Police Officer Peter Liang case study)
- #SCA5 (Chapter 5, California Senate Constitutional Amendment 5 case study)
- #AB1726 (Chapter 6, California Assembly Bill 1726 case study)
- #BlackAAPIaction and #ReleaseMN8 (Chapter 7, 18 Million Rising website—the 2017 Asian American Pacific Islander [AAPI] Immigrant Rights Table and the Release the Minnesota 8 case studies)
- #DontEraseIndia (Chapter 8, 2016 California Textbook Controversy case study)
- #ComfortWomen (Chapter 9, Korean Americans and the World War II comfort women memorials case study)

Tweets containing these respective hashtags were coded for race, ethnicity, gender, issue position (pro, neutral, or con), and location. Multiple steps were taken to determine and verify the race and ethnicity of each tweet's author. The user's profile photo and description, if available, could be effective aids to determine their race. Users of social media platforms such as Twitter and Facebook tend to share personal information, such as photos, that can help determine their race, ethnicity, and gender. Those who use their first and last name in their Twitter handle help to verify this information as well. For those who use a non-name Twitter handle, a user's Twitter address, which is visible next to their Twitter handle, may contain their surname—another clue to their race and ethnicity. The list on the "Following" tab may also help shed light on these three factors.

Tweets for the respective hashtags were also coded for their stances on the case studies. Concerning the former NYPD officer Peter Liang trial, tweets were coded as "For Liang," "Against Liang," or "Neutral." The same was done for California Senate Constitutional Amendment 5 and California Assembly Bill 1726. The "Neutral" category was for tweets that either shared or retweeted news on the case study without any comment or did not advocate one side over another. Tweets that retweeted news with commentary were coded as either for or against the issue.

Finally, tweets were all geocoded for their location. Geocoding is the biggest challenge with tweets. For those tweeting from a desktop computer, the geocode can be located by the user's IP address, a numeric code assigned to every stationary computer. A majority of tweets are from smartphone devices, whose locations are provided by longitude and latitude coordinates. The main problem with this involves getting Twitter to authorize access to this information, which it rarely does even for research purposes.[3] Countries were coded for tweets outside of the United States to illuminate the transnational characteristics of the Asian American community.

The Racial Paradox and Emerging Political Contours of Asian Americans

How Connective Action Challenges and Amplifies Them

Asian Americans are the highest-income, best-educated and fastest-growing racial group in the U.S., with Asians now making up the largest share of recent immigrants. A Pew Research survey finds Asian Americans are more satisfied than the general public with their lives, finances and the direction of the country, and they place a greater value on marriage, parenthood, hard work and career success.

—Pew Research Center, "'The Rise of Asian Americans' Report" (2012, par. 2)

I do not know how to explain why I knew Liang would be found guilty well before the verdict was announced. I cannot adequately describe the conflict in feeling like a race traitor for applauding Liang's conviction while also feeling like a race traitor for questioning it. I know the lifeblood of my conditional whiteness as an educated, upwardly mobile Asian-American lies somewhere in those conflicts. And because it's historically been in the best interests of people like me to never discuss these things, even in private, I lack the vocabulary to discuss it.

—Jay Caspian Kang, "How Should Asian-Americans Feel about the Peter Liang Protests?" (2016, par. 8)

The Unique Position That Asian Americans Occupy in the U.S. Racial Hierarchy

Two coexisting common stereotypes of Asian Americans that still prevail today have shaped their unique racial position in the U.S. racial hierarchy: the forever foreigner and the model minority. The forever foreigner is rooted in the historical treatment of Asian cheap laborers as being from an undesirable, foreign culture, which made them incapable of becoming part of the U.S. citizenry through immigration and citizenship, rendering this racial group as apolitical in American politics (Ngai 2004; Lai 2011). This stereotype dates back to 1849 and the California Gold Rush, in which the first Asian American groups began to enter the United States primarily along the West Coast, an area fraught with xenophobia. Specifically, they were met with anti-Asian sentiment in state-endorsed discrimination in the form of anti-miscegenation laws, alien land laws, and immigration laws in states like California, Nevada, Oregon, and Washington. The entire continental United States was not too far behind. For example, in 1924, the U.S. Congress enacted the National Origins Act, which effectively barred all Asians from entering the United States by prohibiting those whose national origins classified them as aliens ineligible for naturalized citizenship (Chan 1991).

The key law that would determine which national origins group fit this description was the 1790 Naturalization Clause, which declared that only immigrant groups consisting of free White people and those of African descent could legally naturalize as U.S. citizens (Chan 1991). If effect, both the 1790 Naturalization Clause and the National Origins Act of 1924 made early Asian immigrants into outsiders looking in when it came to the essential opportunity of becoming a U.S. citizen—the right to naturalization and the ability to create an established community through immigration. As a result of this anti-Asian sentiment, a common belief manifested in society that members of this group were forever foreigners who were incapable of assimilating and civically participating in U.S. politics. The forever foreigner image has conflated Asian Americans with Asians overseas as a homogenous racial group of outsiders, as seen during the civil rights violations of Japanese American internment during World War II and recently with the swelling of anti-Asian violence toward Asian Americans during the COVID-19 pandemic (Cai, Burch, and Patel 2021).

The depiction of Asian Americans as a model minority in the mainstream media initially began with the January 9, 1966, *New York Times* article "Success Story, Japanese American Style," which equated Japanese Americans' purported socioeconomic success with that of Jewish Americans. The model minority stereotype, which has contributed to the unique status of Asian Americans in the U.S. racial hierarchy (Pettersen 1966), generally frames Asian Americans as the one minority group to be emulated by other racial minority groups, particularly African Americans, due to their cultural values of family, education, and hard work. The end effect is that the model minority image pit Asian Americans against other racial minorities during the civil rights movement era of the 1960. The most vivid example is the December 25, 1966, article entitled "Success Story of One Minority Group in the U.S.," which appeared the *U.S. News and World Re-*

port and examined Chinese Americans' purported success in San Francisco's original Chinatown:

> [Visit] Chinatown U.S.A. and you will find an important racial group pulling itself up from hardship and discrimination to become a model of self-respect and achievement in today's America. At a time when it is being proposed that hundreds of billions be spent to uplift Negroes and other minorities, the nation's 300,000 Chinese-Americans are moving ahead on their own—with no help from anyone else. ("Success Story of One Minority" 1966, p. 6)

The model minority stereotype of Asian Americans continues today. A modern example is the Pew Research Center's 2012 study "The Rise of Asian Americans," which touted the U.S. Census Bureau figures on the average number of years of formal education, divorce rate, and median family income of Asian Americans, who often compare favorably to other groups, including White people. These demographic figures ignore contemporary income and housing inequalities among Asian American national origin groups, which were found to be some of the poorest communities in the United States (De La Cruz-Viesca et al. 2018). As a result of the model minority stereotype, Asian Americans are often comparatively positioned or triangulated with other racial minorities and viewed as honorary White people and/or oppressors of other racial minorities, given that Asian Americans have access to educational and economic institutions and recourses that other racial minorities do not have.

The model minority stereotype emerged during the Cold War and Civil Rights periods as an endorsement of U.S. pluralism and egalitarianism. An effect of the model minority narrative is that it has pitted Asian Americans against African Americans and Latinxs, as witnessed in the conflicts in U.S. inner cities where mostly Korean American small businesses were targeted, looted, and burned down by African Americans and Latinxs during the 1992 Los Angeles riots and the 2015 Baltimore riots due to racial resentment around power and resources. Globalization has further amplified the model minority stereotype but with an added twist: the perception as a digital laborer in high-tech industry, as exemplified by the fact that a majority of H-1B visas are going to immigrants with technology backgrounds in Mainland China and India. For example, in 2016, 82 percent of all H-1B visas issued were from Mainland China and India (Molla 2017). Since 2000, Asian Americans have become the majority of the Silicon Valley workforce.

These stereotypes of Asian Americans are contradictory: while Asian Americans are perceived as forever foreigners, apolitical, and racially undesirable, they are also framed as a highly educated and technologically advanced racial group that should be culturally emulated (i.e., value of education) by other groups, particularly African Americans and Latinxs, as the embodiment of hard work and values that can inevitably lead to the American dream. As a result, Asian Americans arguably transcend and challenge the traditional racial fault lines of a racial minority group experiencing class privilege like their educated White counterparts while at the same time suffering from racial inequities like African Americans and Latinxs.

The common mainstream depiction of Asian Americans is that of a model minority that appears to be successful both educationally and economically. Their purported success is primarily attributed by a cultural lens that personifies hard work and validates the American dream, as captured in this chapter heading's first quote from Pew Research Center's 2012 study "The Rise of Asian Americans." In contrast, this chapter heading's second quote captures this day-to-day invisible yet cerebral, heuristic belief among Asian Americans, immigrant and U.S.-born, who have benefited from White privilege but experienced subtle and explicit forms of racial discrimination, as African Americans and Latinxs have endured. The difference, then, is that Asian Americans have historically lacked the vocabulary to express this unique status of being visible yet invisible, unlike African Americans and Latinxs, who do not generally occupy both social worlds in the U.S. racial hierarchy.

The U.S. racial hierarchy can be seen in the inextricable link between race and the extent of racial stereotypes that exist for non-White groups (Masuoka and Junn 2013). For Asian Americans, as discussed earlier, these stereotypes can be both "positive" and "negative" and have challenged traditional racial fault lines often associated with the process of "othering" or deifying African Americans and Latinxs versus White people (Ngai 2004). Given this socioeconomic context during the post–civil rights period, the focus and challenge for Asian American leadership have been to reframe their purported "success," as often supported by racially aggregated economic and academic achievement data, by disaggregating this data along ethnic and foreign-born statuses that empirically demonstrate intra-ethnic group differences that are more aligned with other non-White groups. As illustrated in the Chapter 7 case study of California Assembly Bill 1726 in 2016, despite these altruistic intentions among progressive Asian American community leaders with regard to pursuing data disaggregation within the diverse Asian American community as a more equitable and holistic policy in the area of education, social welfare, and health care, not all Asian American ethnic groups are in favor of such policies for different reasons. In addition, Asian Americans who challenge the model minority stereotype also argue that they have been perceived as the "forever foreigner," which views the political incorporation of Asian Americans as outsiders rather than insiders (Kim 1999).

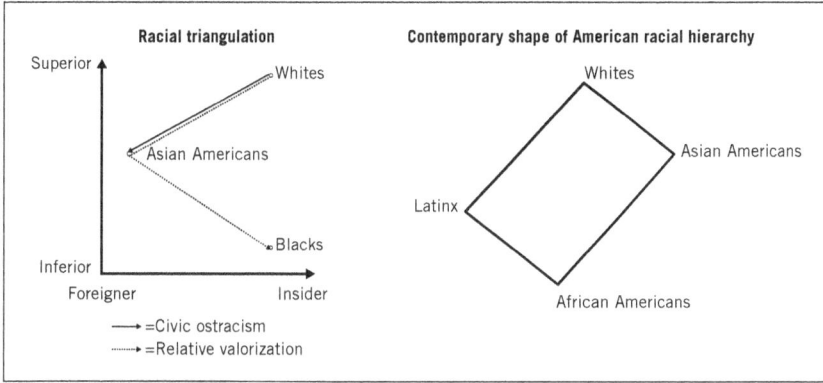

Figure 2.1 Models of Asian Americans within America's Racial Order
([*Left*] Source: Claire Jean Kim, *Politics & Society* [27:1], p. 108, © 1999 by Sage Publications. Reprinted by Permission of SAGE Publications, Inc. [*Right*] Source: Masuoka and Junn 2013, p. 22.)

The absence of a common language, combined with the overwhelmingly foreign-born population, has been divisive among Asian American sub-populations that comprise over twenty-five national origin groups, thereby arguably preventing an Asian American group or panethnic identity from emerging, similar to African Americans and, to a lesser extent, Latinxs (Lai 2011; Lai 2000). Not only is the absence of a common vocabulary among Asian Americans is linguistic but it can also be attributed to previous experiences in their respective native homelands, such as living with an authoritarian government and length of residency (Lien, Conway, and Wong 2004; Ramakrishnan 2005). Given that the national Asian American population has the largest percentage of foreign-born at nearly 70 percent of the entire racial population in 2010, many of these transnational Asian immigrants develop more than one identity due to the movements and experiences between their origin countries and the United States. These identities differ among the Asian ethnic groups with regard to types of immigrants, places of origin, geographic distributions in the United States, patterns of settlement, and population sizes (Shi 2005). While the factors that underlie the racial divisions within the Asian American community are a burden to be contested, they may also serve as a benefit for understanding what issues both panethnic and multiracial coalitions can construct around race, nativity, and class.

Each of the models in Figure 2.1 captures the unique positionalities of Asian Americans within the U.S. racial hierarchy. The "racial triangulation" model developed by Claire Kim is groundbreaking as it conceptualizes the privileges and disadvantages of Asian Americans in relation to White people and African Americans along two interconnected axes: the vertical axis is the model minority as measured by inferior to superior racial group perceptions, and the horizontal axis embodies the forever foreigner as measured by foreigner to insider statuses; this helps us better understand race relations in New York City and Los Angeles within the context of the interracial tension and conflict between Korean American small business owners and African American patrons (Kim 1999). The fact that Asian Americans are valorized over African Americans on the racial group perception axis yet "disadvantaged" when it comes to perceived foreigner status captures the unique positionality of Asian Americans as both a privileged and disadvantaged racial group in the U.S. racial hierarchy. As Kim stated:

> Asian Americans are not, as they are often labeled, a "model minority" whose cultural endowments have allowed them to outstrip other less equipped minorities. However, like whites, they do enjoy a priceless set of structural privileges and immunities, as evidenced by high educational and residential integration and intermarriage rates with whites. They have also been immunized, relatively speaking, from the systemic, routine and often lethal violence exercised by the state against the black community—not just episodes of individual killing, but the institutionalized violence of residential segregation, educational segregation, job discrimination, policing, and mass incarceration. (Kim 2016, par. 5)

The "contemporary shape of American racial hierarchy" model developed by Masuoka and Junn expanded on Kim's racial triangulation model by including Latinxs, resulting in the U.S. racial hierarchy being viewed as a diamond where White people are at the top and, in regard to public opinion and racial stereotypes related to immigration, Asian Americans are viewed more favorably in comparison with Latinxs and African Americans. According to the authors, their model is not static and is highly malleable to public-opinion attitudes that shape immigration policies.

While both models in Figure 2.1 critically reflect the racial representations and hierarchies today through public opinion around immigration and perceived racial group characteristics, they remain isolated and stagnant in other dimensions that are fluid, such as the emergence of social media and how it can be an influential medium in altering racial perceptions and thus hierarchies in both positive and negative ways. The effect is a need to delve deeper into how these racial hierarchies are being challenged by various intersections emerging among political movements, changing identities, new technologies, and changing local contexts.

In Asian immigrant influenced cities that have witnessed dramatic demographic shifts within a short period of time, going from a majority Anglo population to a majority and/or plurality Asian American population has also changed the local identity and culture of these cities, where Asian Americans are perceived by both White people and Asian Americans to be at the top of the racial hierarchy (Jiménez and Horowitz 2013). One visible contemporary example of this phenomenon is in public education, where Asian Americans have changed the curricular focus (i.e., Mandarin or Tamil courses are now common in many Silicon Valley public high schools and viewed more favorably for future employment opportunities in a global economy than French or Italian; math and STEM courses are viewed as more essential than art and music courses).

These dramatic demographic and public education curricular changes have created tensions in such California cities as Fremont and Cupertino, which has resulted in what the *Wall Street Journal* described in a 2005 article as "the new white flight," where White families with children are now leaving Asian-influenced suburban areas to resettle in more White-populated cities (Hwang 2005). None of the above macro-level models takes into consideration any of these dimensions that are becoming part and parcel of transnational, Asian-influenced cities that are emerging not only in California, where the largest percentage of the current Asian American population resides, but also throughout many similarly emerging cities that are rapidly and dramatically changing throughout the major regions of the United States (Lai 2011).

Emerging Political Contours in Asian America

The contemporary Asian American electorate has become increasingly diverse with regard to its political contours, especially as it relates to political partisanship and ideological policy choices due to the variance in socio-class among its diverse national origin groups, which have emerged since the mid-1960s. U.S. immigration policy is at the root this fractured politics among Asian American voters. According to the U.S. Census, Chinese Americans represent the largest Asian American ethnic group in the United States, and one with an extensive history that dates back to the first gold rush laborers in 1849. Even with this long history, a majority of Chinese Americans has arrived since the U.S. Congress passed the Hart-Celler Act of 1965. Since this monumental immigration act, an overwhelming majority of Asian American immigrants have migrated to the United States from over twenty-five nations and many different socioeconomic backgrounds.

The Hart-Celler Act of 1965 and its stringent policy of seven preferences—the third gave immigration preference to "artists, scientists, and those of exceptional ability"—helped not only to shape a burgeoning Asian America but also to create a larger community that was increasingly polarized along ethnic and class lines (Lai 2011). More recent changes in U.S. immigration policy that have continued giving preference to those with special skills and greater economic resources to employ U.S. citizens facilitated the emergence of an Asian American elite class. This class dynamic helped to facilitate a unique status among Asian Americans in the U.S. racial hierarchies: they are racially privileged and disenfranchised at the same time.

The racial group impact of this diversity and unique status can be seen in two diametric and competing ideological movements emerging within Asian America since 1992—the progressive shift of Asian Americans, as symbolized by the gradual rise of Democratic voters (only 31 percent supported Democrat Bill Clinton in 1992, compared to 73 percent for incumbent President Barack Obama in 2012) and the emergence of Asian American immigrant conservative politics, as seen within the highly educated first-generation Chinese American community and its anti–affirmative action lawsuits.

1. The Rise of Asian American Democratic Voters

Democratic shifts have been taking place in both the Asian American and Latinx electorates since 1992. While both racial groups have large immigrant populations (70 percent and 40 percent in 2010 for Asian Americans and Latinxs, respectively), Asian Americans are the only racial group, including African Americans, where their percent of voting Democratic in each successive U.S. presidential election since 1992 to 2012 has increased gradually each presidential election cycle. The reasons for this shift are related to both internal and external dynamics. Internally, the large amount of foreign-born, working-class immigrants have gradually identified with the Democratic Party platform. Externally, the Republican Party has been perceived as anti-immigrant in its rhetoric at state and national levels, as witnessed in California, a majority-minority state containing nearly 40 percent of the national Asian American population, with controversial laws. Examples of such polarizing proposed laws included California's 1992 Proposition 187, which denied social services and public education to undocumented immigrants; the U.S. Congress' House Resolution 4437 in 2006, which increased federal penalties against undocumented immigrants and called for a four-hundred-mile wall along the Rio Grande between the United States and Mexico; and Arizona's 2010 Senate Bill 1070, the Support Our Law Enforcement and Safe Neighborhoods Act, which allowed state law enforcement officers to pull over anyone who appeared to be undocumented. All of these laws were spearheaded by Republican coalitions. While these laws focused primarily on Mexican undocumented workers, the anti-immigrant rhetoric and perception of the Republican Party's leadership behind these laws had a prolonged negative effect on the Asian American community given that this group has the nation's largest foreign-born population.

President Donald Trump's demagoguery toward Latinx and other non-White immigrant groups during the 2016 U.S. presidential election only cemented this perception in the minds of many Asian American voters, as public opinion surveys have revealed. In an April to May 2016 national telephone survey of 1,212 Asian American registered voters, 61 percent of the survey respondents held an unfavorable view toward Trump while only 19 percent held a positive view. In comparison, 62 percent held a favorable view toward Democratic candidate Hillary Clinton and 26 percent held an unfavorable view (APIAVote, Asian Americans Advancing Justice, and AAPI Data 2016).

The pivoting of the Asian American electorate toward the Democratic Party parallels the progressive ideology that has been central to the group's own civil rights movement and a period of racial formation known as the Asian American Movement, from the late 1960s to this day. For Asian Americans, this has been a turbulent period in which Asian American community leaders and activists have sought new modes of equality and opportunity in social services, job employment, and educational opportunities in large metropolitan areas throughout the West Coast. In higher education, Asian American young adults have been central partners in progressive multiracial coalitions for racial minorities that have worked to attain access to and curricular changes in higher education institutions. During this period, an emerging progressive racial consciousness has taken shape among second-generation Asian Americans living in large metropolitan areas, as expressed through the cultural arts, community-based organizations, and educational curricula (Louie and Omatsu 2001).

Asian Americans in the United States during the turbulent social movements of the 1960s and 1970s began to mobilize around a common racial identity as "Asian Americans." Through this process of racial formation, they sought to transcend ethnic differences by finding common struggle with other racial minorities and with progressive White people through the common language of English. With both this common language and a guiding progressive racial ideology, Asian Americans along the West and East Coasts began to mobilize their group interests through "racial projects," which sought influence on domestic and international policies as well as equitable redistribution of resources along racial lines (Omi and Winant 2014). The Asian American Movement was a microcosm of the civil rights and antiwar movements and would define subsequent generations of Asian

American leadership, whether as community-based organization leaders, labor activists, educators, professionals, or elected officials, as these young activists came of age. The Asian American Movement continues today as Asian American activists and civil rights organizations seek to continue one of the movement's core tenets: "uniting all who can be united" by working in multiracial coalitions across a wide range of public policies and social justice issues (Louie 2001).

2. Emanating Conservative Strands among Highly Educated, Affluent Asian Immigrants

Stringent immigration policies and the rise of H-1B visas since the Immigration Act of 1965 have put increased emphasis on educated, technologically trained, and affluent immigrants from East and South Asian countries who tend to live in suburbs that are either majority Asian or have large Asian and White populations (Lai 2011). In 2016, 82 percent of all recent H-1B visas came from either Mainland China or India (Semotiuk 2019). As a result, an emerging strand of conservatism that aligns with the Republican Party has taken shape particularly among first-generation Chinese Americans over the past thirty years (Xiaoqing 2019). Many of these Chinese immigrants may not be familiar or agree with the liberal traditions of the Asian American movement during the late 1960s to the mid-1970s and may have firm beliefs in meritocratic principles that are against group rights (Garces and Poon 2018). While they may be a minority, one would be remiss to ignore or dismiss these conservative ideological strands that are part and parcel of the larger Asian American community and that have been effective recently in utilizing connective action to shape political outcomes in American politics.

While conservative first-generation Chinese Americans have successfully mobilized against a sanctuary city law in the suburbs of Montgomery County, Maryland, and are currently trying to create a referendum on a city council–approved local affordable public housing development in Cupertino, California, perhaps no other policy issue has galvanized this group's local, state, and national mobilization than affirmative action in higher education admissions (Turque 2017; Sarwari 2018; Garces and Poon 2018). As this issue has taken the nation's center stage, first-generation Chinese Americans have mobilized against affirmative action behind the claim that Asian American students have been victims of racial discrimination in the holistic admissions policies and practices at select universities in the Ivy League. One primary example is the nonprofit, 501(c)(3) national organization called Asian American Coalition for Education (AACE), which filed two anti-affirmative federal complaints with the U.S. Education Department's Office for Civil Rights in 2015 and 2016. The coalition includes more than one hundred Asian American organizations, an overwhelming majority of them Chinese American, from nine states including and even other countries such as Vancouver, Canada.[1] In order to mobilize, disseminate information, fundraise, and recruit, AACE has created a website in both English and Chinese and a Facebook page and has posted several of the organization's videos on YouTube. For example, the website provides a link entitled "Call for Discriminated-against Asian American Students to File Individual Complaints" as well as a link to donate money online. Yukong Zhao, president of AACE and a Chinese immigrant who was the primary person behind the complaint and main organizer of the coalition, stated the stereotype of Asian American students not being creative or risk-takers is false: "Nearly half of the tech start-ups in the country were started by Asian-Americans. Everyone is a great example of creativity, and risk-taking and leadership" (Belkin 2015, par. 9).

The contemporary conservative strands and racial narratives are undoubtedly shaped and bound by recent U.S. immigration policies that give preferences to the children of well-educated and wealthier Asian immigrants. Conservative first-generation Chinese Americans are certainly not the only ideological conservatives in the larger Asian American community, but they have found recent and visible success in mobilizing their collective online voices in determining public policy outcomes in their favor through social media platforms like WeChat. The underlying political motivation is concern about their children's future and their belief in meritocratic values in determining life opportunities. According to Donghui Zhang, a Chinese American immigrant community activist in New York who helped to mobilize the Chinese community against New York Mayor Bill de Blasio's controversial policy to reform the meritocratic admission policies of city's specialized high schools: "Today there are no politicians or leaders. We are all ordinary parents but we should believe in our power. As long as we fight together, we are able to fight for the future of our children" (Xiaoqing 2019, par. 2). The rise of Chinese conservatism, guided by this political motivation along with their effective use of connective action, is vividly illustrated in Chapter 4 ("Case Study 1: The 2016 Trial of New York Police Department Officer Peter Liang and the Connective Action Mobilization by First-Generation Chinese Americans") and Chapter 5 ("Case Study 2: The Asian American Community's Online and Offline Affirmative Action Battle over the 2012 California Senate Constitutional Amendment 5 Bill").

The effect of both competing ideological movements challenges the traditional tenets of Asian American panethnicity. Historically, panethnicity among Asian Americans has often been viewed as solely progressive coalitions, as seen with the Asian American Movement of the 1960s and 1970s. A central question of previous research on Asian American panethnicity has been whether Asian ethnic groups can come together as a racial group or go it alone (Lai 2000). Diversity was once seen as a factor of tension for creating a progressive panethnic coalition. However, this may no longer solely be the case, as multiple coalitions may form along the entire progressive-conservative continuum due to intersectional identities emerging in the contemporary Asian American community. It is now possible to witness multiple panethnic coalitions forming among various ideological and class segments within an Asian ethnic group or among other ethnic groups and competing against each other around issue stances. Connective action is a critical component to understanding contemporary prospects for Asian American panethnicity because it provides all segments of the Asian American community the ability to create a consensus and to mobilize regardless of their size, naturalization status, and ideological perspectives.

Challenging the Traditional U.S. Racial Hierarchy and Race Relations

Connective action may allow Asian Americans opportunities to reframe existing racial tropes and hierarchies that are rooted in racial inequality, as often depicted in both mainstream media and larger society. Specifically, Asian American connective action has the potential to challenge both the model minority and the forever foreigner stereotypes that have been foregrounded in the public arena. For example, for non–Asian Americans, the public protests that result from connective action as covered by the news media may challenge their stereotypical assumptions of this group as a model minority and/or a forever foreigner. Connective action can help shed a light on an invisible community regarding their diverse perspectives that would otherwise be closed to Asian Americans. These virtual observations have the potential to take on existing racial stereotypes that non–Asian Americans may hold of Asian Americans and thereby challenge the traditional racial hierarchy along social, economic, and political lines.

The outcome of these changes can also have a great impact on the ideologies, identities, and thus politics within the Asian American communities themselves. As is discussed in the next section, demographic shifts can challenge existing ideologies that have defined the historical and contemporary politics of the Asian American community at the local, state, and national levels. In the case of Asian Americans, a progressive ideology has been central to the Civil Rights Movement of the 1960s to the Asian American Movement of the 1960s and 1970s. Because many Asian Americans today have arrived in the U.S. as immigrants during the past thirty years with no connection to or understanding of the roles that Asian Americans played in these social movements, it has challenged the progressive ideology that has served as a foundation within many Asian American communities established pre-1965. Moreover, established perceptions ranging from a common racial experience to public opinions on key aspects are now in flux as new immigrants, particularly those who are motivated with key resources at their disposal, begin to exert themselves within the larger racial discourse of American politics.

Connective action also allows Asian Americans to challenge and reposition themselves as both "outsiders" and "foreign" within the traditional U.S. racial hierarchy through civic engagement around various campaigns, regardless of the ideological perspective. On one hand, the outsider or apolitical stereotype of Asian Americans not wanting to engage or make political waves in the public arena are shattered by rapid, organized protests and swift political action. This is due, in part, to traditional organizations no longer having sole access to critical information. Instead, such information can be shared widely through various social media platforms. Moreover, issue groups and forums can be created to allow for recruitment, dialogue, and planning of organized protests. National news accounts of racial minority group movements throughout the nation, such as Black Lives Matter, illustrate the profound effects of social media activism. As is illustrated in the forthcoming case studies, a similar dynamic is developing among the growing online Asian American community.

Connective action can also serve as a precursor to other forms of civic engagement, such as voting, among minority groups with large immigrant populations, including Latinxs and Asian Americans. This belief was evident in May 2006, in the early stages of social media, during the "Day without an Immigrant" protests, which involved over two million Latinxs across the continental United States and were primarily coordinated through social media including Facebook and MySpace and various Spanish media (television, digital radio). Today, the mobilization continues with Deferred Action for Childhood Arrivals (DACA) protests and demands for pathways to citizenship; we also see social media networks on smartphones used by local emergency response teams to dispatch trained witnesses to document potential civil rights abuses by Immigration and Custom Enforcement (ICE) agents attempting to apprehend potential undocumented suspects. Like Asian Americans, Latinxs are viewed as outsiders and foreigners among their respective documented and undocumented populations. Both minority groups' abilities to mobilize in campaigns around social justice can ultimately serve as a foundation for future civic engagement, as previous studies have shown.

While connective action offers the potential for Asian Americans to challenge the larger, traditional U.S. racial hierarchy as well as specific group stereotypes pertaining to them, it can also be dangerous in promoting a self-interested group stereotype, especially when polarizing public policy issues are at the center. In short, the ability for Asian Americans of all ideological backgrounds to pursue a connective action strategy may, in effect, also shape how other racial groups perceive them around polarizing issues. A zero-sum perspective may develop in such a condition among the multiracial landscape, which is always challenging, as Asian Americans, Latinxs, and African Americans have historically tried to create and sustain multiracial coalitions in local and state politics since the Civil Rights Movement.

The accessibility of social media affords all groups the ability to mobilize, channel, and voice their opinions through the sharing of information on the internet, but in doing so it may also create increasingly separate and insulated online chambers, occupied by various segments of a racial group, that reward those who are more vociferous and who have greater resources to mobilize in effective ways that extend beyond the internet. This belief was particularly evident in this book's first three case studies (justice for former NYPD Officer Peter Liang, California Senate Constitutional Amendment 5, and California Assembly Bill 1726). Factions within the national Chinese American community were politically successful in mobilizing in each of these three campaigns; many who participated saw these movements as a perceived threat to their ethnic group interests and thus viewed them as social injustices despite contrary evidence and support from other segments of the same ethnic population. As a result, from the perspective of other racial groups such as African Americans and Latinxs, as well as from the larger progressive Asian American community, who understood the multiracial landscape, the actions of these segments of the Chinese American population were construed as mere self-interest. The significance of these high-profile and public campaigns, whether fair or not, is that Asian Americans are perceived as a racial group based on the connective actions of a small segment that is focused only on self-interest at the expense of other racial groups. This is a very dangerous perception for any group in states like California, where there is no longer a majority racial group, which requires nuanced approaches to building majorities in support of policies that benefit the larger multiracial populations.

Past studies on racial conflict highlight the challenges of building progressive, multiracial coalitions. In *Bitter Fruit: The Politics of Black-Korean Conflict*, Claire Kim analyzes the tensions between Korean American fruit stand owners and African American patrons in New York City by examining the early 1990 boycotts by African Americans of Korean American businesses in their neighborhoods and how they challenged the traditional Black-

White racial power paradigm (Kim 2000). Kim argued that the Black-Korean conflict was the result of a "racial order" and "racial power" in the contemporary United States. Kim defined racial power as "systemic tendency that expresses itself through myriad processes, some of which involve intentional domination and some of which do not" (Kim 2000, p. 9). The effect of racial power is that it creates social interactions between racial groups and determines how conflicts get resolved and, ultimately, the U.S. racial hierarchy. The significance of this theoretical argument is that it often pits Asian Americans against other racial groups because of their placement within the U.S. racial hierarchy. As illustrated in Figure 2.1 by Claire Kim's racial triangulation model, Asian Americans are disadvantaged in relation to African Americans when it comes to being political insiders due to their permanent alien stereotype but are advantaged in other ways when it comes to perceived group valorization due to their model minority stereotype. Thus, if there is no attempt to create a bridge across the echo chambers that often develop, connective action could further exacerbate this racial triangulation in instances when a vocal minority within the larger Asian American community mobilizes against another racial group. This key point in particular is addressed in the final chapter, in addition to ways to mitigate this effect.

Conceptualizing a Model for Asian American Connective Action

Traditional Models of Collective Action and Their Limitations for Marginalized Groups

Two traditional models of collective action have emerged in the American politics literature: the socioeconomic model and the group incentives model. One common narrative found in the socioeconomic model literature is that minorities and marginalized groups do not participate in the political process (e.g., voting, contacting a candidate) because they lack the most common characteristics of the general population of voters such as education and income (Brady, Verba, and Schlozman 1995). Those with socioeconomic resources are more likely to be engaged in electoral politics and to protest (Brady, Verba, and Schlozman 1995; Van de Donk et al. 2004). The socioeconomic model underlies the most common explanation for the relatively low political participation rates of Asian Americans in comparison with other racial groups.

An alternative literature to the socioeconomic model is the group incentives model, which argues that collective action is based on group political motivation. For example, Olson, in his classic *The Logic of Collective Action*, argues that even with common incentives, individuals do not automatically collaborate without the presence of formal organization structures that are central for locating, motivating, and coordinating the actions of those who choose to take collective action (Olson 1965). Recent studies have addressed the theoretical void of the group incentives model through a multitiered approach that expands political motivation to take into consideration the various political inequalities that exist between mainstream White voters and underrepresented minority voters such as African Americans, Latinx, and Asian Americans (Han 2009).

The above traditional models of collective action are limited in their understandings of civic engagement in the age of social media. Why? Social media has altered the relationships between citizens, information, and civic engagement by opening up what some scholars refer to as "virtual spaces" that bypass the traditional gatekeepers (Luttig and Cohen 2016, par. 5). The rise of new technology and participatory media have challenged the formal organizations aspect by making them available to individuals and by allowing such new modes of communication technologies to take on various aspects of formal organizations (Bimber, Flanagin, and Stohl 2005). As a result, the public and private planes have been blurred by new communication technologies that were once clearly demarcated. Thus, when two or more people in conjunction cross the private and public boundary with the goal of seeking a public good, connective action is said to have occurred. In summary, the authors argue that three components exist that allow for this transcendent moment of connective action: (1) the ease of transforming private discourse to public discourse through social media platforms and smartphones, without any specific dependence on central organization; (2) the absence of a central organization; and (3) the internet serving as a vehicle for crossing public and private boundaries (Bimber, Flanagin, and Stohl 2005).

Social media and mobile technologies have provided new affordances to marginalized groups who limited political and economic capital such as age, U.S. citizenship, and access to formal political organizations to begin leveling the playing field during the pursuit of public goods (Han 2009; Bimber, Flanagin, and Stohl, 2012; Earl and Kimport 2011). The logic of connective action challenges the socioeconomic model by allowing people from all different socioeconomic classes, particularly those who are less affluent, to build consensus through social media networks and to mobilize offline around common interests and ideologies with community-based organizations provided that there is political motivation. The ability to provide new affordances through social media networks to amplify political voices mitigates the socioeconomic limitations during traditional collective action. As a result, local movements can manifest into national and even international movements among historically muted and underrepresented racial groups. This belief is clearly evident with the national Black Lives Matter movement, which began as a local hashtag movement and now seeks national police reform and accountability for the racial profiling of and violence against African Americans.

Recent studies conducted by the MacArthur Research Network on Youth and Participatory Politics (YPP) have found that social media has a direct and positive effect on how youth involve themselves in politics (Kahne and Middaugh 2012; Kahne, Lee, and Feezell 2012; Cohen and Kahne 2012). Based on the YPP national survey of youth between fifteen and twenty-nine, which included an oversampling of African Americans, Latinxs, and Asian Americans during 2011, 2013, and 2015, the following two findings were found regarding young minorities: (1) they are the biggest consumers of new online forms of political media (i.e., websites created by and for minorities); and (2) those from socioeconomically disadvantaged homes are more likely to get their political information from new online sources (Luttig and Cohen 2016). Other findings from the YPP surveys suggest that young people generally consume political information from traditional sources (i.e., newspapers and television) in roughly equal percentages and that those with greater socioeconomic backgrounds are more likely to get their political information from these traditional sources (Luttig and Cohen 2016).

A study on connected civics among youth found that through shared civic practices, members of affinity networks lower barriers for entry and increase opportunities for young people to engage in civic and political action by opening up lower points of entry when they may not otherwise participate in institutional politics (Ito et al. 2015). The case studies and interviews done in this study revealed that young people were able to construct hybrid narratives by mining the cultural contexts that they are embedded in and can relate to civic themes of social concern. The same study also found that young people, working with adults, can institutionalize their efforts to transform what began as loosely affiliated networks into something that is socially organized and self-sustaining (Ito et al. 2015). A vivid example is DREAMactivist.org, which was founded by students who met in person after the site was created and consists of thirty sponsor organizations that coordinate other programs such as the National DREAM Graduation in addition to petitions and fundraising on a national level (Zimmerman 2012). As a result, we can see the mobilization effects of social media on the civic engagement of African Americans and Latinxs, but can the same be said about Asian Americans, and how does it differ?

Conceptualizing Asian American Connective Action

Figure 3.1 captures the two typologies of Asian American connective action—predominantly crowd-led and predominantly organization-led networks—and their respective characteristics and corresponding book case studies. All six case studies in this book featured aspects of both typologies but were primarily characterized by the typologies listed above. Predomi-

Asian American connective action	Asian American connective action
Predominantly crowd-led networks	**Predominantly organization-led networks**
• Crowd-led coordination of political action and civic engagement around goals • Asian language–focused social media networks (e.g., Facebook, Twitter) through smartphone apps (e.g., WeChat, WhatsApp, KakaoTalk, and Line) • Communication content centers on personal action frames around political goals, public policies, and/or social justice issues • Large-scale personal access to multi-layered and multilingual social technologies regardless of English proficiency • Personal and multilingual expression with other Asian ethnic members shared over social media platforms	• Coordination of political action and civic engagement • Organization provides social technology via web-based or smartphone-based platforms • Communication content centers on organizationally generated inclusive personal action frames around political goals, public policies, and/or social justice issues • Large-scale personal access to multi-layered and multilingual social technologies regardless of English proficiency • Personal and multilingual expression with other Asian ethnic members shared over social media platforms

Book Case Study Examples:
• Chapter 4: Peter Liang
• Chapter 5: SCA 5 and Affirmative Action
• Chapter 6: AB 1726 and Data Disaggregation
• Chapter 8: California Textbook Controversy
• Chapter 9: Comfort Women Memorials
	Book Case Study Examples:
	• Chapter 7 (18 Milion Rising online organization):
	    (a) Black AAPI Action for a Clean Dream Act; and
	    (b) Release Minnesota 8 campaign

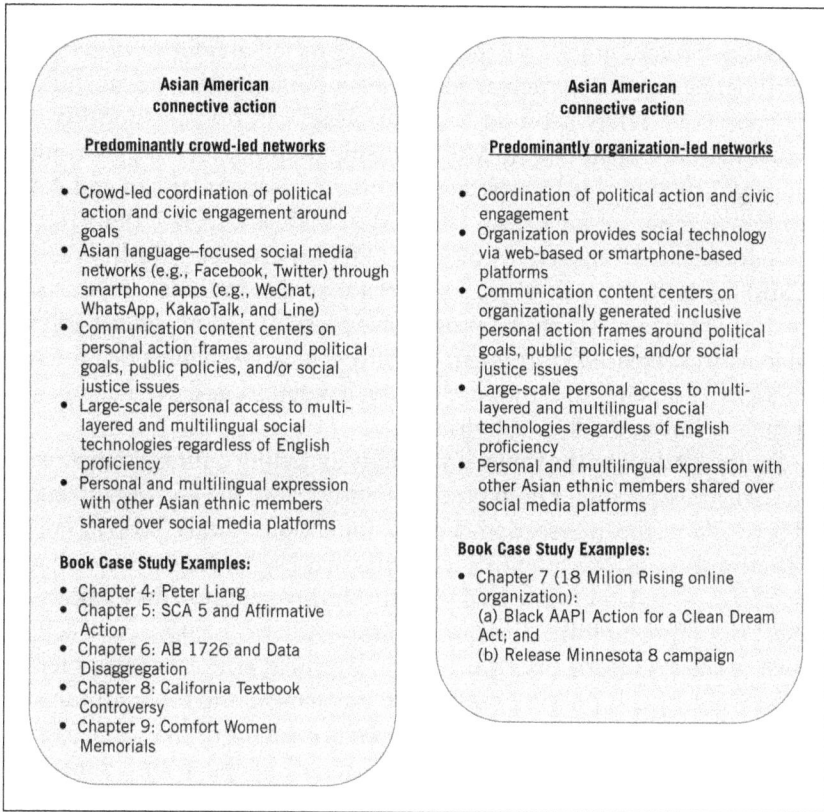

Figure 3.1 Typologies and Aspects of Asian American Connective Action Networks
(Source: The above typologies and their aspects were modified from Bennett, W. Lance, and Alexandra Segerberg. 2013. *The Logic of Connective Action: Digital Media and the Personalization of Contentious Politics.* Figure 1.1: Defining Elements of Connective and Collective Action Networks, p. 47.)

nantly crowd-led networks involve little to no formal organization involvement. Instead, the primary driving forces are inclusive personal, multilingual action frames involving a public policy and/or social justice issue through online social network platforms and smartphone apps. One critical aspect of Asian American connective action is the importance of native-language-based apps and platforms to communicate in their respective ethnic languages, which is critical given the large foreign-born and LEP populations, as mentioned earlier. Case studies that were primarily characterized as crowd-led are reviewed in Chapters 5 (Peter Liang), 6 (SCA 5), 7 (AB 1726), 9 (California Textbook Controversy), and 10 (comfort women memorials).

Predominantly organization-led networks are primarily driven by Asian American ethno-racial organizations, which coordinate and generate both the online social network platforms and the inclusive personal frames around a social justice and/or policy issue(s). This allows for later forms of personal, multilingual expressions across social network platforms. A case study in this book that vividly captures an Asian American organization-led network is found in Chapter 8 (18 Million Rising website), covering two online campaigns that involved this website: (1) the African American and AAPI coalition to mobilize for a clean DREAM Act (#BlackAAPIAction) and (2) the Release the Minnesota 8 campaign (#ReleaseMN8). 18MillionRising (18MR) has created a web-based social platform that features various Asian American campaigns that tout progressive perspectives on policies and social injustices. Website visitors can civically engage by clicking on an Asian American campaign that they are willing to support and participate with through online and offline activities.

Figure 3.2 depicts the three dimensions underling online Asian American connective action for both predominantly crowd-led and organization-led networks as the intersection of three dimensions: Goals (Motivation for Collective Action), Medium (Social Media and Digital Ethnic Media), and Site (Asian American Influenced Cities). All three of these dimensions intersect in online mobilization during Asian American connective action, which produces offline political action. A critical element that underlies connective action is political motivation for shaping and determining outcomes such as responsive policies, elected representation, and social justice. It is important to note that connective action can happen simultaneously with and/or separately from traditional forms of political action such as contacting local and state elected representatives. Below is a discussion of each of the three dimensions of online Asian American connective action.

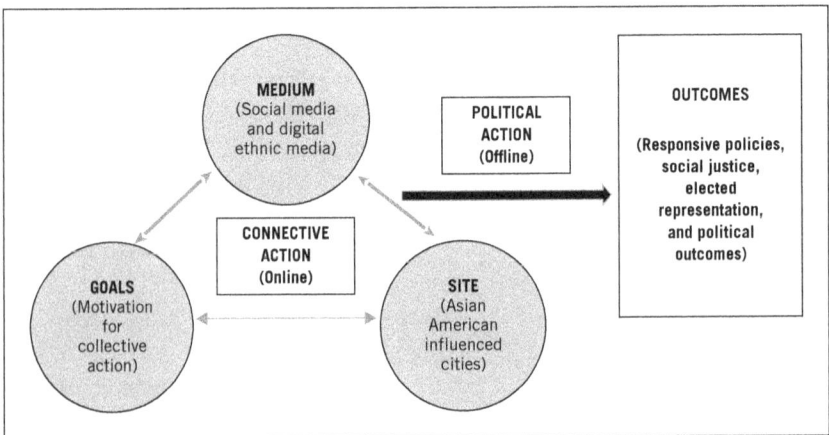

Figure 3.2 The Three Dimensions of Online Asian American Connective Action (Crowd- and Organization-Led Networks)

1. Medium Dimension: Social Media and Digital Ethnic Media

The medium dimension of Asian American connective action, particularly in Asian-influenced suburbs across the continental United States, may involve the interaction of social media and digital ethnic news media that facilitate the articulation, organization, and dissemination of information to pursue a policy or political outcomes. Formal organizations, unlike collective action, are no longer necessary because these new technologies serve as a surrogate for them. As a result, these new technologies have challenged the traditional models of political participation in two important ways: (1) the belief that immigrants must follow a linear process to participate by naturalizing as U.S. citizens, registering to vote, and then participating through the ballot and other forms of involvement; and (2) the belief that those who participate politically typically have high socioeconomic status.

Social media in the form of smartphones, computers, and tablets allow organizations, individuals, nongovernment and government organizations, and businesses to view, create, and share information through virtual communities and networks. As illustrated in Table 3.1, there are many types of messaging apps that are preferred among different Asian national origin groups based on where the apps were created, as seen with KakaoTalk (South Korea), Line (Japan), WhatsApp (United States), and WeChat (Mainland China). As a result, these messaging apps cater to various Asian national origin groups with regard to language preferences and adaptation in their respective homeland countries. They also serve as a form of ethnic media among users by connecting them to their native homelands via information in their respective native languages, thus serving as a cultural bridge between Asian immigrant communities and U.S. society.

Other ubiquitous forms of social media networks within the transnational Asian/Asian American diaspora include the Chinese Twitter-like website Sina Weibo, where predominantly Chinese users with profiles can anonymously create and post in subject forums as well as upload videos for discussion to the website from a laptop or smartphone. Within all of these social media networks, language no longer poses as a barrier for both access and communication during connective action. For example, ethnic social

TABLE 3.1 MOST COMMON SMARTPHONE MESSAGING APPS BY ASIAN ETHNIC GROUPS				
	KakaoTalk	Line	WeChat	WhatsApp
Origin Country	South Korea	Japan	Mainland China	United States
Launch Date	March 2010	June 2011	January 2011	May 2009
Number of Users	75 million	100 million	3 billion	More than 1 billion
Main Markets	Korea	Japan and Taiwan	Mainland China, Southeast Asia	India
Source: Data provided by each company.				

media platforms like WeChat and Sina Weibo are common in the United States among transnational Chinese and Taiwanese Americans.

2. Goals Dimension: Motivation for Collective Action

The goals dimension embodies the motivation underlying Asian American collective action for the purpose of influencing a particular policy or a political outcome at the local, state, or national level. Previous studies have illustrated that at the local level, recently immigrated and U.S.-born Asian American–influenced cities undergo regional racial formations by shaping the established regional identities and spaces as Asian Americans make these cities their homes (Cheng 2013; Lai 2011; Chang and Amam 2010). Whether it is the need for public-funded Chinese-language schools or the unlawful firing of an Asian American teacher because of her accent, these issues serve as a vehicle for collective action. The advent of new mobile phone and social media technologies has allowed the Asian American community to go local, state, national, and even global during the process of traditional political action by connecting other Asian-influenced cities throughout states and the continental United States. In effect, Asian American connective action both coincides with and alters traditional Asian American political action.

Recently, successful Asian American candidates in Asian American suburbs have utilized social media to mobilize both old and new Asian American voters around their respective campaigns in local politics. A prime example is first-time candidate Shannon Peng, who ran for an at-large seat on the school board of Edison, New Jersey, during its November 2016 elections. New Jersey was home to the sixth-largest Chinese American community in the nation in 2015, according to the U.S. Census Bureau (Cui 2017). Peng, a mother of two elementary school children who emigrated from Mainland China and currently works as a senior software engineer at MetLife, decided to run for the school board in the emerging Asian American suburb of Edison, where Asian Americans made up 37.5 percent of the total population in 2010. Her school board campaign received no support from any political or civic organizations. Instead, she exclusively used WeChat to recruit volunteers and fundraise from local, state, and national Chinese American communities. According to Peng:

> We built the entire campaign through a WeChat group that began two years ago among a group of parents who had children enrolled in our local Chinese language school. We just kept adding more parents to the WeChat group and it ended up being close to 300 members. We had 80 plus volunteers from the WeChat group. The volunteers were broken up into five or six subgroups each with different roles and func-

tions. Every subgroup had their own WeChat group with assigned leaders for each. All of the voter data they collected was shared through the WeChat groups. I also fundraised through my University of Chicago alumni groups on WeChat that had chapters in Western and Central New Jersey. I was able to post my campaign statement and get approximately 50 percent of my campaign contributions through these alumni WeChat groups. It was a very efficient and effective organization run exclusively through WeChat. Since I was running as a broader candidate representing all residents, we reached out to the Indian community of Edison through WhatsApp to advertise my campaign and field questions about my policy stances.[1]

Peng eventually finished second for the three open seats by receiving nearly twelve thousand votes—a quarter of the total votes casted. She largely credits her election to her strategic use of WeChat. For example, during her campaign, volunteer groups organized on WeChat performed various tasks. One was to identify approximately 10,000 addresses (out of Edison's 100,000 residents) of registered voters who participated in previous elections to be targeted for door-to-door campaigning (Cui 2017). In addition, Peng was able to get 500 members from the WeChat group to plant lawn signs in front of their homes (Cui 2017). The effective mobilization and sharing of data through the messaging app likely played a role in mobilizing voters during the competitive election.

Peng is certainly not the only Chinese American candidate in New Jersey who utilized WeChat to achieve successful election results. During the same election cycle, in Livingston, New Jersey, George Shen ran for the school board and primarily utilized WeChat to promote his candidacy and to find Chinese American volunteers to distribute campaign signage throughout the city. Examples such as Peng and Shen illustrate how social media has become a necessary component for Asian American candidates to mobilize all segments of the Asian American community, particularly the largest segment, which consists of immigrants. As a result, the connective action model, which incorporates social media platforms like WeChat, provides a glimpse of how a largely immigrant community that lacks resources and access to formal, traditional institutions can still participate politically in the digital era of mobile technologies such as smartphones and tablets.

3. Site Dimension—Asian American Suburbs as the Primary Node During Connective Action

The site dimension is the geographic context where Asian American connective action takes shape and where community formations have mostly taken shape during the past three decades, in cities across the continental United States that predominantly range from small to medium-size suburbs with significant percentages of Asian American populations. Regional racial formation in the local context of Asian American suburbs, for example, can both challenge and alter traditional racial, social, economic, and political orders that previously existed in these cities (Cheng 2013; Jiménez and Horowitz 2013; Lai 2011). These redefinitions and reconfigurations in Asian American suburbs have been rapid and have concomitantly come with growing pains such as contemporary White flight and racially charged local campaigns (Lai 2011). The ability to mobilize the community through social media platforms as a racial group and/or an ethnic group beyond local boundaries is especially critical for a minority group like Asian Americans, given their relatively small population in comparison with other racial groups.

In order to understand the importance of the site dimension for Asian American connective action, one must understand this racial group's contemporary community formation patterns. Asian Americans are the fastest growing racial minority group in the nation according to the U.S. Census findings from 2000 to 2010. In 1965, Asian Americans were less than 1 percent of the population. Today, that figure is nearing 6 percent and rapidly trending upward. The number of Asian Americans jumped from 11.9 million in 2000 to 17.3 million in 2010, a 46 percent growth rate that outpaced and surpassed Latinxs as the largest racial group immigrating to the United States in 2009. As this majority foreign-born population, now estimated at 70 percent, enters the United States and begins the long process of U.S. naturalization, little is known about where they choose to live and form communities and how they are transforming the communities they now call home.

Large Asian American–populated suburban cities in states across the continental United States constituted the nodes that form this transnational community's larger network. Northern and Southern California suburbs, where nearly 30 percent of the national Asian American population resides in 2017, remain significant nodal destinations for community formation patterns, and the Golden State is not alone. Like a majority of all Americans, Asian Americans are choosing to live in small to medium-size suburbs throughout the continental United States (Lai 2011). During the last decade, Asian American population growth in small to medium suburban cities has reached nearly 1.7 million, four times the rate of those in large central cities at 770,000 (Frey 2011). This mimics national population settlement trends, in which a majority of Americans identified living in a suburb with minorities, accounting for 35 percent of suburbs' populations (Oliver and Ha 2007; Frey 2011). In 2000, 51 percent of Asian Americans nationally lived in small to medium suburbs, compared to 33 percent of African Americans, 45 percent of Latinxs, and 54 percent of White people (Jones-Correa 2004).

Activating and Connecting the Nodes: How a Local Issue Becomes National during Connective Action

Like all racial groups, the process of Asian America connective action has the ability to materialize among the network of cities or nodes that make up the larger community of Asian national origin groups throughout the Continental United States, which has developed over the past three decades. This is a salient point for Asian Americans who often lack the large aggregate populations that are necessary to sustain a larger movement or political voice when it comes to their mobilization around a particular social justice issue. As discussed earlier, while the Asian American community is growing in all major regions of the United States, there exist geographic variations among the diverse Asian national origin groups.

Figure 3.3 provides a vivid example of the site dimension for the top nine Asian national origin groups (Asian Indian, Cambodian, Chinese, Filipino/a, Hmong, Japanese, Korean, Vietnamese, and Other Asian) in regard to the top five Asian ethnic group populations within the top twenty metropolitan areas according to the 2010 U.S. Census. The first thing that one notices is how spread out in various major cities throughout the continental United States the Asian ethnic groups are, and how their respective ethnic populations vary by these locations. Imagine these Asian ethnic communities in cities/nodes linked by online and smartphone social media networks in which critical information and dialogue on a policy or social issue affecting them are shared instantaneously in their respective ethnic languages during crowd- and organization-led Asian American connective action.

Local issues can rapidly evolve into national issues through social media networks within and among these Asian ethnic groups and/or the larger Asian American group. As discussed earlier, small to medium-size (ranging from 10,000 to 250,000) U.S. cities are where the fastest and most significant growth has taken place among these Asian national origin groups. These cities are central to the development of the transnational cities/nodes among the Asian national origin groups throughout the continental United States, which is distinctly different from their pre-1965 community settlement patterns in large gateway cities such as New York, Los Angeles, Seattle, and San Francisco (Lai 2011). Each of these cities could connect in ways that were more than just settlement patterns but provided a larger network of connected communities during Asian American connective action. The Peter Liang case study, in which demonstrations at a local Brooklyn, New York, event spurred similar demonstrations in thirty cities, many with significant Chinese American populations, illustrates this belief.

Since the 1970s, the Asian American community has taken on both global and local dimensions in the continental United States because of glob-

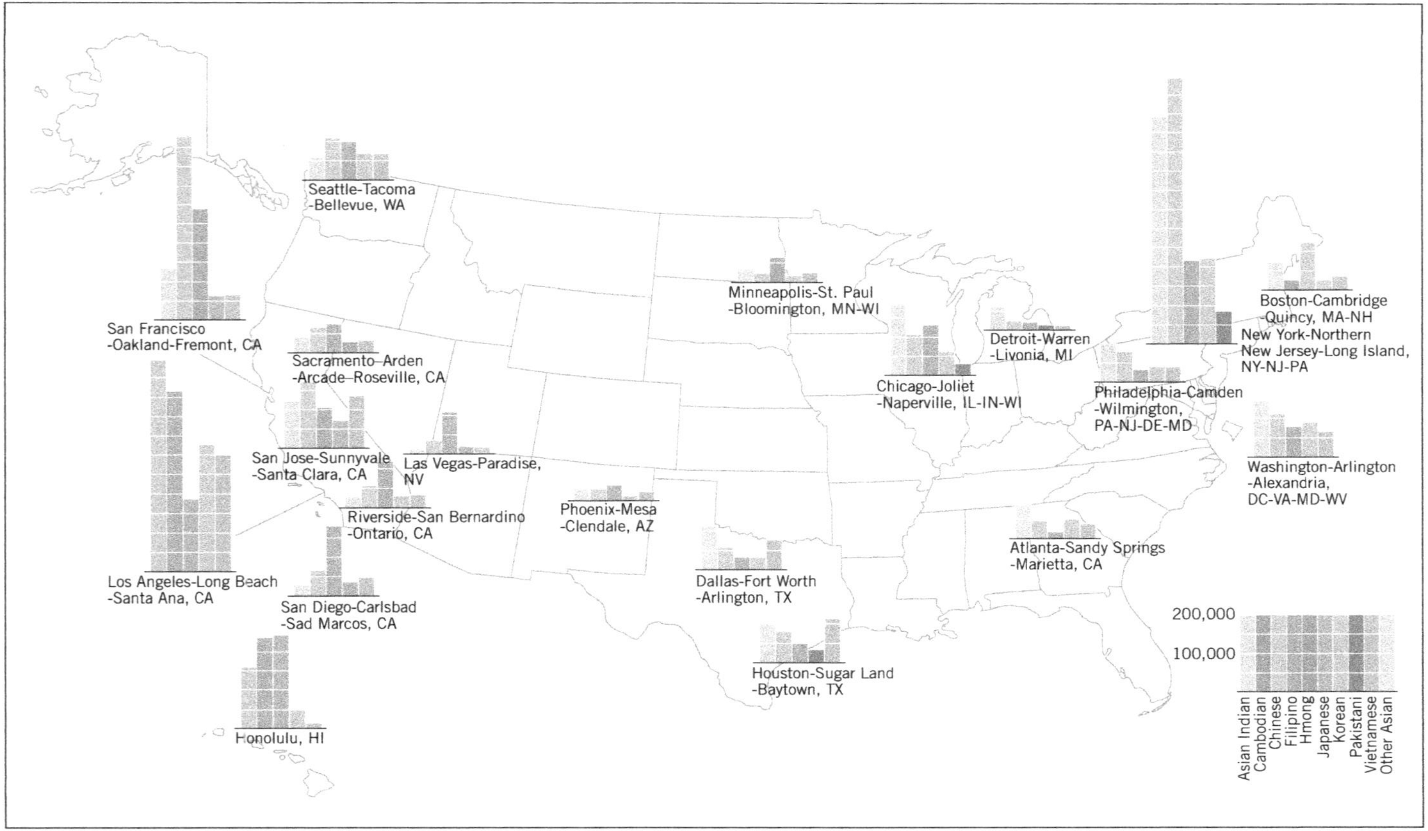

Figure 3.3 The Top Five Largest Asian Ethnic Group Populations in the Top Twenty Metropolitan Areas, 2010 (Source: U.S. Census Bureau, 2010 Census special tabulation.)

alization, transnationalism, and cosmopolitanism. In specific, the term *trans-nationalism* is defined as "the process by which immigrants forge and sustain multi-stranded social relations that link their societies of origin and settlement" (Basch, Schiller, and Blanc 1993, p. 1). The embodiment of this transnational dimension among Asian Americans can be seen in the rise of Asian American immigrant-influenced suburbs or ethnoburbs, which often contain plurality or majority Asian American populations. These suburbs are typically small to medium-size cities with populations ranging between 35,000 and 110,000 (Skop and Li 2005; Lai 2011). Some scholars have referred to this as both global and local, or "glocal," culture, which has in some ways shaped the myriad of political participations and racial/ethnic identities of the large Asian immigrant population that has taken on the "Trans-Pacific" commute, as people and capital flow back and forth throughout the Pacific Rim (Chang and Amam 2010).

Gravitational migration has been a central force creating these suburbs since 1965, as Asian immigrants have gravitated to specific suburbs throughout the continental United States due to various reasons ranging from emerging ethnic economies to strong public schools. Listings of home for sale that emphasize their communities' strong public schools are typically found in ethnic newspapers that cater to transnational readers in Seoul, Ho Chi Minh City, Mumbai, and Taipei, which further facilitates the gravitational migration. Class issues, as a result, have less effect on settlement patterns among recent Asian immigrants who reside in these suburbs. According to one study, more-affluent Asian immigrants choose to move directly to the suburbs as opposed to metropolitan areas due to their desire and ability to afford newer homes in safer neighborhoods with better public schools. Less-affluent Asian American immigrants choose to live in rental homes or apartments in the outer rings of these small to medium-size suburbs in order to have access to amenities such as award-winning public schools, religious institutions, ethnic economies, and ethnic language schools (Kwong 1996; Li 1998; Miller 2004).

One result of heavy Asian gravitational migration to specific suburbs has been the emergence of Asian American majority and plurality cities, a recent phenomenon that has provided an important critical mass for collective action. During the 1970s, only one Asian American majority area existed in the continental United States: Monterey Park, a small suburban city located in the San Gabriel Valley region of Los Angeles County that was labeled as the "first suburban Chinatown," with a predominantly Chinese American majority population—nearly 56 percent in 1990 (Fong 1994). Nearly twenty years later, based on the 2010 U.S. Census, over a dozen California cities contained Asian American majority populations (Lai 2011). Each is small to medium size, with total populations ranging from 30,000 to 110,000. Outside of California, the dramatic shifts are equally noticeable.

For example, in the suburbs of Northern Virginia, outside of Richmond, the Asian American population has doubled during the past decade, according to the 2010 U.S. Census.

Suburban areas represent the primary site of the current and future Asian American connective action theoretical framework. One scholar defines this network of cities as "global neighborhoods that expand beyond jurisdictional boundaries of the state comprising the homeland nation and each of its diaspora sites" (Laguerre 2010, p. xx). In many ways, these suburbs reflect demographic characteristics of the national Asian American community, which is the largest immigrant cohort in the United States as of 2009 with regard to percentage and currently has the largest foreign-born population in the nation at nearly 60 percent. Such an examination helps reveal the impact that globalization and Asian American dimensions of ethnicity, class, and nativity may have on the outcome of local and state-level policies during collective action. Given the diversity of viewpoints that globalization can bring, the political behaviors of Asian American immigrants in these suburbs may not always fit the ideologies or interests of the progressive, multiracial coalitions that have developed since the Civil Rights Movement of the 1960s, which have included Asian Americans. Because social media allows for all ideological viewpoints to be expressed, emerging identities are likely to be articulated across a broader range of political ideologies during connective action than has been witnessed during traditional forms of participation such as voting, as this book's case studies reveal.

Social media and smartphones may act as transmitters of information that is shared across the vast digital social networks of Asian-influenced cities/nodes. One scholar argues that these exist among Asian national origin groups that comprise the larger "cosmonation," defined as "global neighborhoods that expand beyond jurisdictional boundaries of the state comprising the homeland nation and each of its diaspora sites" (Laguerre 2010, p. xx). Asian American connective action is not bounded solely by the local context but may develop at one, both, or all of the three levels. This is particularly critical for a relatively small racial group like Asian Americans, as the ability to build coalitions beyond a local community with larger statewide and national communities may increase their political power and influence in the outcomes of public policies or social justice issues. As a result, local issues can quickly become statewide, national, and transnational as well due to the network of nodes that comprise the larger, interconnected Asian immigrant communities. Ethnic digital media (i.e., ethnic newspapers, satellite channels), which are local, national, and transnational, may play a critical role in transmitting community issues beyond city limits through their vast digital networks that link other city nodes, allowing for collective action on local issues in ways not seen before.

Case Study 1

The 2016 Trial of New York Police Department Officer
Peter Liang and the Connective Action Mobilization
by First-Generation Chinese Americans

If we didn't come out, today it's Peter Liang. Tomorrow it's
Peter Lee. After that it's Peter Chan. We've borne it long enough.

—JOHN CHAN, who founded a civil rights organization
   after the Liang incident

Chinese community in North America is always too quiet. Let us
speak up, protest, and donate for #PeterLiang #FreePeterLiang
#Justice4Liang.

—MEI ZHANG, February 21, 2016, via Twitter

"One Tragedy, Two Victims": Why and How
Chinese American Immigrants Mobilized

On the evening of November 20, 2014, a tragedy unfolded in the dark stairwells of the New York City Housing Authority's (NYCHA) Louis H. Pink Houses in Brooklyn. New York Police Department (NYPD) rookie officers Peter Liang and Shaun Landau were on a "vertical patrol," a controversial NYPD procedure of having a pair of officers patrolling public housing units from top to bottom, looking for any criminal activities. Akai Gurley and his girlfriend had entered the seventh-floor stairwell, a floor below Liang and Landau at the time. Liang, who is left-handed, took the lead, carrying a flashlight in his right hand and a 9mm Glock pistol in his left hand as the two officers descended to the next floor. Liang stated in his testimony that he was doing what the NYPD had taught him—that is, to open the door with his shoulder, with his gun drawn—as he descended toward the seventh-floor stairwell, which was pitch dark due to a broken light. Neither Liang nor Gurley could see each other. During the trial testimony, Liang stated he heard a "quick sound" to his left; he immediately turned, and his gun "just went off and my whole body tensed up" (Lartey 2016, par. 8).

The bullet ricocheted off the wall in the stairwell and then struck Gurley on the left side of his chest. Testimony indicated that Liang and Landau argued with each other as Gurley lay shot. Neither Liang nor Landau provided any emergency medical support and argued over who was going to call for an emergency ambulance (Nir 2016a). Gurley died several minutes later. It was later discovered, after Landau's testimony, that he did not feel confident to provide cardiopulmonary resuscitation because he felt that he had not been trained properly.

In the immediate aftermath of the tragic shooting death of Gurley, NYPD Police Commissioner Bill Bratton declared Gurley to be a "total innocent" and that the shooting was an accident (Wilson 2014). As the news spread, much justified anger and frustration over Gurley's death at the hands of a police officer took shape within the local and national African American community, coinciding with the larger Black Lives Matter movement protests facilitated by Black Twitter and connective action.

On February 10, 2015, a grand jury found there was enough evidence to warrant an indictment of Officer Liang for second-degree manslaughter and misconduct, making him the first NYPD officer in a decade to be indicted. The news spread rapidly among Chinese Americans in New York City through the Chinese social media networks facilitated by WeChat, the ubiquitous smartphone app used in China. Two hundred protesters, mostly Chinese Americans, immigrant and U.S.-born, who had never previously spoken or acted out in public on political issues and race relations in the United States, organized and marched peacefully in Brooklyn for Peter Liang and their quest for social justice. Among the protesters were working-class immigrants who decided to speak out against what they viewed as a racial injustice.[1]

For many of the Chinese Americans who supported Liang, the issue was whether he was a racial scapegoat and a victim of injustice. As of December 2014, there have been 179 NYPD-related deaths with only three cases resulting in indictments of NYPD officers; Liang's was the most recent case (Yee 2016). During this period, the first indictment was in 2000 and involved a group of three NYPD officers who shot Amadou Diallo forty-one times on his doorstep, thinking he was a rape suspect, after he tried to pull out his wallet from his back pocket. The indictment resulted in all three NYPD officers being acquitted (Yee 2016). The second indictment involved an undercover NYPD officer disguised as a postal worker, who shot Ousmane Zongo four times (two in his back) in a warehouse during an investigation into an illegal CD piracy outfit. The officer was convicted of negligent homicide but was found innocent of second-degree manslaughter, the same charge as Liang. It carried a maximum prison sentence of fifteen years; however, the officer served no jail time and was placed on five years of probation (Yee 2016). These incidents drew the ire of Liang supporters who felt that Liang was a racial scapegoat to atone for the wrongdoings of White police officers against African Americans.

On February 11, 2015, the city prosecutor charged Liang with second-degree murder, reckless endangerment, and two counts of official misconduct (Chung 2015). Liang pleaded not guilty to the charges. Liang's trial began on January 25, 2016, with both national and international media coverage. Liang was convicted on February 11, 2016, of official misconduct and second-degree manslaughter, which could have resulted in a maximum jail sentence of fifteen years (Nir 2016b). Brooklyn city council member Margaret Chin, the first Asian American elected to the seat, lauded the grand jury's conviction but asked for a more lenient sentence (Leonard 2016).

The high-profile trial of Peter Liang would leave an indelible mark on the larger Asian American community's progressive ideology amid the conservative immigrants who shared their concerns and mobilized in support of Liang through social media platforms. More than three thousand politically disenfranchised Chinese American immigrants who had never attended a political rally before in the United States protested in support of Liang at New York City Hall in March 2016, the month following the grand jury indictment (Shyong 2016). Many carried bilingual signs that read "One Tragedy, Two Victims" and "Equal Justice: No Scapegoats" while Black Lives Matter protesters held signs that read "Akai Gurley: Murdered by Peter Liang." In April 2016, over a thousand of mostly Chinese American protesters marched across the Brooklyn Bridge in support of Liang.

In addition to public protests, Chinese Americans mobilized support to bolster Liang's defense fund. For example, one woman gave a $1,000 check to support Liang's legal defense (Levitt 2016). Eddie Chu, the senior director of the Ling Sing Association in New York City,[2] stated that a petition had been signed by over five hundred people calling on Brooklyn State Supreme Court Justice Danny Chun, a Korean American who presided over the Liang trial, to reduce the grand jury's conviction with a lessened sentence of probation (Levitt 2016). For many Chinese American protesters, Liang's conviction was a symptom of a larger historical problem between White officers and Black suspects. As one anonymous Chinese protester poignantly wrote in a letter to a weekly independent newsletter entitled the *NYPD Confidential*:

> His case represented an opportunity for those jurors to assuage their conscience after multiple instances of unjust policing activities against black suspects. . . . And this jury decided that someone must be punished for all the police shootings of unarmed black men. This jury did not have the open-mindedness to weigh this case on its own merits but chose to make Peter Liang's conviction an opportunity for a national referendum on policing and race relations. Unfortu-

nately for Peter Liang and Asian Americans everywhere, the verdict that the jurors handed down is that Asians are an easy minority to scapegoat for the unresolved racial prejudices that continue to hamper our judicial system. (Levitt 2016, par. 13)

The belief embodied in the above letter is that White people have scapegoated Asian Americans to assuage the historical racial prejudices against African Americans in the U.S. judicial system. Many raised Liang's precedent of being the first NYPD officer to be convicted of a shooting in the line of duty in over a decade as a reason to raise the question of whether he would have been on trial if he were White. Others pointed to previous examples that contradict the jury indictment of Liang, such as the outcome in another high-profile NYPD case involving the choking death of Eric Garner. A witness's smartphone captured NYPD officer Daniel Pantaleo holding Garner from behind, despite Garner exclaiming several times, "I can't breathe." A Long Island grand jury failed to indict Pantaleo of any charges.

For a majority of the Chinese American protesters, the racial scapegoating belief resonated with their everyday experiences of perceived or real prejudice, whether as the model minority stereotype that paints them as a monolithic, successful racial group or as forever foreigners who are unconsciously viewed as non–U.S. citizens. This highlights the challenge that Asian

Figure 4.1

Figure 4.2

Figure 4.3

Figures 4.1–4.3 Activating the Nodes: The Chinese American Community's Support of Peter Liang Goes National. (*Previous page*) Peter Liang Supporters in Brooklyn, NY (Source: Pacific Press Media Production Corp./Alamy Stock Photo); (*top*) San Francisco, CA (Source: Alexander Zhu/Alamy Stock Photo); (*bottom*) and Los Angeles, CA (Source: Xinhua/Alamy Stock Photo)

Americans face in the U.S. racial hierarchy as they move from outsiders to insiders within American politics.

The national mobilization among the Chinese American protesters after the February 16, 2016, jury indictment of Liang appeared to have an impact on Brooklyn State Supreme Court Justice Danny Chun's decision to examine the jury's verdict of Liang being guilty of second-degree manslaughter, which carried a fifteen-year jail sentence. On April 19, 2016, Judge Chun decided to reduce the verdict to criminally negligent homicide that required no jail time but rather a five-year probation and eight hundred hours of community service. Judge Chun believed that there was no evidence to suggest that Liang was aware of Gurley's presence in the pitch-black stairwell: "Given the defendant's background and how remorseful he is, it would not be necessary to incarcerate the defendant to have a just sentence in this case" (Kim 2016, par. 5).

The trial of Peter Liang came to a close on August 15, 2016, after nearly two months of negotiations, when New York City officials announced the settlement of a wrongful death claim filed by Akai Gurley's family in the amount of $4.1 million. In addition, NYCHA, which manages the Pink Houses where the tragedy unfolded, agreed to contribute an additional $400,000 to a trust fund created for Akai Gurley's daughter, Akaila. Peter Liang also agreed to pay Akaila's mother, Kimberly Ballinger, an additional $25,000 (Rankin 2016).

The above photos capture Mainland Chinese American protesters in Brooklyn, the original protest site, San Francisco, and Los Angeles, which were among the thirty-eight U.S. and three Canadian cities that hosted national public demonstrations in support of Liang on February 20, 2016.[3] Connective action through online networks facilitated by social media platforms was central in the mobilization and organization of these protests. Facebook and email networks were utilized to connect Chinese Americans in cities across the continental United States; a digital flyer entitled "Support Peter Liang in 40 U.S. Cities" was circulated widely on Facebook and Twitter. The flyer contained a graphic of two columns of rectangles. Within each rectangle, a state, date, and WeChat name of the organizer was provided, allowing one to participate in WeChat forums for each of these geographic locations.

The significance of the connective action process for the political empowerment of Asian American immigrants, who often feel like outsiders in U.S. politics, was captured in a personal essay posted on a personal blog on February 19, 2016, entitled "Tomorrow They Will Come Out Like Ants," by Xujun Eberlin:

Ever since former NYPD policeman Peter Liang's guilty verdict last Thursday plans for rallies all over the nation have been developed through grassroots campaigns on WeChat. Watching the efforts in full swing on a cellphone is no less breathtaking than an action movie. All kinds of voices, rational and irrational, calm and angry, fair-minded and extreme, can be "heard" on the palm-size screen. What a mass movement! (Eberlin 2016, par. 3)

WeChat is one of the primary social media platforms used among the transnational Chinese American immigrant community due to the fact that China banned social media platforms such as Facebook and Twitter along with other smartphone messaging apps such as Line, which was created in Japan. Users can post videos and messages, link to articles and websites, and create groups. The WeChat community is large and vibrant but subjected to state monitoring, particularly those groups that involve sensitive discussions about politics (Rauhala 2016).

WeChat provides a critical alternative public space or counter-public to the larger public sphere for conservative Chinese American political culture and identities. This is different from other predominantly English-based social media platforms that Asian Americans use such as Facebook and Twitter. This is important for conservative, well-educated Chinese American immigrants who choose to contest public issues and voice their concerns over what they view is social justice, even if they are not ideologically aligned with other Asian American voices as well as other racial minorities.

During the 2016 Liang demonstrations, over a hundred chat groups throughout U.S. cities were created on WeChat. For example, the Los Angeles protest march organizer, Tian Wang, issued a statement on WeChat calling on Chinese people to participate in the February 20 national protests to show that although the incident happened in New York City, it had a national impact on Chinese Americans. In addition, Wang stated that the protests were not about only Chinese Americans but about everyone because the right to equality and a fair justice system is universal (Chen 2016). Finally, Chinese American activists created digital petitions, circulated through the social media networks, to obtain signatures in support of Liang. An example was two petitions created on February 12, 2016, on WE *the* PEOPLE, the White House's website for grassroots petitions, one of which garnered seventy-six thousand signatures in only two days. A minimum of one hundred thousand signatures per petition is needed to generate an official response by the White House (Chen and Xiaoqing 2016).

As previously discussed in Chapter 3 (Table 3.1), Asian American digital news media are also essential aspects of this global, transnational community in the United States and can serve as important sources of news and information during group connective action. Asian American digital news media were critical in providing a myriad of news reporting regarding the

Liang case and the community's responses, which would be shared among Chinese Americans through social media platforms across the many cities. For example, one Chinese ethnic newspaper story entitled "Helping Peter Liang, How and Why" was reposted over 100,000 and received more than 2,000 likes on Facebook (Rauhala 2016).

On the international level, as the digital activism among Chinese American immigrants in the United States was beginning to emerge, Chinese blogging websites such as Sina Weibo hosted forums and provided news about Liang, giving people the ability to follow the events in the Chinese American communities from as far away as Mainland China and a digital space to articulate their thoughts.

Emerging Divisions within the Asian American Community around Peter Liang

The Asian American community is socially, economically, and politically diverse, as illustrated during the Liang national protests. The photo in Figure 4.4 captures the divisions within the Asian American community around the national Black Lives Matter movement, reflecting a body politic emerging in neoliberal politics, where Asian Americans are often portrayed as a successful example of multiculturalism and racial assimilation vis-à-vis the model minority image, which in turn masks systemic racial inequalities (Liu 2018). Progressive Asian American activists and national organizations seek to resist this body politic in favor of fostering future multiracial coalitions. For example, more than fifty national Asian American and Pacific Islander groups signed an online open letter to call for justice and support for Akai Gurley (CAAAV 2014). The text of this open letter read:

> As Asian and Pacific Islander community leaders and organizations from across the country, we strongly oppose calls coming from some members of the Asian American community to drop charges against NYPD Officer Peter Liang for the death of Akai Gurley. This demand is misguided and utterly hurtful to Akai Gurley's family and to communities that have been subjected to discriminatory and often deadly policing practices across the country. We stand with Akai Gurley's family and all those who have lost loved ones to police violence. We firmly believe that Peter Liang must be held accountable for his actions. (CAAAV 2014, p. 1)

On Twitter, hashtags such as #APIs4BlackLives, which supported the Gurley family and the larger Black Lives Matter movement, were being

Figure 4.4 Cleavages in the Asian American Community. Approximately twenty Asian American protestors in front of the New York City courthouse demonstrating for justice for Akai Gurley. The Chinese sign reads, "Black people's lives are also important" as another way of saying "Black Lives Matter." (Source: Maura Ewing.)

tweeted and retweeted. Underlying their belief is that Asian Americans must understand and stand against anti-Black prejudices within both the Asian American and mainstream communities. In particular, the younger generation of Asian American activists, in addition to older ones who participated in the social movements of the 1960s and 1970s, believed that many of Liang's Chinese American supporters were misguided based on self-interest and threatened the possibility of any progressive multiracial coalition. Perhaps the most eloquent commentary in support of this perspective came from Annie Tan, the niece of Vincent Chin, an icon in the Asian American community for institutional racism and social justice in the 1980s to the present. Tan wrote an opinion editorial for the *Huffington Post* website:

> I understand people's instinct to stand by others in their community, but the anger and protests in support of Officer Peter Liang are misplaced. The only time I'd ever seen such a large rally of Asian Americans was in footage of the Vincent Chin case. At the height of Detroit's auto-industry crisis in 1982, Vincent, a Chinese American

man, was having his bachelor party, when a group of White laid-off autoworkers called Vincent a "motherfucker," mistaking Vincent as Japanese, and blaming Vincent for taking their jobs. Two autoworkers, Ronald Ebens and his stepson, Michael Nitz, chased Vincent down and beat him to death with a baseball bat. Unlike Peter Liang, the two men, Ebens and Nitz, walked away from the case. Ebens and Nitz never served time for killing my uncle Vincent. . . . I bring Vincent up because a freelance writer, Shirley Ng, referenced Vincent Monday in a *NY Post* op-ed comparing Officer Liang to Vincent. . . . She further stated Asian Americans were "united" behind Officer Liang. Her article was insulting and wrong. Vincent Chin has far more in common with Akai Gurley than with Peter Liang. Like Akai Gurley, my uncle Vincent was killed because he was a person of color. Like Akai Gurley's family, my family continues to mourn the death of a son. Ng does not speak for me, nor does she speak for the entire Asian American community. Injustice is injustice. (Tan 2016, pars. 3–16)

The heated rhetoric between the progressive camp led by African Americans and the conservative camp of Chinese Americans prevented them from seeing potential common ground. One commonality is that Liang, like Gurley, was an immigrant in the United States. Liang and Gurley ended up in New York City from Hong Kong and the U.S. Virgin Islands, respectively.

Another commonality is that African Americans and Asian Americans have previously been pitted against each other in a competitive and exploitative economic superstructure rather than seeing themselves as potential coalition partners for change. For example, in inner cities like Los Angeles, Korean American small-business owners have opened up stores in predominantly blighted, underserved African American communities to fill the void in food deserts as a result of the absence of chain grocery stores. This relationship bubbled up and boiled into interracial conflicts and scapegoating that culminated in the 1992 Los Angeles uprising, where nearly half of the $1 billion in damage due to fires and looting was suffered by Korean American businesses that were targeted by African American and Latinx looters. The African American perception was that Korean American businesses owners were disrespectful and discriminatory toward their patrons, which made them a target of their anger after the acquittal of the LAPD officers who had beaten Rodney King. The same parallels can be drawn with Liang, who is seen as the face of the state legal apparatus, and Gurley, the innocent victim. In the perspective of Korean Americans, the 1992 Los Angeles riots left an indelible mark on the collective psyche of the Korean American experience. Among the opinion editorials that were written on the meaning of the Liang case for Asian Americans, Korean American Jay Caspian Kang reflected this point poignantly in the *New York Times Magazine*:

> The Liang protests mark the most pivotal moment in the Asian American community since the Rodney King riots, when dozens of Korean-American businesses were burned to the ground. . . . This long history has erased any possible nuance Saturday's protests might have brought to our understanding of what happened to Liang. Which is tragic, because there is much ugly, essential nuance to be examined. (Kang 2016, par. 4)

The "long history" that Kang refers to above is the dual contradicting stereotypes discussed in Chapter 2, in which Asian Americans experience a sense of conditional citizenship due to being seen as the "other" or "outsider" with the forever foreigner stereotype and being celebrated as successful and equal with the model minority stereotype. The unequal outsider feeling is historically rooted in the early nineteenth-century experiences of Asian immigrants, who were legally classified by the U.S. Congress as aliens ineligible for naturalized U.S. citizenship; this would be federal law until the McCarran-Walter Act of 1952, which finally allowed Asian immigrants to have the right to naturalize.

Online Connective Action Findings

1. Analysis of Twitter Hashtags #PeterLiang, #FreePeterLiang, and #Justice4PeterLiang

Twitter is one of the most commonly used social media platforms in the United States. On it, users can share their thoughts and opinions on any issue through tweets that were, in the beginning, limited to 140 characters (currently, it is 280 characters) using a computer and/or mobile device such as a smartphone. On Twitter, tweets are primarily organized by hashtags that may go viral, or become a trend on the internet, with other users including the same hashtags in their respective tweets. While other forms of connective action were certainly occurring on other social media platforms at the time of the Peter Liang trial, specifically examining Twitter hashtags can provide a glimpse into those within the Asian American community who were sharing information and their opinions. For example, was it only Chinese American males who tweeted about Liang? Or was it a broader panethnic participation that included Asian American women?

To address the above questions, content analysis of the two most common hashtags used among Chinese Americans during the Peter Liang trial

(#PeterLiang and #FreePeterLiang) were coded for the following categories: race, ethnicity, gender, issue orientation, and date. While there were many months of tweets and retweets that followed the Peter Liang–Akai Gurley case, the time frame for the Twitter hashtags that were coded starts on February 11, 2015 (the date when Liang was indicted by a grand jury for second-degree manslaughter and official misconduct) and goes through April 19, 2016 (the date Judge Chun reduced the verdict to a criminally negligent homicide). This time frame was chosen because it best reflects the height of the connective action efforts for and against Liang within the Asian American community.

The total number of tweets that included #PeterLiang during this period were 3,990. Asian Americans accounted for the largest percentage at 39.1 percent (1,560 tweets), followed by African Americans at 25.6 percent (1,022 tweets), Not Determinable at 16.4 percent (654 tweets), White people at approximately 16.2 percent (648 tweets), Latinxs at approximately 2.5 percent (100 tweets), and Native Americans at 0.2 percent (6 tweets).

The above findings of Asian Americans using #PeterLiang on Twitter illustrate the crowd-led characteristics of Asian American connective action through Twitter as well as how Asian Americans felt compelled to share their personal action frames and opinions that would eventually lead them to mobilize politically in their own respective ways. African Americans also utilized crowd-led connective action as the Liang-Gurley incident related to the larger Black Lives Matter movement.

Table 4.1 shows the findings of #PeterLiang tweets for race and gender by issue stance from February 11, 2015, to April 19, 2016. Among the 1,560 Asian American tweets, females accounted for a majority with 54 percent (839 tweets) while males accounted for 46 percent (718 tweets). In contrast, among the 1,776 non-Asian tweets, males accounted for a majority at 56.6 percent (1,006 tweets) while females accounted for 43.3 percent (769 tweets).

For the issue stance variable, tweets were coded for the following categories: positive comments were coded as "For Peter Liang," negative comments were coded as "Against Peter Liang," and those comments that were retweeted news stories without comment were coded as "Neutral."

The findings for race and gender by issue stance illustrate that a majority of both Asian American males and females using #PeterLiang supported Liang. Thus, gender did not have any effect on the sample. As found in Table 4.1, a majority of these tweets were from Chinese Americans. Among Asian American males, 71.7 percent (515 tweets) were "For Peter Liang" compared to 12.5 percent (90 tweets) that were "Against Peter Liang" and 15.7 percent (113 tweets) that were "Neutral." Among Asian American females, 67.2 percent (564 tweets) were "For Peter Liang" compared to 19.5 percent (164 tweets)

TABLE 4.1 #PETERLIANG TWEETS FOR RACE AND GENDER BY ISSUE STANCE
(2/11/15 TO 4/19/16)

	For Peter Liang (Percent of Total)	Against Peter Liang (Percent of Total)	Neutral (Percent of Total)	Total
Asian American	1,078 (69.1)	256 (16.4)	226 (14.5)	1,560
Male	515 (71.7)	90 (12.5)	113 (15.7)	718
Female	564 (67.2)	164 (19.5)	111 (13.2)	839
Not Determinable	0 (0)	2 (66.7)	1 (33.3)	3
Non-Asian	74 (4.2)	857 (48.3)	845 (47.6)	1,776
Male	39 (3.9)	584 (58.1)	383 (38)	1,006
Female	35 (4.6)	273 (35.5)	461 (59.9)	769
Not Determinable	0 (0)	0 (0)	1 (100)	1
Not Determinable	15 (14)	40 (37.4)	52 (48.6)	107
Male	5 (13.5)	17 (45.9)	15 (40.5)	37
Female	4 (12.9)	6 (19.4)	21 (67.7)	31
Not Determinable	6 (15.4)	17 (43.6)	16 (41)	39
Organization/Media	57 (10.4)	188 (34.4)	302 (55.2)	547
Total	1,218 (30.5)	1,340 (33.5)	1,424 (35.7)	3,990

that were "Against Peter Liang" and 13.2 percent (111 tweets) that were "Neutral."

In contrast to Asian Americans, non-Asians generally either opposed Liang or were neutral in their tweets. Among the total 1,776 non-Asian tweets of #PeterLiang, 48.3 percent (857 tweets) were "Against Peter Liang" compared to 47.6 percent (845 tweets) that were "Neutral" and only 4.2 percent (74 tweets) that were "For Peter Liang." For non-Asian males, a majority of 58.1 percent (584 tweets) was "Against Peter Liang" compared with 38 percent (383 tweets) that were "Neutral" and only 3.9 percent (39 tweets) that were "For Peter Liang." The findings for non-Asian females show that a majority at 59.9 percent (461 tweets) were "Neutral" while 35.5 percent were "Against Peter Liang" and only 4.6 percent (35 tweets) were "For Peter Liang."

As one would expect, given that the Liang trial was in New York City, many local news media outlet reporters as well as community organizations were tweeting using #PeterLiang on a daily basis. An overwhelming majority of the media outlet reporter tweets provided factual information about the Liang trial, as seen in the 55.2 percent (302 tweets) that were "Neutral." Tweets by African American organizations were coded as "Organization/

Media" and showed 34.4 percent (188 tweets) were "Against Peter Liang" and 10.4 percent (57 tweets) were "For Peter Liang."

Among the 280 total tweets by Chinese Americans that included #Free-PeterLiang from February 11, 2015, to April 19, 2016, those whose location was "Not Determinable" made up the largest group with 167 tweets for 59.6 percent. Among those whose location was determinable, thirteen U.S. states and Canada were represented. Among the thirteen U.S. states, New York had the most with 42 tweets for 15 percent, followed by California (16 tweets for 5.7 percent), Texas (6 tweets for 2.1 percent), Massachusetts (5 tweets for 1.8 percent), New Jersey (5 tweets for 1.8 percent), North Carolina (4 tweets for 1.4 percent), Florida (3 tweets for 1.1 percent), Georgia (3 tweets for 1.1 percent), Pennsylvania (2 tweets for 0.7 percent), Washington (2 tweets for 0.7 percent), Arizona (1 tweet for 0.4 percent), Connecticut (1 tweet for 0.4 percent), and Illinois (1 tweet for 0.4 percent). Washington, DC, accounted for 4 tweets at 1.4 percent. Canada (Vancouver) was the sole country outside of the United States that was represented in the findings, with 11 tweets for 3.9 percent.

2. The Lack of Asian American Panethnic Support for Liang during the Trial

Since Twitter can represent a vehicle for personal action frames on contentious issues, it offers one opportunity to examine how those Asian Americans who took to Twitter viewed the Liang trial. The overall findings for the two Liang hashtags (#PeterLiang and #FreePeterLiang) raise the panethnic identity question as to whether non-Chinese ethnic groups viewed the Liang case as a racial case involving all Asian Americans or a Chinese case. While it is clear from the overall Peter Liang hashtag findings that an overwhelming percent of Chinese American males and females supported Liang, the findings also suggest that Asian American panethnicity among the Peter Liang tweets was not largely present.

A large number of Asian American progressives, including Chinese Americans, between the ages of eighteen and fifty who tweeted any of the three Peter Liang hashtags were against Liang. Fei Mok, a Chinese American female in California, tweeted on March 24, 2016, "This is B.S. Prosecutors will not seek prison sentence for #PeterLiang." Audrey Kuo, a Chinese American female in California, tweeted on April 13, 2016, "#PeterLiang chose to be there. He chose to become a police officer and be on the vertical sweep. He chose to draw his weapon." This perspective was also shared among non-Chinese American females. Joo-Hyun Kang, a Korean American female in New York, tweeted on April 13, 2016, "#PeterLiang should be held accountable for killing #AkaiGurley."

Asian Americans saw the Liang case as a racial wedge, as illustrated in the many tweets that continued to use #PeterLiang well after his trial's conclusion. For example, Aree Worawongwasu, a Chinese-Thai American female in New York, tweeted on April 12, 2017, "Selective outrage is unacceptable. While we demand justice for #DavidDao, let's also condemn the #PeterLiang supporters in our communities." David Dao was a Chinese American physician who was physically assaulted on a United Airlines flight for refusing to give up his seat; the incident caused an international uproar.

The above examples highlight one of the reasons why Asian American panethnicity was not strong among the Liang tweets: there is an emerging generational and ideological divide within the Asian American community that has been developing between U.S.-born progressives who have a link to the Civil Rights Movement and policies and, more recently, highly educated and affluent Asian immigrants who do not have any such connection to this period. Asian American progressives viewed the Liang case as a racial wedge and threat to multiracial coalitions with other minority groups such as African Americans and the Black Lives Matter movement.

Bridging the Racial Divide between First-Generation Chinese Americans and African Americans

One of the collateral effects of first-generation Chinese American connective action during the Liang trial was the racial divide it created with African American activists within the Black Lives Matter movement both in the public and on social media sites like Twitter. This was clearly evident when Black Twitter reacted to the April 19, 2016, decision by Justice Danny Chun to reduce Liang's sentence. For example, one poignant tweet captured Black frustrations and where Asian Americans fit within the U.S. racial hierarchy:

> White privilege—Kill a black man. Never see trial.
> Asian privilege—Kill a black man. Never see jail.

Efforts to mitigate this racial divide were taken on by both communities at the grassroots level in New York City. For example, on March 28, 2016, a forum entitled "Race Relations and Collaboration between Asian American and African American Communities after the Peter Liang Case" was cosponsored by the Asian American Business Development Center and One Hundred Black Men, Inc. The event included two-person panels with one Asian American and one African American speaker, such as "Different Community Reactions to the Case of Peter Liang: Two Perspectives" and "Exploring Common Issues Facing the Two Communities."

The primary message from these forums was that while the public images captured in the mainstream media during the Liang trial focused on the tensions between the first-generation Chinese American and African American protesters, misunderstanding, not ignorance, was at the root of the Peter Liang-Akai Gurley tragedy. During one panel, the late CUNY Professor Emeritus Peter Kwong gave a talk where he outlined the challenges with recent Chinese immigration into multiracial cities throughout the New York City boroughs:

> The current Chinese population is quite diverse. . . . Marginalized and invisible to most Americans, they often live and work inside of ethnic enclaves. Their interactions with Blacks are minimal. There are, however, racial conflicts between them. The Chinese often complain of being the victims of crime and racial attacks in schools and businesses located in Black neighborhoods. Blacks complain about the Chinese squeezing them out of schools, jobs, and business opportunities. These two groups rarely verbalize their issues in public. However, this situation is fast changing. As new immigrants begin to settle in, and as second generation working class Chinese search for job opportunities, they often look to public sectors such as the municipal and health care profession. In doing so, they come right into competition with African Americans who had made their inroads into those areas decades earlier. The Chinese believe that Blacks have unfairly used their seniority to block Chinese entry and promotion. These two groups also come into conflict competing for affordable housing in public housing projects. With the large influx of Chinese in some African American neighborhoods, the Chinese are now seen as "gentrifiers." . . . We need to be engaged with each other—most of all making the effort to understand each other. The Peter Liang case offers new ways in which we can work together, including demanding reforms of the New York City's grand jury system, making it more consistent, more transparent, and more just, particularly in the case of police killing civilians. (Kwong 2016, p. 88)

The overall picture that Professor Kwong's speech painted shows that differences and competition exist between the recent Chinese American immigrant working class and small-business entrepreneurs and the African American working class. Along the lines of Asian businesses in African American neighborhoods, the following March 26, 2016, tweet from the Twitter account of *Racial Justice News* captures these tensions: "As Black People we have supported Asian Businesses in our neighborhoods! No more. #BoycottAsianBiz BC [Because] #PeterLiang."

The above tweet reflects the historical tensions between Asian small-business entrepreneurs and African American patrons in the inner cities of metropolises such as South Central Los Angeles during the 1992 riots and the Baltimore during the 2015 riots, where Korean American merchants, in both instances, suffered the most damages. Such tensions can be mitigated only if both communities attempt to understand the commonalities between them. Examples of these similarities include the historical U.S. experiences of Chinese Americans and African Americans with regard to not being allowed to have citizenship at some point in their respective histories, anti-miscegenation laws that prohibited them from marrying White people, and segregated public housing and education institutions.

The challenge to these efforts at understanding similarities between the Chinese American and African American communities is that social media platforms can exacerbate the tensions by emphasizing group self-interest, zero-sum politics, and/or victimization by the other in the context of online echo chambers. The significance of this is the slippery slope that exists between social media usage and connective action.

Building any multiracial coalition requires a convergence of common interests and common ideologies among its members (Sonenshein 1994). The slogans "Two Victims, One Tragedy" and "Justice for All" were more than just two of the most common placards seen at Peter Liang rallies. These two slogans represented a framing of those activists who believed that both Peter Liang and Akai Gurley were victims of a racially oppressed system. Through these two narratives, common interests and ideology were articulated between first-generation Chinese Americans and African Americans during the Liang trail. On one hand, Peter Liang was a rookie Chinese American officer who was assigned by the NYPD to perform the racial-profiling procedure known as "vertical patrols." This procedure put Liang in a dangerous situation where a rookie should not be in the first place, given his lack of experience. On the other hand, Akai Gurley and his family were innocent victims as well. Gurley was not breaking any laws and was in the building where he lived. His death was yet another symbol of the racially oppressive strategies of the city police departments. By recognizing this perspective, Chinese American protesters were attempting to reframe the shooting and killing by Liang both as accidental and as racial scapegoating, two separate and distinct points. Racial scapegoating is an issue that African Americans understand and share common interests and ideology around.

Two reasons help to explain why efforts to create a coalition did not come to fruition between the Liang supporters and the Black Lives Matter activists during the Liang trial. First, there was the presence of a faction within the Chinese American Liang supporters who held signs at the public protests that declared perspectives such as "Two Victims, One Tragedy" and

"No Selective Justice." This vocal segment repeated this perspective on We-Chat forums as they mobilized. Second, the mainstream media heightened the tensions between Peter Liang supporters and the Black Lives Matter protesters because the optics of two minority groups pitted against each other fueled sensationalism. Progressive factions within the Asian American community felt compelled to challenge these optics with the formation of #Asians4BlackLives to protest side by side with the larger Black Lives Matter protesters during the Liang trial. Historically, this was the case during the 1992 Los Angeles uprising as the media sensationalized the growing tensions and violence between Korean American small-business owners and African American patrons in historically African American inner cities (Chang 1993).

One legitimate critique of Liang supporters' "Two Victims, One Tragedy" argument is that it denies that Liang had any culpability in Akai Gurley's death. The only indisputable fact is that Gurley was the victim of Liang's accidental shooting. Many Black Lives Matter and Akai Gurley supporters have argued that Liang is not a victim because he was criminally negligent, as supported by the fact that he spent several minutes talking with his union representative after shooting Gurley rather than trying to administer CPR or call in for medical help. As Seattle-based Black Lives Matter activist Ijeoma Oluo eloquently stated:

> The protest against Liang's conviction seems to be aware that there is a problem, but completely misguided about what the problem actually is. I think too that this is an opportunity to see that perhaps the Asian American community, in contrast to the model minority myth, has real grievances with White Supremacy that don't get much light. . . . I think a lot of non-Asian people are scratching their heads trying to figure out what it's about. But I think the fact that we don't know has a lot to do with how little the black and Asian communities mix. . . . And I think that it's right to recognize the disparity—that one of the very few convictions would be of an Asian American man when the vast majority of White perpetrators go free—but I don't think the solution is that everybody gets to murder brown and black people without consequence. I worry too that this will feed into the narrative that the Asian American community is basically a part of White Supremacy, when this same troubled thinking is found everywhere. (Oluo 2016)

The effect of the Chinese American protesters supporting Liang and claiming he was a victim like Gurley is denying justice for Gurley and his family. Many of those in the Asian American community who supported

Akai Gurley believed that the Liang supporters should focus their attention on the NYPD and why Liang was being tried, unlike past White officers who had killed unarmed Black citizens. In effect, the efforts of Asian Americans to support Liang hampered any efforts at coalition building between African Americans and Asian Americans, two racial minorities who have experienced historical and contemporary forms of racism. Progressive Chinese American activist Kat Yang-Stevens wrote in her powerful essay "Reframing the Conversation":

> Support for Liang creates a highly visible spectacle that does more to further harm Black people—and our chances of organizing in solidarity with Black people—than it does to highlight the ways that Asian Americans continue to experience racism, oppression, and domination under white supremacy. . . . Simply put, Asian Americans frustrated with racism should invest energy into supporting Black and indigenous struggles not institutions of white power. (Yang-Stevens 2016, pars. 38 and 40)

If both sides are to move forward in the future, the issues at the heart of incidents such as the Peter Liang protests must be first addressed and understood. On one side, Asian Americans historically felt they have been scapegoats to mask and serve as a racial wedge against other minority racial groups to maintain systemic racism in the United States (as seen with the model minority stereotype). The Peter Liang trial was an example of this belief given that Liang was one of the few NYPD officers convicted for the killing of an innocent civilian while on duty. On the other side, African Americans historically viewed Chinese Americans as benefactors and perpetrators of White privilege given their relatively higher socioeconomic backgrounds. An example of the latter point is what Asian American progressives criticize the #JusticeforPeterLiang protesters for as enablers of police brutality, and thus White supremacy, by failing to understand the macro issue that those in the Black Lives Matter movement are taking on through their protests (Yin 2016). Ultimately, this divide is bridgeable, as both groups want police reform, justice, fairness, and equality. This interracial challenge represents the unique status of Asian Americans within the traditional U.S. racial hierarchy as well the emerging and distinct political identities materializing within this diverse community.

Case Study 2

The Asian American Community's Online and Offline Affirmative Action Battle over the 2012 California Senate Constitutional Amendment 5 Bill

The state must play a more active role to ensure equal access to higher education. After having reformed K-12 education funding last year to focus on low-income and English language learning students, it is time for a thoughtful debate about what can be done to ensure that all hardworking students have access to a state university education. This means taking a hard look at recruitment and retention activities to ensure that our campuses provide opportunities for students from underrepresented communities, as is the common practice in our nation's elite private colleges.

—CALIFORNIA STATE ASSEMBLY MEMBER PHIL TING'S
  STATEMENT ON SCA 5

Dear Congressman Maienschein: I am eight years old. I am in second grade. I like school a lot and I work hard. I want to be able to go to college in California when I grow up. Please help stop SCA-5. I don't think it's fair if I can't go to college in California just because I am Asian American.

—ANONYMOUS LETTER EMAILED TO CALIFORNIA CONGRESSMAN
  BRIAN MAIENSCHEIN

Asian Americans and the Racial Politics of Higher Education Admissions

On December 3, 2012, California State Senator Edward Hernandez introduced the California Senate Constitutional Amendment (SCA) 5 bill, which would allow California voters to determine if they should or should not eliminate the controversial 1996 Proposition 209, which passed with 55 percent of the statewide vote during Republican California Governor Pete Wilson's administration and specifically banned the use of race, sex, color, ethnicity, or nationality in the recruitment, admissions, and retention programs at the University of California and the California State University systems. SCA 5 was an attempt by Senator Hernandez and his California Democratic Party coalition to wipe away the long-standing law, which was a major sore spot in the declining admissions of the state's racial minority students, especially African Americans and Latinxs.

Proposition 209 had a negative impact on the number of African American and Latinx first-year students admitted to the University of California system. For example, at the University of California at Berkeley, Latinx and African American first-year admissions decreased by 50 percent immediately after Proposition 209 went into effect in the fall of 1998. In 2019, African American and Latinx students were 3 percent and 25 percent, respectively, of the first-year class at the University of California at Berkeley despite the fact that African American and Latinx students accounted for 4 percent and 45 percent, respectively, of California high school seniors who met University of California eligibility requirements. In comparison, Asian Americans and White people accounted for 42 percent and 23 percent, respectively, of first-year students at the University of California at Berkeley in 2019. The same year, in the entire University of California system, Asian Americans accounted for the largest racial group of first-year students at 30 percent, followed by White people at 20 percent, Latinxs at 16 percent, and African Americans at 3 percent (Koseff 2020).

While racial diversity among incoming first-year college students in the entire University of California system has been relatively stymied since Proposition 209, California has become a majority minority state with the largest minority population in the United States; the largest racial group is Latinxs at 39 percent followed by White people at 34 percent, Asian Americans at 15 percent (the largest of any state), African Americans at 7 percent, multiracial (two or more races) at 4 percent, and American Indians at 2 percent. Given this opposite trend, is this racial gap in admissions feasible and sustainable for the future of the nation's most racially diverse state, and can Asian Americans argue that they are being discriminated given their population size and percentage representations on the University of California campuses? These questions were posed, and their answers represented the underlying perspective that has fueled the progressive coalition in the California state legislature to reintroduce race through SCA 5 as one of hundreds of variables that go into considering higher education admissions.

The Asian American Divide on Affirmative Action

Perhaps no other policy issue has divided the Asian American community more than affirmative action, which has historically been a source of contention among those Asian Americans nationally, not only in California, citing data that show a racial bias in admissions against Asian American students with perfect SAT scores and well over 4.0 grade point averages at the elite universities throughout the Ivy League. One the most influential studies on this topic is by Thomas J. Espenshade and Alexandria Walton Radford in their book *No Longer Separate, Not Yet Equal: Race and Class in Elite College Admission and Campus Life*. The study specifically examined compiled data of SAT scores and grade point averages of applicants to certain elite private universities across admitted racial groups. The authors found that compared to a White peer and an African American peer, an Asian American student hypothetically had to score an additional 140 points and 450 points, respectively, on the SAT to obtain admission probability (Espenshade and Radford 2015). Critics of the study point out that while this data is comprehensive, the findings represent only data from select private universities and are not reflective of all national private universities as well as public universities. In particular, the study's data overvalues race while deemphasizing hundreds of other holistic criteria used by private and public universities in the admissions process. Nevertheless, the Espenshade and Radford study's findings have been cited often in various anti–affirmative action lawsuits.

The narrative of the disadvantaged Asian American applicant continues to be fostered both within and outside of the Asian American community. For example, in a 2016 book by Greg Jay Kaplan entitled *Earning Admission: Real Strategies for Getting into Highly Selected Colleges*, he argues that students should decline to state their racial background if they identify with a group that is overrepresented at that particular university, even if their surname suggests an affiliation (Kaplan 2016). The *Boston Globe* ran a 2015 story in which a professional college counselor was interviewed and stated that he regularly advised his Asian American clients to "appear less Asian when they apply" (English 2015, par. 2).

Despite this public perception that affirmative action policies harm Asian American students, a 2014 analysis of the Field Poll data of California's Asian American registered voters found that 69 percent favored affirmative action programs in higher education, compared to 61 percent in 1996 (Ramakrishnan and Lee 2014). At the national level, a 2014 survey found that 69 percent of sampled Asian American voters were in favor of affirmative action programs in higher education (APIAVote and Asian Americans Advancing Justice 2014). Asian Americans have also joined the recent legal fray surrounding affirmative action policies in higher education institutions, most notably a recent federal lawsuit against Harvard University for discriminatory practices against Asian American applicants, which ended on October 1, 2019, with the federal judge ruling in favor of Harvard.[1]

California's First-Generation Chinese Americans Recoil and Lash Out at SCA 5

Word about SCA 5 began to spread quickly, first among the social media networks of the Chinese American immigrant communities in the San Francisco Bay Area and Southern California. Social media platforms such as WeChat and Facebook and personal email networks were primarily used among first-generation Chinese Americans to voice their concerns and became very effective platforms for sharing and spreading information that culminated in both local and statewide mobilization efforts against SCA 5.

Two critical factors, among several, underlying the concerns among affluent, highly educated, racially isolated Chinese American immigrants were an exam-focused culture and systems of selective college admissions in China (Garces and Poon 2018). Thus, a perception that many Chinese American immigrants transplant with them as they settle in the United States is the belief of meritocracy as a fundamental rule that they had to overcome personally to reach their current status despite other ethno-racial prejudices that they may have experienced. This is why affirmative action reflects a difficult policy for many highly educated Chinese immigrants to embrace.

The Chinese American immigrant communities in the San Francisco Bay Area and in Southern California were able to mobilize against SCA 5 in three effective ways: one, taking the individual voices of dissent and parlaying them into collective online affinity groups that would disseminate information and protests around SCA 5; two, establishing an effective online campaign that controlled the narrative that portrayed SCA 5 as racially discriminatory against Asian Americans by even quoting civil rights leader Dr. Martin Luther King Jr., which in turn facilitated group resentment against the policy that would lead to group mobilization; and three, developing a coordinated outreach and political action campaign primarily through WeChat forums and email networks with a focus on public protests and targeting Asian American elected officials in the California State Senate and Assembly, where the legislative debate on SCA 5 would take place.

1. Creating Online Groups among the Anti-SCA 5 Protesters

Previous studies on connective action among online groups illustrate the importance of consolidating the diffused voices of communities of shared interests on the internet into organized and self-sustaining political power (Ito et al. 2015). The official website, Say No to SCA 5, was created by the online group Extremely Concerned Californians to serve as such an online organization to disseminate information and to mobilize against SCA 5. In addition to this website, a Say No to SCA 5 Facebook page was created that received 184 likes during the time it was available. On its Facebook front page, a link was provided to an online petition that the affinity group created on Change.org entitled "Vote No to SCA 5!" The petition was addressed to the California State Assembly members and framed the issue against SCA 5 thus: "This will unfairly roll back the clock to discriminate a student simply on her/his race" (Extremely Concerned Californians 2014, par. 3). According to the "Say No to SCA 5!" Change.org petition, 116,332 online signatures were recorded along with the "Victory" icon that showed that the petition was successful in helping to get SCA 5 tabled in the California State Assembly.

Another online group in the San Francisco Bay Area that played a pertinent role in defeating SCA 5 was United Asian Americans for Activism (UAAFA), which was originally created in 2013 by a group of Chinese Americans to protest a controversial skit on the *Jimmy Kimmel Live* show that asked this question to a group of children: "How do we deal with America's $1.3 trillion debt to China?" It was intended to be humorous but resulted in the controversial response by a five year old to "shoot cannons all the way over and kill everyone in China" (Duke 2013). In response to the incident, UAAFA created a website as well as a Facebook page. While it boasts no formal members, it has seven members on a board of directors. Chris Zhang, one of the founders of UAAFA, stated, "We needed another issue to connect the Chinese and Asian American community to community activism. I first heard about SCA 5 through an online Chinese discussion board when an anonymous poster stated that the bill would result in discrimination against Chinese American students. It was not only then that I finally joined WeChat because of how many of my Chinese American friends were using it. Now I can't live without it."[2]

Online groups such as Say No to SCA 5 and UAAFA are necessary in consolidating diffuse Chinese American voices into one self-sustaining voice with the focus of defeating SCA 5. Members primarily received information through social media websites such as the "Say No to SCA 5" Facebook page during the critical stages of statewide mobilization coordination efforts. Smartphone applications such as WeChat were instrumental in rapidly sharing informational updates on protesters and links to articles to Say No to SCA 5, and for recruiting.

Finally, a traditional Bay Area organization, Silicon Valley Chinese Association (SVCA), utilized what was described in Chapter 3 (Figure 3.1) as organization-led connective action to effectively mobilize and frame the issue of SCA 5 through online efforts that culminated in public forums against SCA 5, such as a December 10, 2017, forum that featured Edward Blum, the key conservative leader who had linked up with Chinese American parents in a discrimination lawsuit against Harvard University. According to Jason Xu, a member of SVCA, his personal opinion of why SVCA stood against SCA 5 was the following:

> First of all, Asian parents are known to push their kids to do well in schools, seeing that as a way to earn a decent living. Therefore, Asians don't want the University of California system to put a cap on Asian admissions. Second, a majority of recent immigrants from China all have U.S. graduate degrees, so to them, equal access to higher education is vital to them. Third, doing well in school go some immigrants to escape from Mainland China where they may not have the same opportunities as in the United States.[3]

Given such concerns with SCA 5, Chinese American organizations' battle against it would shift to creating the personal and organizational action frameworks to shape online perceptions of SCA 5. The next section will address how this was done effectively through crowd- and organization-led connective action.

2. Creating an Effective Online Perception of Racial Discrimination

Numerous videos were created and uploaded on YouTube to establish the perception that there would be racial discrimination if SCA 5 were to pass. For example, an affinity group named No2SCA5 created and uploaded a YouTube video entitled "Say No to SCA 5" that was linked to their Facebook website. The video opens with the voice of Dr. Martin Luther King Jr. and his famous "I Have a Dream" speech, with a map of Washington, DC, then an image of the San Francisco Golden Gate Bridge, followed by an aerial image of the University of California at Berkeley's Sather Tower. The video then goes specifically into text that explains Proposition 209 with the following words: "The State shall not discriminate, or grant preferential treatment to, any individual or group." All of the words are in white with the exception of "shall not discriminate," which is in red. An image of the California State Capitol is followed by the words "Say No to SCA 5." The video then shows an SCA 5 activist at a public protest declaring, "Asian Americans are not silent, and we are going to stand up and have our voices heard!" The words "Act Now!!!" follow, with a screen shot of the organization's Change.org petition, and ending with the caption "No on Skin Color Act 5" below the organization's website URL.

The above example illustrates how Asian American protesters against SCA 5 were extremely effective in coordinating a broad-based movement against affirmative action policy. According to Paul Fong, a former California assemblyman (D, District 28), who chaired the California Asian Pacific Islander Legislative Caucus at the time SCA 5 was being debated, stated, "The Chinese opponents of SCA 5 were so effective in framing the narrative around SCA 5 that its proponents, including myself, in the State Legislature, could do thing to change this perception once it got out."[4] The Chinese opponents of SCA 5's effective narrative of linking Dr. Martin Luther King Jr.'s color-blind appeal with the group's rearticulation of SCA as meaning "Skin Color Act" instead of "Senate Constitutional Amendment" is a sophisticated strategy that appealed to preexisting Asian American fears about racial discrimination. In addition, the "Skin Color Act" gave many of its opponents in the Chinese American community a meme that they could rally diffuse voices around into a consolidated interest that was sustainable and organized.

3. Developing a Coordinated Outreach and Political Action Campaign through Online and Smartphone Discussion Group Applications

As was the case during the coordination of national protests in forty-one U.S. and Canadian cities in support of Peter Liang, first-generation Chinese American protesters against SCA 5 exclusively used WeChat to perform outreach and coordinate political action in expedient and effective ways with regard to public forums and contacting Asian American state elected officials. Two California examples of connective action that were inextricably linked in the form of creating public forums and protests on SCA 5 took place in Cupertino and Monterey Park, located in the San Francisco Bay Area and Los Angeles County, respectively. Both of these two suburbs witnessed both demographic and political shifts during different decades (Monterey Park in the 1980s and Cupertino in the 1990s), in which both became Asian American majority cities with significantly large immigrant Chinese American populations (Lai 2011). Thus, it is not surprising to see both suburbs as the two primary local sites that were activated during the connective action of immigrant Chinese Americans during the anti-SCA 5 protests.

The first high-profile public gathering by first-generation Chinese Americans against SCA 5 took place in Cupertino (California) City Hall during the afternoon of March 2, 2014. The primary sponsor of the town hall was the Bay Area chapter of the nonpartisan organization Asian Pacific Islander American in Public Affairs Association (APIAPAA), which coordinated a balanced discussion of SCA 5 by inviting two proponents (California State Assemblyman Bob Huff and President of Community Advocates David Lehrer) and two opponents (UC Berkeley Professor Ling Chi

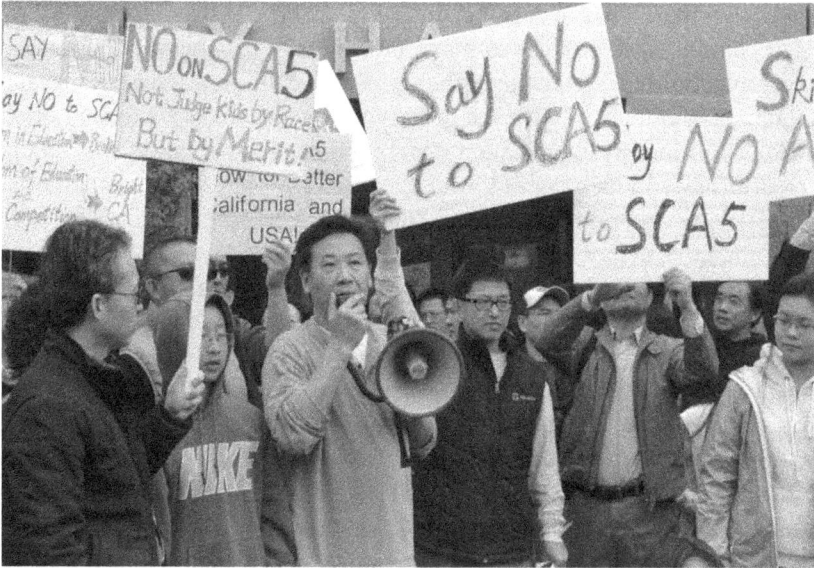

Figure 5.1 Anti-SCA 5 Protest Takes Place Outside of Cupertino City Hall. Chinese Americans voice their opposition to SCA 5 to Cupertino city leaders on March 17, 2014. The same day, the California State Legislature announced that it would table SCA 5 indefinitely. (Source: Kasey Fang, *Harker Aquila*.)

Wang and former Director of Chinese for Affirmative Action Henry Der) of the controversial bill. The panel's format was intentionally designed to be as fair and balanced as possible. Hundreds of Chinese Americans of all ages, in addition to other Asian Americans, packed the Cupertino City Hall building to voice their concerns with SCA 5. According to Chris Zhang, "We packed the City Hall building. While we hoped to have a balanced and fair discussion on SCA 5, it did not happen as many of the audience members would applaud only the opponent speakers and openly disagreed with the proponent speakers. I think we could have moderated the event better to prevent such reactions during the panel."[5]

As the debate around SCA 5 continued in the state capitol, Chinese American activists in the majority Asian suburb of Cupertino began their final push to let their voice be heard in Sacramento. Once again, the social media platform WeChat would be instrumental during their mobilization efforts. Approximately two weeks after the March 2, 2014, town hall on SCA 5 in Cupertino, a public hearing was coordinated by a coalition of Chinese Americans and Asian Indians on March 17, 2014, in the Cupertino City Hall chambers. More than three hundred protesters showed up.

Former Cupertino Mayor Gilbert Wong had the difficult task of presiding over the public hearing while trying to limit the growing list of speakers to three minutes on the dais. According to Wong, "As I walked to the City Hall chambers, there were so many protesters everywhere. . . . I became more and more a target of them [the anti-SCA 5 coalition] since I didn't take a public position on it."[6] The list of sixty-nine scheduled speakers included various community organization leaders and members such as Chris Zhang (an attorney and member of UAAFA), Alex Li (a high school sophomore), and Richard Dai (member of Fair Education Alliance) as well as the field representative of local California Congressman Ro Khanna (D) from California Congressional District 17, the only Asian American majority district in the continental United States. All of the speakers spoke of their respective concerns about how SCA 5 would negatively affect the University of California college admissions of Asian American students. Two minutes into the meeting, Wong told the audience that about an hour earlier SCA 5's primary author, California State Senator Edward Hernandez, had requested that California Senate Assembly Speaker John A. Perez send SCA 5 back to the State Senate without having the State Assembly vote on it, effectively tabling the bill. After the bombshell announcement sunk in, applause erupted among the crowd of anxious protesters. A small political victory was achieved by arguably a statewide group of political outsiders to the California State Legislature, consisting of immigrant activists mostly located in Cupertino and Monterey Park, and primarily organized through social media networks. For many of these protesters, it was their first entry into civic affairs.

The Cupertino public forum was emblematic of the most vociferous and active segment of the first-generation Chinese American community's reaction to the larger issue of affirmative action in that it is primarily guided by self-interest and intolerance of opposing views. This is not to say that all first-generation Chinese American activists who publicly spoke out against SCA 5 were guided by self-interest. As Chris Zhang, who attended the Cupertino public forum and was against SCA 5, pointed out, "I believe in the need to give people with disadvantages also some merit. This is where I differ from other Chinese Americans who only look at test scores and GPA. The process needs to be holistic. You have wealthier African Americans in Silicon Valley compared to poor Southeast Asians in Oakland. I consider myself a moderate. I see arguments on the other side."[7]

Social Media Influencers, Cyberbullying, and the Echo Chamber Effect

Social media presents a double-edged sword when it comes to its ability to connect individuals around contentious issues. The Chinese American SCA

5 opponents were passionate about their opinions and perspectives on this State Senate amendment, and social media platforms like WeChat forums, Twitter, and Facebook were an outlet for them to share their perceptions with each other in their own language and to facilitate national political action. However, at the same time, it was clear that the Chinese American individuals who were doing the influencing in the various WeChat forums were also using the social media platforms to subject individuals, particularly those who disagreed with them, to possible personal attacks with a few taps on the screen. This form of cyberbullying was definitely present during the SCA 5 connective action process. According to OiYan Poon, an education professor at the University of Illinois at Chicago, "SCA 5 was the rocket fuel and WeChat was the pipeline. It really set people off" (Pomfret 2017, par. 9).

Outspoken Asian American activists who went online to challenge the first-generation Chinese American opposition could be subjected to various amounts of cyberbullying in the form of personal attacks against them. For example, Diane Wong, a university professor and activist who was outspokenly in favor of SCA 5, indicated that she was subjected to gender-based attacks, the spreading of false information about her background, and the sharing of personal contact information for others to attack her. According to Wong, "A number of them targeted and doxxed me on their Reddit threads by posting my personal information to the public."[8]

At the heart of this issue is whether social media platforms will be used during Asian American connective action as a way of amplifying a consensus around an issue and/or as a platform for mob mentality against those who disagree. For those mostly immigrant Chinese Americans and other Asian American protesters against SCA 5, social media networks amplified extreme views by creating digital echo chambers where participants' views went unchallenged, as they viewed only content that reinforced their perspective on the issue. This belief was most evident on the hundreds of WeChat forums that were created to discuss and distribute information against SCA 5. Many of the expressed beliefs focused on a presumed meritocracy that many Chinese immigrants experienced firsthand where test scores were the most important way of determining what one's place society would be, from the type of university one could attend to one's occupation.

A critical issue of social media lay not with the individuals' perspectives based on their experiences but with the echo chamber effect on social media platforms such as WeChat where those who either completely disagreed with the protesters' views or took on a moderate stance on SCA 5 were weeded out or attacked. On WeChat, any member can create a forum and invite only those within their personal circles to join the discussion—unlike Twitter, for example, which can be viewed and commented on by any member. The reason for this restriction is because China heavily monitors the discussions and the design of WeChat to localize, not nationalize, any controversial discussions that are critical of the government. Public figures and anonymous posters who disagreed with the anti-SCA 5 protesters' views on user forums often found themselves banned and attacked on these WeChat forums. As a result, a digital echo chamber of extreme views on affirmative action could emerge among the anti-SCA posters on WeChat without any balanced, open discussions in these forums, as the only perspectives that were highly critical of SCA 5 as a threat to Chinese Americans were discussed.

The potential power of Asian American connective action lies in its ability to link communities or nodes together around group interest. On March 7, 2014, in the heavily transnational Asian suburbs of San Gabriel Valley, located outside of Los Angeles County, Chinese American activists organized their own public forum/rally against SCA 5. Similar to the Cupertino public forum/rally, the San Gabriel Valley forum featured approximately eleven Asian American and non-Asian local and state elected officials (including State Senator Ed Hernandez, D-West Covina, who sponsored SCA 5) from San Gabriel, Monterey Park, San Marino, Claremont, and Walnut, all majority Asian American suburbs located in San Gabriel Valley (Vuong 2014). Also, similar to Cupertino, the event's Chinese American organizers and attendees utilized WeChat to mobilize turnout.

Another similarity that the San Gabriel Valley forum shared with the Cupertino forum was that while it was also intended to be a balanced discussion about the pros and cons of the controversial state amendment, the focus quickly swung to the negative effects of SCA 5. Senator Hernandez stated at the forum "that every student that gets accepted either to the community colleges, Cal States, or the UCs will only be admitted by the merits of them as a quality student, whether it be SAT (score), extracurriculars, grades—all of this will be taken into account. . . . What makes a country and a society better is its diversity and how we interact" (Vuong 2014, pars. 8 and 18). This perspective was clearly in the minority as other speakers began to weigh in. Among them was Olivia Liao, president of the Joint Chinese University Alumni Association, who offered her insights on the issue at the forum: "[Legislators] feel like the Chinese-American community isn't paying attention to politics. We are concerned citizens. We need to stand up when things are not right; we need to be heard. We shouldn't have any [exceptions] related to race. After all, America is a free country" (Vuong 2014, par. 3). Other prominent Asian American elected officials and organization representatives that spoke at the event were U.S. Congresswoman Judy Chu (D-Pasadena) and State Assemblyman Ed Chau (D-Monterey Park), and members of the Chinese Consolidated Benevolent Association, the Southern California Council of Chinese Schools, and the Taiwan Benevolent Association.

Taking It to the State Capitol: Anti-SCA 5 Protesters Target Asian American California State Representatives

First-generation Chinese American activists also began to target the growing number of Asian American elected representatives in both houses in the state capitol through mass emails, letters, and calls to their capitol and district offices. Ironically, the elected representation of Asian Americans in the California State Legislature was linked to the gradual political incorporation of Asian American immigrants throughout the state (Lai and Geron 2006; Lai 2011). In 1991, no Asian American had either served on or been elected to the California State Assembly since 1981, when S. Floyd Mori was elected to his sixth term. In 2016, the Asian Pacific Islander Legislative Caucus (APILC) consisted of twelve members (ten in the State Assembly and two in the State Senate).[9] Many of them initially supported SCA 5, a fact that was not lost on many of SCA 5's loudest critics in the Chinese American community. One of these critics is S. B. Woo, who served as Delaware lieutenant governor from 1985 to 1989. Woo, who is president of the 80-20 Initiative, one of the main Chinese American organizations fighting SCA 5, voiced his displeasure with the support for SCA 5 among the APILC members: "Asian American politicians have been spoiled by new immigrant immaturity toward politics. . . . In Chinese culture, elected officials must be the great scholars and you respect them like parents. . . . That's a feudal way of thinking" (Huang 2014, pars. 15 and 17).

This tension among new immigrants and elected leaders within the Asian American community that Woo referenced would underlie the tug-of-war between the anti-SCA 5 Asian American constituents and their Asian American elected representatives in the State Legislature. Prominent Asian American state representatives at the time who supported SCA 5 were State Assembly members Paul Fong (D-District 28) and Ed Chau (D-District 49). Thus, when it came time to mobilize against SCA 5 through ethnic social media networks, these Asian American elected leaders, many of whom were elected from districts containing cities with significant Asian American populations, became logical targets for protest.

The statewide mobilization efforts would move the needle in favor of the anti-SCA 5 protesters in regard to how their California Asian American elected representatives would vote for it. For example, California Assembly Representative Ed Chau from District 49, which contains large portions of Asian American majority populated suburbs such as Monterey Park, Rosemead, El Monte, and Alhambra, issued a press release on February 25, 2014, that stated, "SCA 5 is a very important Legislative Measure that has the potential of having a significant impact on students pursuing higher education. . . . I am grateful to have received a great deal of information and suggestions from various sources in the last few days. . . . Based on the information . . . I have concluded that I cannot support SCA 5 in its current form" (Ed Chau Press Release 2014).

In the California State Senate, Carol Liu (D-Glendale), Leland Yee (D-San Francisco), and Ted Lieu (D-Redondo Beach) all voted in favor of supporting SCA 5 but later expressed reluctance for supporting it once they received mass emails and letters from the anti-SCA 5 protesters and constituents. Senator Lieu wrote a letter to Senator Ed Hernandez, author of SCA 5, to delay the bill "until he has an opportunity to meet with affected communities and to build a consensus" (Kleinfeld 2014, par. 4). Senator Yee stated, "I believe in affirmative action, and I believe it is an important tool to bring diversity. I don't want anyone to believe that SCA would negatively impact any community, and I asked [Hernandez and Perez] to have a discussion so that people are all on the same page" (Kleinfeld 2014, par. 8).

Political backlash began to surface over SCA 5 between members of the California Asian Pacific Islander Legislative Caucus and members of the California Latino Legislative Caucus and the California Legislative Black Caucus. For example, Senator Ted Lieu's turnaround on SCA 5 would result in him losing six fellow state representative endorsements (State Senators Ricardo Lara of Bell Gardens, Norma Torres of Pomona, and Holly Mitchell of Los Angeles; State Assembly members Lorena Gonzalez of San Diego, Anthony Rendon of Lakewood, and Jose Medina of Riverside) during his campaign as one of eighteen candidates seeking to win retired Henry Waxman's congressional district (Merl 2014). The move was believed to be political payback for Lieu by several members of the Latinx and Black caucuses. In an interview with the *Sacramento Bee*, when asked if other candidates would receive treatment similar to what Lieu was given if they did not support affirmative action, State Senator Holly Mitchell, who heads the California Legislative Black Caucus, stated that similar future political actions could happen if members feel that "there is a lack of commitment to a core Democratic party priority" (White 2014, par. 9).

Another example of tensions in the state capitol among the three California legislative caucuses of color occurred when State Assemblyman Al Murasutchi's Assembly Bill 2013, which would expand the number of electric vehicles able to use the high-occupancy lanes, fell eleven votes short of the number needed to pass on the Assembly floor after several members from the California Latino Legislative Caucus and the California Legislative Black Caucus withheld their votes (White 2014).

The California Republican Party leaders saw a great opportunity to capitalize on the political tensions between the minority caucuses in two ways: one, to allow affirmative action to be an issue that would galvanize the state's dwindling GOP voter base; and two, to broaden their voter base with conservative and moderate factions within the state's growing Asian American population, which is nearly 14 percent—the second largest racial minority group. Sensing a political opportunity to gain Republican votes among Asian American voters, top Republican leaders in both chambers came to the Stop SCA 5 forum at the Cupertino City Hall. Republican Ward Connerly, the controversial former University of California regent who was behind Proposition 209, which SCA 5 would overturn, said the following at the Cupertino public forum: "It would be a serious mistake to let the Latino Caucus to secure the votes of all Democrats. . . . I guarantee you the number of Asians will be diminished and the number of Latinos will be increased" (Noguchi 2014, pars. 3 and 7). Assembly Minority Leader Connie Conway (R-Visalia) quipped to the protesters, "Why work hard when that hard work will not be rewarded?" (Noguchi 2014, par. 12) The significance of this GOP strategy was to use Asian Americans as a racial wedge group to advance their anti–affirmative action perspectives while at the same time trying to expand their voter base by reaching out to the anti-SCA 5 protesters.

The reverberations of the anti-SCA 5 movements in Northern and Southern California instigated an equally vociferous counter movement on social media among Asian American activists and scholars who attempted to refocus the debate away from race-baiting and misinformation. This belief could clearly be seen among the vast Asian American blogosphere, which tends to be more progressive and multiracial in ideological orientation, during the anti-SCA 5 movement. While mainstream media outlets (television, radio, and print) focused exclusively on the anti-SCA 5 Chinese American protesters, progressive Asian American activists took to social media sites to clarify the discussion.

One vivid example was Loyola University Higher Education Professor OiYan Poon's 2014 guest post essay entitled "Hate, Fear, and Lies: How Anti-Affirmative Action Haters Are Shoveling Bullsh*t about SCA 5" on the progressive website Angry Asian Man (Poon 2014). Poon argues that "there are two key ways the anti-affirmative action haters are shoveling a lot of bullsh*t about SCA 5. First, they claim SCA 5 is 'anti-Asian.' Second, they hold an assumption that tests and grades are race neutral, reliable, and the only valid considerations in selective admissions practices. In the meantime, while they're too busy in a fear mongering campaign, they're missing a great opportunity to really fight to expand college opportunity for all of the highly qualified students in the state" (Poon 2014, par. 2). Poon then went on to list the hundreds of holistic factors that go into the complex admissions process at the University of California at Berkeley.

Online Connective Action Findings

1. Analysis of Twitter Hashtag #SCA5

The most popular hashtag to go viral on Twitter for the debate on California Senate Constitutional Amendment 5 was #SCA5. Those who were for or against SCA 5 who took to Twitter universally included this hashtag. The time frame that was examined for content analysis was from December 3, 2012, the date that California State Senator Edward Hernandez introduced the Senate amendment, to March 17, 2014, the date that Senator Hernandez tabled the bill.

Of the 349 total tweets with #SCA5 during this period, Asian Americans accounted for the largest racial group with 294 tweets for 84 percent of the total, followed by White people with 26 tweets (7.4 percent), African Americans with 14 tweets (4 percent), Latinxs with 12 tweets (3.4 percent), and those whose race was "Not Determinable" with 4 tweets (1.1 percent).

A broad representation of ten Asian national origin groups were represented among the #SCA5 tweets. Chinese Americans were the largest with 234 tweets (66.9 percent), followed by Japanese Americans with 16 tweets (4.6 percent), Vietnamese Americans with 11 tweets (3.1 percent), Hmong Americans with 9 tweets (2.6 percent), Filipino/a Americans with 8 tweets (2.3 percent), Korean Americans with 7 tweets (2 percent), Laotian Americans with 4 tweets (1.1 percent), Asian Indians with 2 tweets (0.6 percent), Guamanian Americans with 1 tweet (0.3 percent), and Other South Asian Americans with 1 tweet (0.3 percent).

Table 5.1 illustrates the total number of #SCA5 tweets for race and gender by issue stance between December 3, 2012, and March 17, 2014. With regard to racial groups, Asian Americans were generally "For SCA 5" with 181 tweets for 61.6 percent compared to those "Against SCA 5" with 102 tweets for 34.7 percent and those who were "Neutral" with 11 tweets for 3.7 percent. Among non-Asians, a plurality was "For SCA 5" with 22 tweets (42.3 percent) compared to those "Against SCA 5" with 17 tweets (32.7 percent) and those who were "Neutral" with 13 tweets (25 percent). Those whose race was "Not Determinable" were split among the three categories: those "For SCA 5" had 2 tweets (50 percent) compared with those "Against SCA 5" and "Neutral" with 1 tweet (25 percent) each. Among those that were coded as "Organizations/Media," a majority was "For SCA 5" with 26 tweets (60.5 percent) compared with those "Against SCA 5" with 10 tweets (23.3 percent) and those "Neutral" with 7 tweets (16.3 percent).

When examining for race and gender by issue stance, the findings reveal intra-racial group differences between males and females with regard to their stances on SCA 5. A majority of Asian American males were "Against SCA 5" with 80 tweets (54.1 percent) compared to those "For SCA 5" with

TABLE 5.1 #SCA5 TWEETS FOR RACE AND GENDER BY ISSUE STANCE (12/3/12 TO 3/17/14)				
	For SCA 5	Against SCA 5	Neutral	Grand Total
Asian American	181 (61.6)	102 (34.7)	11 (3.7)	294 (100)
Male	68 (45.9)	80 (54.1)	0 (0)	148 (100)
Female	113 (77.4)	22 (15.1)	11 (7.5)	146 (100)
Non-Asian	22 (42.3)	17 (32.7)	13 (25)	52 (100)
Male	16 (47.1)	13 (38.2)	5 (14.7)	34 (100)
Female	6 (40)	3 (20)	6 (40)	15 (100)
Not Determinable	0 (0)	1 (33.3)	2 (66.7)	3 (100)
Not Determinable	2 (50)	1 (25)	1 (25)	4 (100)
Male	1 (100)	0 (0)	0 (0)	1 (100)
Female	1 (50)	0 (0)	1 (50)	2 (100)
Not Determinable	0 (0)	1 (100)	0 (0)	1 (100)
Organization/Media	26 (60.5)	10 (23.3)	7 (16.3)	43 (100)
Grand Total	231 (58.8)	32 (8.1)	130 (33.1)	393 (100)

68 tweets (45.9 percent). In contrast, the opposite was the case for Asian American females, where an overwhelming majority was "For SCA 5" with 113 tweets (77.4 percent) compared to those "Against SCA 5" with 22 tweets (15.1 percent) and those "Neutral" with 11 tweets (7.5 percent).

For non-Asians, a plurality of males and females were "For SCA 5" with 16 tweets (47.1 percent) and 6 tweets (40 percent), respectively. Non-Asian males "Against SCA 5" accounted for 13 tweets (38.2 percent) compared to non-Asian females with 3 tweets (20 percent).

2. Geocode Analysis of Twitter Hashtag #SCA5

Figure 5.2 captures the 349 total #SCA5 tweets from Chinese Americans by state between December 3, 2012, and March 17, 2014. Overall, nine U.S. states, including Washington, DC, and three countries (Australia, China, and Canada) are represented. Among the U.S. states, California leads the way with 87 tweets for 24.9 percent of the total, followed by Colorado with 16 tweets (4.6 percent), Illinois with 10 tweets (2.9 percent), New York with 8 tweets (2.3 percent), Michigan with 4 tweets (1.1 percent), Texas with 4 tweets (1.1 percent), Massachusetts with 2 tweets (0.6 percent), Florida with 1 tweet (0.3 percent), and Pennsylvania with 1 tweet (0.3 percent). Washington, DC, had 9 tweets for 2.6 percent. Outside of the United States, Canada

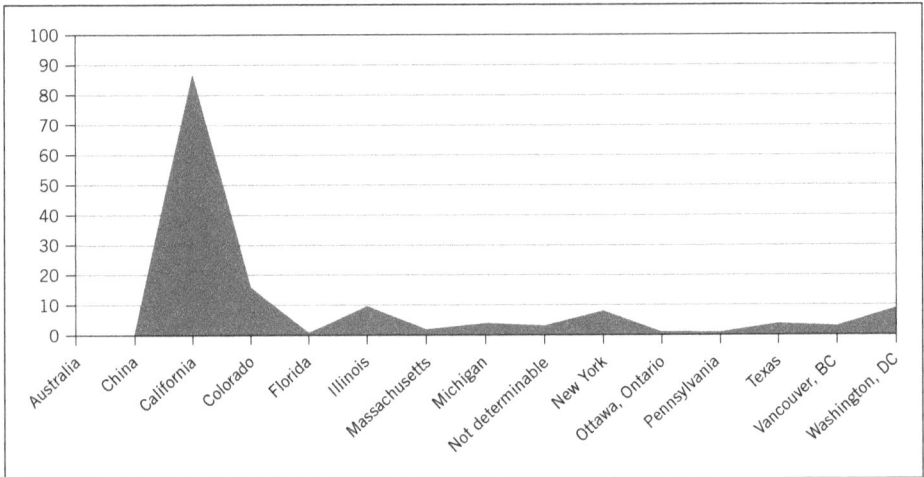

Figure 5.2 Total #SCA5 Tweets for Chinese Americans by State (12/3/12 to 3/17/14)

accounted for the most with 3 tweets for 0.8 percent followed by China and Australia with 1 tweet (0.3 percent) each.

Similar to the Peter Liang hashtag findings, the Chinese American community mobilizes through connective action on local, state, national, and global levels when it comes to affirmative action issues. U.S. states with significant Chinese American communities connect through online civic engagement, as seen with the #SCA5 findings on Twitter. The significance of these findings suggests that first-generation Chinese Americans will mobilize collectively if there is political motivation. Thus, one should not view a local or statewide issue or policy such as SCA 5 as parochial or pertaining only to California when it comes to highly educated, wealthy Chinese American immigrant communities and connective action. The ability to influence such policies will be determined by both the scale and the speed at which groups can mobilize both online and offline. The findings suggest that the ability to mobilize in both areas is beginning to emerge, facilitated by connective action, which connects local, state, and national Chinese American communities.

A total number of 64 tweets with #SCA5 were tweeted by non-Chinese Asian national groups between December 3, 2012, and March 17, 2014. Eight Asian national origin groups (Hmong, Filipino/a, Laotian, Indian, Japanese, Korean, Other South Asian, and Vietnamese Americans) were from seventeen states including Washington, DC. Among the top states, California led the way with 28 tweets for 43.8 percent of the grand total. Japanese Americans in California had the most with 8 tweets (12.5 percent) followed by

Hmong Americans with 6 tweets (9.4 percent), Filipino/a Americans with 5 tweets (7.8 percent), Laotian Americans with 3 tweets (4.7 percent), and Korean Americans with 3 tweets (4.7 percent). Tweets where the locations were "Not Determinable" accounted for the second largest group with 16 tweets for 25 percent. Both Hmong Americans and Vietnamese Americans accounted for the largest group with 5 tweets (7.8 percent) each. Japanese Americans accounted for 2 tweets (3.1 percent) followed by Laotian, Indian, Korean, and Other South Asian Americans with 1 tweet (1.6 percent) each. Colorado was the third-largest state with 6 tweets for 9.4 percent of the grand total. Japanese and Korean Americans both accounted for 2 tweets for 3.1 percent each, followed by Hmong and Vietnamese Americans with 1 tweet (1.6 percent) each. Michigan was the fourth-largest state with 4 tweets for 6.3 percent of the grand total. Both Japanese and Vietnamese Americans had 2 tweets for 3.1 percent each. Illinois was the fifth-largest state with 2 tweets for 3.1 percent of the grand total. Guamanian and Japanese Americans had 1 tweet (1.6 percent) each. New York (Korean American) and Indiana (Filipino/a American) each had 1 tweet for 1.6 percent of the grand total. Washington, DC, had 4 tweets for 6.3 percent of the grand total. Hmong, Filipina/o, Laotian, and Japanese Americans each had 1 tweet (1.6 percent).

Despite the efforts of the SCA 5 supporters to combat the negative narrative and messages via social media, it was too late. Chinese American immigrants who were against SCA 5 were successful because of their three-tiered mobilization strategy, discussed earlier: one, taking the individual voices of dissent and parlaying them into collective online affinity groups that would disseminate information and protests around SCA 5; two, establishing an effective online information campaign that portrayed SCA 5 as racially discriminatory against Asian Americans, which in turn created group resentment against it that would lead to group mobilization; and three, developing a coordinated outreach and political action campaign primarily through smartphone discussion group applications (WeChat), with a focus on public protests and targeting elected Asian American officials in the California State Senate and Assembly. In the end, this three-tiered strategy was both swift and effective in framing the major narrative surrounding SCA 5 that would shake up the top of the California State Legislature power structure and create an outcome in favor of the anti-SCA 5 side.

ACA 5 (Proposition 16) and the California November 2020 Election

After the defeat in 2014, the proponents of SCA 5 in the State Assembly retrenched and reassessed the political landscape to determine when it would be strategic to introduce another version. Nearly six years later, they would make a concerted effort to reintroduce affirmative action in California's higher education, state contracting, and hiring with ACA 5, and it passed in both the California State Assembly and Senate; it was on the November 2020 statewide ballot as Proposition 16. Key endorsers of ACA 5 include California Governor Gavin Newsom, the California Federation of Teachers, and a bevy of progressive Asian American organizations (Huang 2020). Conservative Asian American immigrants, predominantly Chinese American led, created a Facebook page entitled "No ACA 5" and the registered website stopprop16.org in addition to emailing and writing California state representatives. Misinformation has already circulated on WeChat that Prop. 16 would result in racial quotas and nearly half the number of Asian American undergraduates admitted to the University of California system (Savidge 2020).

Similar to SCA 5, the central sites for offline political mobilization among Chinese American immigrants were Asian influenced suburbs. For example, on July 3, 2020, a public rally took place in the Asian American majority suburb of Cupertino, California, that featured key speakers such as Ward Connerly, founder and chairperson of the American Civil Rights Institute; Ritesh Tandon, a South Asian American candidate for Congressional District 17; Cupertino city council member Lian Fang Chao; and Cupertino School Board candidate Sudha Kasamsetty. The nearly one hundred crowd members held signs that read "No on ACA 5" and "Racial Quotas: The Hidden Agenda of Prop. 16." California State Assembly member Evan Low, whose district contains Cupertino, has again become the target of anti-ACA 5 Chinese American immigrants. One graphic that was posted on the "No on ACA 5" Facebook page prior to ACA being voted on in the State Assembly featured Low's photo with the caption "If ACA 5 passes, University of California will likely admissions of 40 percent Asian students to just 15 percent. ACA 5 will be voted this week. Will your Assemblyman Evan Low betray you?" According to Low, during the week of the ACA 5 vote, his office received 99 calls and emails in support and 3,700 in opposition to ACA 5 (Huang 2020).

California voters rejected Proposition 16 by 57 percent on November 3, 2020. One of the contributing factors for this outcome was voter outreach and education particularly to the state's Latinx voters. In a September 2020 poll conducted by Latino Decisions for a report by the Latino Community Foundation, it was found that only 39 percent of Latinxs in California understood the proposition would reinstate affirmative action (Wolf and Abraham 2020). Another September 2020 statewide poll conducted by the Public Policy Institute of California found that only 46 percent of Democratic likely voters across all regional, demographic, and racial/ethnic groups (Latinxs at 41 percent; other racial/ethnic groups at 40 percent; and

White people at 26 percent) would vote yes on Proposition 16. In contrast, a majority of Republican (71 percent) and independent (58 percent) likely voters said that they would vote no (Baldassare et al. 2020). Given these statewide poll findings and the anti-affirmative protests by conservative Asian Americans, the electoral outcome of Proposition 16 was likely due to Asian American voters joining White voters to oppose it. According to Yu-kong Zhao, president of the Asian American Coalition for Education (AACE) in New Jersey, "Going forward, I'd like to warn liberal politicians in California and nationwide: focus your efforts on devising measures to improve K–12 education for Black and Hispanic children, instead of introducing racially divisive and discriminatory laws time and again.... Asian Americans will fight fiercely and defeat your racist policies wherever and whenever tried" (Jaschik 2020, par. 12). In contrast, progressive Asian American organizations such as Asian Americans for Advancing Justice (AAAJ) commented after the November 3, 2020, election, "The ban on affirmative action in California has been devastating for all communities of color, including Asian American subgroups. The reality is that racism and sexism continue to warp and restrict educational and economic opportunities for people of color and women. We need to acknowledge that reality in order to fairly evaluate an applicant's accomplishments and contributions.... We will continue to fight for equal opportunity for all of our communities" (*IndiaWest* 2020, pars. 13 and 14).

Regardless of issue stance, one thing is certain: the affirmative action divide remains within the Asian American community. Social media and connective action will continue to contribute to this divide. As the battle continues, the future of affirmative action policies in public higher education institutions in California and other racially diverse states will likely be determined by which side can more effectively utilize social media and connective action for voter outreach and education across the multiracial electorate that will prominently involve Asian Americans on both sides.

*Data Disaggregation and the 2016 California
Assembly Bill 1726—How Connective Action
Helped Determine the Narrative and Outcome*

*Any race-based preferential policy is not only unreasonable but
also unconstitutional. #AB1726 is blatant RACISM.*
—Twitter Post by "Vincent"

*They see AB 1726 as a backdoor to try and overturn Proposition
209. Asians, especially Chinese, are more politically aware after
2014 and the last fight over SCA 5.*
—Mei Mei Huff, spouse of California Senator Bob Huff

Shifting Battlegrounds: From Higher Education to Data Disaggregation

In the latter days of August 2016, Asian American activists who were predominantly first-generation Chinese Americans mobilized across California against Assembly Bill 1726 (hereinafter AB 1726), officially designated as the Accounting for Health and Education in Asian Pacific Islander Demographics Act, a controversial bill that was introduced by primary sponsor California Assemblyman Rob Bonta (D, California Assembly District 18). AB 1726 would require the California Department of Public Health to disaggregate data along Asian national origin groups and not apply to other state agencies that are connected to state public universities, unlike the original bill (Fuchs 2016b). The intent behind data disaggregation for Asian Americans is that they would be better served in the areas of health care, employment, and education with nuanced data that takes into account the intergroup differences that are emerging among its diverse Asian ethnic groups rather than conflating the data and treating them as a monolithic group.

AB 1726 was an amended bill of AB 176, which was also introduced by Assemblyman Bonta the previous year and required separate categories for Asian national origin groups that often get lost in the category "Other Asian," such as Hmong, Indonesian, Malaysian, Pakistani, Taiwanese, Fijian, and Tongan. AB 176 passed both houses in the California State Legislature but was vetoed by Governor Jerry Brown, who stated in an October 7, 2015, letter to the members of the California State Assembly, "I am returning Assembly Bill 176 without my signature. . . . To be sure, there is value in understanding data on race, ethnicity, gender, or other aspects of identity. On a broad level, these demographic data can signal important changes in society. On a practical level, they can help elucidate how our laws and programs can be shaped to reflect a changing population. Despite this utility, I am wary of the ever-growing desire to stratify. Dividing people into ethnic or other subcategories may yield more information, but not necessarily greater wisdom about what actions should follow. To focus just on ethnic identity may not be enough" (Office of the Governor 2015, pars. 1, 3, and 4).

AB 1726 differed from its predecessor, AB 176, in that it initially asked the University of California, California State University, and California Community College systems to collect data on Asian American "at-risk groups" such as Native Hawaiians and Pacific Islanders in addition to ten new ethnic groups. The bill also required these higher education systems to issue reports on admissions and graduation rates of these groups (Fuchs 2016b). The higher education focus of AB 1726 would come under intense and rapid scrutiny by parts of the Chinese American community through connective action. Many opponents of AB 1726 saw it as a continuation of SCA 5, which they had defeated the previous year, as seen in the Chapter 6 case study. Eventually, Bonta would amend AB 1726 to address the opponents' concerns by specifically addressing data disaggregation within the Asian American community with regard to health care. According to a public statement on AB 1726, "For example, certain AAPI subgroups are more susceptible to certain health risks and more accurate data is desperately needed. The most dramatic increase in uterine cancer has been among Chinese women, while Korean men and women have some of the highest incidences of colorectal cancer rates" (Zhu 2016, par. 12).

After undergoing several amendments within the California State Assembly, the final version of AB 1726 focused on allowing the Department of Public Health to collect and release disaggregated demographic data for the following populations: Bangladeshi, Hmong, Indonesian, Malaysian, Pakistani, Sri Lankan, Taiwanese, Thai, Fijian, and Tongan Americans. The data collected would include rates for major diseases, leading causes of death, pregnancy rates, and housing numbers. According to a press release from Bonta:

> I believe good data drives good policy. One way to get good data is through disaggregation. Disaggregating data means breaking it down into smaller subgroups and assessing specific trends that were

previously hidden. The population of California is uniquely diverse, especially within the API community. There are more than 23 distinct communities within the Asian American population and 19 within the Native Hawaiian and Pacific Islander population. AB 1726 will give us a clearer pathway to formulate policy focused on positive outcomes for our specific API communities. It's critical that our policy leaders understand this diversity and are sensitive to the fact that APIs are not all the same. While we share some of the same challenges, such as language access issues, racial discrimination, and obstacles born of immigration, each of our diverse communities has different social and economic outcomes that need to be addressed appropriately. (Bonta 2016a, pars. 3–6)

The amended AB 1726 unanimously passed the California Senate by a 39-0 vote (Fuchs 2016b). On September 26, 2016, California Governor Jerry Brown signed AB 1726 into law. While the proponents of AB 1726 won the political battle, its opponents could claim a small but significant political victory that was central to their connective action efforts, which was the removal of the higher education component that was part and parcel of the initial AB 1726. That was their major concern in the many online discussions and petitions that were circulated. In many ways, this third case study of data disaggregation represents a continuation of the previously examined SCA 5 case study, as illuminated by the above quote from Mei Mei Huff, the Chinese American wife of California Senator Bob Huff, an outspoken opponent of both SCA 5 and AB 1726.

While the two case studies are interconnected, AB 1726 stands on its own because of how the issue was framed by opponents and proponents. The opponents primarily framed their discontent with data disaggregation around meritocracy rather than race as the bill focused only on Asian Americans, a common bond shared with their arguments against SCA 5. They claimed that such attention to difference, whether it was around race or ethnicity, would result in unfair penalties against any of the Asian national origin groups when it came to public policies involving higher education such as California's Proposition 209 and SCA 5. In contrast, the proponents of AB 1726 argued that it was a twenty-first-century civil rights issue for Asian Americans, as this community has historically been disenfranchised by ineffective state and federal policies that have treated this diverse racial group as monolithic by conflating over thirty national origin groups with unequal socioeconomic backgrounds into a single statistic such as median family income. The significance of analyzing this case study is that it provides another measuring point for comparisons with the second case study of SCA 5 pertaining to how, if at all, the process and perspectives of connective action have changed among the predominantly first-generation Chinese American protesters during the year interval between both protest campaigns. Moreover, the AB 1726 case study sheds light on whether the SCA 5 movement was an anomaly or whether it is a sign of future similar connective action from the larger Asian American community as their political identities and interests continue to develop in local and state politics.

Firing the First Social Media Salvo—California's First-Generation Chinese Americans React to AB 1726

When news of AB 1726 and its focus on data disaggregation within California's higher education systems first broke on social media platforms such as WeChat, the same first-generation Chinese American activists who were fresh off their protests against SCA 5 began to plan a similar mobilization strategy that included the following: (1) targeting Asian American elected officials, particularly those who publicly supported AB 1726, in the California State Legislature through email correspondence and public protests; (2) disseminating information, recruiting, and mobilizing through WeChat forums and email lists; and (3) creating and circulating online petitions through various social media platforms, particularly WeChat, Facebook, and email lists.

1. Targeting Asian American Elected Officials through Correspondence and Public Protests

The Chinese American protesters mobilized and targeted Asian Pacific Islander American elected officials who voted in support of AB 1726, a strategy similar to the anti-SCA 5 movement. On March 25, 2016, dozens of protesters rallied against AB 1726 outside of the Cupertino office of California Assemblyman Evan Low (D-District 28), who, along with Assemblymen Phil Ting (D-District 19) and David Chu (D-District 17), voted for AB 1726. Kai Zhu, a Bay Area attorney and one of the protesters, stated:

> We believe [AB 1726] is more focused on education so they have data supporting the affirmative action and make preferential policies in college admissions for some Asian American subgroups, like Malaysians and Cambodians. Therefore, the Chinese Americans, Asian Indians or Korean Americans, those so-called "over-represented" groups, will become a target. We should promote meritocracy. Any race-based preferential policy is not only unreasonable but also unconstitutional. (Zhu 2016, pars. 5–6)

While the ability to mobilize through connective action is powerful, the intent underlying this mobilization must also be examined. The conflation of AB 1726 with college admissions, as raised by Zhu, is something that others in the Asian American community have incorrectly challenged. For example, the prominent San Francisco–based organization Chinese for Affirmative Action (CAA) issued the following statement on March 25, 2016, that gets at the underlying policy intent of AB 1726:

> CAA strongly supports Assembly Bill 1726 . . . a critically needed effort to unmask Asian American and Pacific Islander (AAPI) subgroups, and to identify the unique health, educational, and economic disparities faced by certain ethnic communities. . . . CAA also cautions against any efforts that may confuse or misrepresent the intentions of AB 1726. It is legally and factually inaccurate to conflate AB 1726 with any issues related to college admissions criteria. (Chinese for Affirmative Action Statement on Assembly Bill 1726 2016, pars. 1 and 4)

One of the dangers of social media, as we discussed earlier with the proliferation and dissemination of fake news, is that public policy issues and intents may be misconstrued and/or falsely propagated for group self-interest or those outside of a particular group who are ideologically opposed to a policy, for the sake of defeating it through a campaign of misinformation. In this case, the Chinese American activists who opposed AB 1726 were incorrectly conflating the issues of disaggregated data collection and college admissions, when the real intentions were getting to health care disparities among Asian American subpopulations. Was this misunderstanding a result of the echo chambers that often plague social media sites and forums?

2. Disseminating Information, Recruiting, and Mobilizing through WeChat Forums

Lily Ding, a Chinese immigrant who came to the United States over twenty years ago, was one of the many faces in the crowd who were protesting against AB 1726 in August 2016 on the steps of the state capitol. Ding, like many of the Chinese immigrant protesters at the rally, had never attended a political rally until she'd heard of former NYPD Officer Peter Liang and his second-degree manslaughter conviction. Learning of the Liang trial through WeChat prompted Ding to attend a San Francisco rally to protest his conviction (Fuchs 2016b). According to Ding, "For me, it was a wakeup call. I have always thought that the U.S. had been very fair" (Fuchs 2016b, par. 3).

Social media platforms such as WeChat, Facebook, and Twitter were again instrumental during the mobilization by the first-generation Chinese American community throughout the San Francisco Bay Area and Southern California regions who were either against or in favor of AB 1726 for various reasons. This belief was clearly seen with the creation and dissemination of online petitions from both sides. For example, in Sunnyvale, California, a suburb in the San Francisco Bay Area, a group calling themselves United Californians initiated an online petition via the website Change.org entitled "Vote No on AB-1726." As of December 2016, 15,253 supporters, well short of the 25,000 signature goal that was needed, had signed the petition. Had the petition succeeded, it would have been delivered to California Governor Brown and the California State Legislature. The petition declared the following:

Honorable Governor Brown:

Despite the strong opposition from many Asian American organizations, California legislature passed *AB-1726* (Bonta) this month. AB-1726, in essence, is a *duplicate* of *AB-176* (Bonta) that you vetoed last year. We applaud your previous decision and we urge that you take the same action this time again.

Regrettably, AB-1726 is equally *divisive, unfair, unscientific*, and *infeasible*. We believe that your concern over its predecessor bill AB-176 holds true in this current case: "Dividing people into ethnic or other subcategories may yield more information, but not necessarily greater wisdom about what actions should follow. To focus just on ethnic identity may not be enough."

AB-1726 is clearly divisive and unfair. It does not stipulate the collection of similar racial data from any group other than the Asian American Pacific Islanders. The bill, for example, does not require Cuban Americans or Mexican Americans to report their ethnicities other than the generic "Hispanic." Similarly, it does not require Jewish Americans, Arab Americans, or Irish American to report ethnicities other than the generic "White." It is indisputable that those subgroups within the Hispanics and Whites are ethnically and culturally diverse. Singling out Asian Americans for stratification is not only unfair to Asian Americans but also to all Americans.

AB-1726 is unscientific. It confuses ethnicities with national origins. For instance, China as a country officially recognizes 56 ethnic groups among its citizens, including, for example, Korean, Hmong, Muslim, and Mongolian. So identifying oneself as "Chinese" or

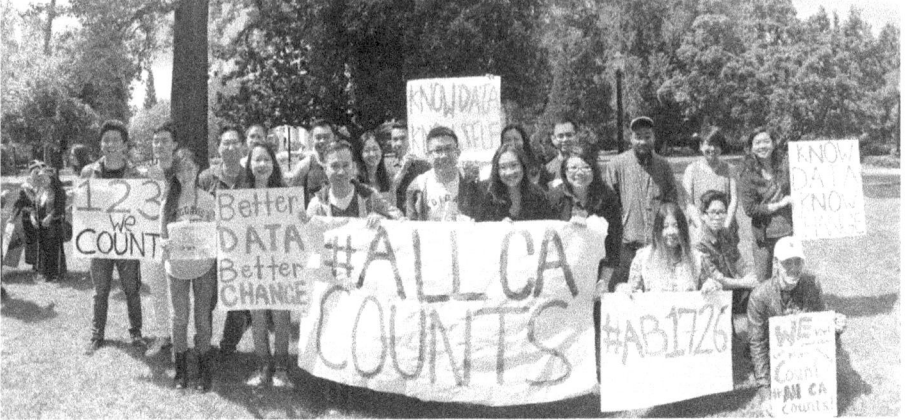

Figure 6.1 Asian Americans Rally for the California Assembly Data Disaggregation Bill. Southeast Asian American protestors gather to support AB 1726
(Source: Jonathan Ronald Tran for Southeast Asia Resource Action Center.)

"Taiwanese" doesn't disclose that person's true ethnic and possible cultural background. Furthermore, the impact of the citizenship of one's ancestry—and in many cases multiple citizenships within the family tree—is not necessarily a deciding factor of that person's genetic makeup or socioeconomic situation and educational status. Therefore, such stratification tactics encoded by AB-1726 wouldn't have been a useful factor in allocating educational or health resources of California.

In addition to all the problems above, this bill cannot be realistically implemented. Besides putting substantial costs on California taxpayers, the system is not intended to, nor is it able to, monitor and verify the accuracy and integrity of the self-identified data generated under this bill.

California does not need a bill that could only *divide* our communities. California does not need more heightened *racial tensions*. Please veto AB-1726. (United Californians 2016)

In contrast to the United Californians online petition "Vote No on AB 1726" a pro-AB 1726 online petition entitled "Governor Brown: Make All AAPI Communities Visible! #AllCACount" was created by 18MillionRising .org, a social activist website and portal for the Asian American community. According to this petition:

As AAPIs, we are made up of 48 diverse groups. When data clumps us all under "Asian," it can overshadow the specific challenges faced by Southeast Asian American, Pacific Islander students and refugee communities. *By not accurately reflecting these AAPI communities' experiences, we become invisible to policy makers—which can reinforce the model minority myth. . . . In California, the economic, health, and educational data of 5 million Asian American, Native Hawaiian, and Pacific Islander students and families is not accurately collected to reflect their unique challenges. . . .* Significant challenges such as high poverty rates, limited English proficiency, and cultural barriers (for these groups) would finally be made visible to the public and policy makers. *Tell Governor Brown and the CA State Legislature to sign AB 1726 so that certain AAPI communities are no longer invisible.* (18MillionRising.org 2016a)

The 18 Million Rising petition collected 1,874 signatures, short of its 3,200 signature goal. Regardless of this outcome, an overwhelming majority of Asian Americans who filled out a petition on a social issue were doing so online as opposed to a hard copy, which is exactly the strategy that both opponents and proponents of AB 1726 were effectively doing.

Both of the above online petitions and their respective texts offer a glimpse into the chasm that existed between both sides of AB 1726. Those who opposed it believed that the bill was a backdoor way of potentially targeting Chinese Americans by introducing affirmative action into higher education. For example, "Vincent," who was one of the most vocal protesters of AB 1726, tweeted on September 23, 2016, "#AB1726 collect the type of racial profiling data used by Congress in the passage of the Chinese Exclusion Act of 1882" (Vincent 2016).

The perception among AB 1726 protesters was that the bill was racist because it targeted only Asian Americans and that it would harm them because it could potentially be a back doorway of introducing affirmative action policies into higher education admissions. In Vincent's brazen tweet, he erroneously equated AB 1726 to racial exclusionary laws such as the Chinese Exclusion Act of 1882, in which the U.S. Congress purposely excluded the emigration of Chinese laborers into the United States based on racial xenophobia and economic competition under the guise of this group's inability to become naturalized U.S. citizens. This is hardly equitable to AB 1726, which sought to provide greater racial equality in higher education to historically underrepresented racial groups in California. Nonetheless, the significance of this example is that it illustrates not only how issues can be distorted from reality on social media platforms like Twitter; it also demonstrates how echo chambers within social media among those of a particular perspective can amplify through the use of dangerous rhetoric without any factual check. Those who are followers of Vincent on Twitter may retweet the same tweet to their followers, who in turn may accept that the comparison is legitimate when it is in fact far from being correct.

On the proponent side of the AB 1726 debate was progressive Asian and Pacific Islander American organizations that mobilized as fast as the opposition on the same social media platforms. On Twitter, the most common hashtag used among proponents of AB 1726 was #AllCACounts. For example, on August 19, 2016, the organization Empowering Pacific Islander Communities (EPIC) tweeted, "We need #AB1726 so we can give our families the very best that we can. Support#AB1726!" (Empowering Pacific Islander Communities 2016). Another example is Lange Parks Luntao, who tweeted on August 12, 2016, "#AB1726 gives ALL API communities visibility. Visibility = equity = opportunity . . . Support #AllCACounts" (Luntao 2016).

In addition to progressive Asian American organizations, Asian American elected officials also voiced their support of AB 1726 on Twitter. Current District 4, Los Angeles City council member David E. Ryu, the first Korean American to be elected to the Los Angeles City Council, tweeted on August 23, 2016, "It's crucial for policymakers to have more info re: the communities they serve. Proud to support #AB1726 . . . #AllCACounts" (Ryu 2016). Current California State Assemblyman Rob Bonta tweeted on March 28, 2016, "The path to good public policy is paved with accurate data! #AHEADAct #caleg #AB1726 #API" (Bonta 2016b).

Online Connective Action Findings

1. Analysis of Twitter Hashtag #AB1726

To examine the impact of Asian American connective action during the AB 1726 case study, the Twitter hashtag #AB1726 was coded and analyzed from the period of January 28, 2016 (the date that it was introduced in the California State Assembly by Assembly member Rob Bonta), to September 25, 2016 (the date in which California Governor Jerry Brown signed AB 1726 into state law). This hashtag was the primary one used by both opponents and supporters of the bill.

Of the 370 total number of #AB1726 tweets by racial groups during this period, Asian Americans were the largest group with 335 tweets for 90.5 percent of the grand total, followed by White people with 14 tweets (3.8 percent), African Americans with 11 tweets (3 percent), Latinx with 9 tweets (2.4 percent), and those whose race was "Not Determinable" with 1 tweet (0.3 percent).

Among the eleven Asian national origin groups that tweeted using #AB1726, Chinese Americans were overwhelmingly the largest with 284 tweets for 76.8 percent of the grand total, followed by Filipina/o Americans

TABLE 6.1 #AB1726 TWEETS FOR RACE AND GENDER BY ISSUE STANCE (1/28/16 TO 9/25/16)				
	For AB 1726	Against AB 1726	Neutral	Grand Total
Asian American	165 (49.3)	170 (50.7)	0 (0)	335 (100)
Male	78 (42.4)	106 (57.6)	0 (0)	184 (100)
Female	87 (57.6)	64 (42.4)	0 (0)	151 (100)
Non-Asian	29 (85.3)	4 (11.8)	1 (2.9)	34 (100)
Male	15 (75)	4 (20)	1 (5)	20 (100)
Female	14 (100)	0 (0)	0 (0)	14 (100)
Organization/Media	154 (93.3)	3 (1.8)	8 (4.8)	165 (100)
Grand Total	348 (65.2)	9 (1.7)	177 (33.1)	534 (100)

with 17 tweets (4.6 percent), Vietnamese Americans with 8 tweets (2.2 percent), Asian Indians with 5 tweets (1.4 percent), Cambodian Americans with 5 tweets (1.4 percent), Lu Mien Americans with 4 tweets (1.1 percent), Tongan Americans with 4 tweets (1.1 percent), Japanese Americans with 3 tweets (0.8 percent), Polynesian American with 2 tweets (0.5 percent), Hawaiian Americans with 2 tweets (0.5 percent), and Korean Americans with 1 tweet (0.1 percent).

Table 6.1 captures the findings for 534 total tweets with #AB1726 for race and gender by issue stance from January 28, 2016, to September 25, 2016. Of the 534 grand total tweets, Asian Americans had the most with 335 tweets for 62.7 percent, followed by "Organizations/Media" with 165 tweets for 30.9 percent, and non-Asians with 34 tweets for 10.1 percent. Among the 335 total tweets by Asian Americans, a slight majority (170 tweets for 50.7 percent) was "Against AB 1726" compared to those "For AB 1726" with 165 tweets for 49.3 percent. Asian American males and females differed in their overall views. For Asian American males, a majority was "Against AB 1726" with 106 tweets for 57.6 percent, compared with those "For AB 1726" with 78 tweets for 42.4 percent. In contrast, among Asian American females, a majority was "For AB 1726" with 87 tweets for 57.6 percent compared with those "Against AB 1726" with 64 tweets for 42.4 percent.

Of the 34 total tweets by non-Asians, a majority was "For AB 176" with 29 tweets for 85.3 percent compared with those "Against AB 1726" with 4 tweets for 11.8 percent and those "Neutral" with 1 tweet for 2.9 percent. Both non-Asian males and females were overwhelmingly "For AB 1726." Among the 20 total tweets from non-Asian males, a majority was "For AB 1726" with

15 tweets (75 percent) compared to those "Against AB 1726" with 4 tweets (20 percent) and those "Neutral" with 1 tweet (5 percent). All 14 (100 percent) of the total tweets by non-Asian females were "For AB 1726."

For those tweets identified as being from "Organizations/Media," an overwhelming majority of them was "For AB 1726" with 154 tweets (93.3 percent), compared with those "Against AB 1726" with 3 tweets (1.8 percent) and those "Neutral" with 8 tweets (4.8 percent).

2. Geocode Analysis of #AB1726

Figure 6.2 captures the 283 total #AB1726 tweets of Chinese Americans by state from January 28, 2016, to September 25, 2016. Four U.S. states (California, Illinois, Massachusetts, and New York) and Washington, DC, and two foreign countries (China and Canada), were represented. Chinese Americans whose location was "Not Determinable" accounted for the most with 141 tweets for 49.8 percent of the grand total.

Among the four U.S. states, Chinese Americans in California tweeted with #AB1726 the most, with 111 tweets for 39.2 percent of the grand total, followed by New York with 4 tweets (1.4 percent), Massachusetts with 3 tweets (1.1 percent), and Illinois with 1 tweet (0.4 percent). Chinese Americans in Washington, DC, accounted for 17 tweets (6 percent). Outside of the United States, there were 4 tweets (1.4 percent) in China and 1 tweet (0.4 percent) in Canada (Ontario).

Among the 51 total tweets with #AB1726 from other Asian national origin groups by state from January 28, 2016, to September 25, 2016, a total of two U.S. states (California and New York) and Washington, DC, and one foreign country (China), were represented. Other Asian national origin groups whose location was "Not Determinable" accounted for the largest group with 23 tweets for 45.1 percent of the grand total.

For the two U.S. states, California was the largest with 22 tweets for 43.1 percent of the grand total. Of the 22 total California tweets, Filipino/a Americans were the largest with 9 tweets for 41 percent, followed by Tongan Americans with 3 tweets (13.6 percent), Hawaiian Americans with 2 tweets (9.1 percent), Asian Indians with 2 tweets (9.1 percent), Japanese Americans with 2 tweets (9.1 percent), Vietnamese Americans with 2 tweets (9.1 percent), Lu Mien Americans with 1 tweet (4.5 percent), and Polynesian Americans with 1 tweet (4.5 percent). In New York, a Tongan American provided 1 tweet (100 percent). Washington, DC, had 3 total tweets with the largest from Filipino/a Americans with 2 tweets (66.6 percent) and a Vietnamese American with 1 tweet (33.3 percent). A total of 2 tweets came from China, a Filipino/a American and a Vietnamese American with 1 tweet (50 percent) each.

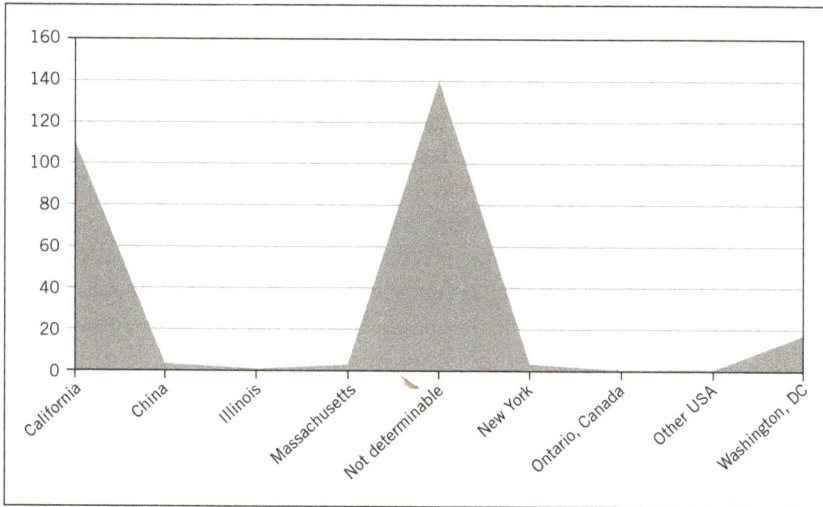

Figure 6.2 #AB1726 Tweets by Chinese Americans and Location (1/28/16 to 9/25/16)

Two Competing Frames: Chinese Group Self-Interest versus a Panethnic Asian American Coalition

The overall findings for AB 1726 on Twitter suggest that there were two competing frames, each backed by different interest groups that existed within the Asian American community. One frame viewed AB 1726 as a backdoor policy that would bring back affirmative action vis-à-vis SCA 5 and threaten Asian American group interests, particularly those of Chinese Americans. As discussed earlier, this perspective is historically grounded in Chinese American organizations' assertions that other prestigious universities, such as the Ivy Leagues, have discriminated against them in their admissions criteria. A second frame was the narrative that viewed AB 1726 as a crucial step to obtaining nuanced and equitable public policies when it comes to socioeconomic diversity within the Asian American community through data disaggregation. Both camps within the two frames clashed with one another on social media platforms like Twitter. Ultimately, the pro-AB 1726 side won due in large part to a broad and powerful panethnic Asian American coalition behind it that used social media to influence California legislators in addition to Governor Brown, as seen earlier.

As discussed earlier in this chapter, many of the Chinese American immigrants viewed AB 1726 as a threat to their group self-interest when it came to the ability of their children to gain admission to the University of California system. Thus, like with SCA 5, the common narrative in this camp viewed AB 1726 as racially discriminatory for singling out Asians in favor of other racial minority groups. This group's self-interest perspective was vividly demonstrated in their anti #AB1726 tweets. An example was Roy You, a Chinese American, who tweeted on August 24, 2016, "No matter how you spin it, #AB1726 is a racist bill. It either try [*sic*] to 'benefit' Asians ONLY or try to divide Asians. Shame on its supporters" (You 2016). At the heart of this tweet is the incorrect belief that AB 1726's call for data disaggregation was going to either benefit or harm Asian Americans by specifically focusing on them as opposed to including other racial groups. The problem with this and similar perspectives is that it fails to understand the reasons argued for data disaggregation when it comes to health and economic disparities within the Asian and Pacific Islander communities that are masked by statistics that conflate them together as a racial group. Thus, a main challenge of the coalition that supported AB 1726 was to educate the public through social media as to why it was necessary within the Asian and Pacific Islander communities.

A panethnic Asian American coalition of activists, elected leaders, and organizations consisting of twelve Asian national origin groups were effective in mobilizing support by explaining the health and economic reasons for AB 1726 on social media platforms such as Twitter. Two key coalition partners among these groups included at-risk Southeast Asian and Pacific Islander groups whose social and economic struggles have often been neglected by California policy makers because historically they have been racially lumped in with more established Asian national origin groups.

The ability to form a successful panethnic Asian American coalition of supporters behind AB 1726 stemmed primarily from how they framed the issue to the public. One of the key online slogans that emerged during the AB 1726 campaign was "All Californians Count," which eventually became #AllCACounts on Twitter. The focus of this digital campaign emphasized educating the public about the social, economic, and ethnic differences within the Asian American community and the need for data disaggregation to address these disparities. An example of the health care focus came from Dr. Tung Nguyen, a Vietnamese American, who tweeted on April 26, 2016, "Our @UCSFCancer @UCD_Cancer study showing lay health care workers increase colon cancer screening in Hmong" (Nguyen 2016). The tweet linked to a University California, Davis press release of the findings.

This belief that a panethnic coalition was behind AB 1726 included Asian American organizations as well. Because these organizations tend to be panethnic in their clientele and focus, many of them found common interests with AB 1726. An example was the legal and civil rights organization Asian Americans Advancing Justice–Los Angeles (Advancing Justice–LA), which provides a wide array of legal services and advocacy for the larger Los Angeles Asian American Pacific Islander community. As discussed previously in the findings from Table 6.1, Advancing Justice–LA was coded in the "Organization/Media" category that accounted for the second-largest number of #AB1726 tweets among all groups, with 165 tweets for 30.9 percent of the grand total. Among these organization and media tweets, an overwhelming majority (154 tweets for 93.3 percent) was "For AB 1726."

What can we learn from the successful outcome of AB 1726 and the construction of a vibrant panethnic Asian American coalition? Perhaps the most important lesson is that the ability to frame an issue as the major narrative on a policy on social media may likely determine the outcome. In the case of SCA, its opponents, mostly Chinese American immigrants, were able to seize control of the narrative on social media and mobilize in an expedient and effective manner both online and offline. This narrative immediately put the proponents of SCA 5 in the California State Assembly, including Asian American state elected officials, on the defensive. A former California State assemblyman, one of the few Asian Americans in the State Assembly who supported SCA 5 despite pressure from his Chinese American constituents, stated:

> Being able to control the message was what eventually determined the fate of SCA 5. Those of us [State Assembly members] who endorsed it were immediately put in a defensive position after all of the public demonstrations by Chinese Americans and the way they portrayed the amendment on social media, having to explain why we supported the bill as opposed to what it was about.[1]

In contrast to the defeat of SCA 5, the successful outcome for AB 1726 was due in large part to its supporters' ability to get in front of the opposition early in framing the message about why it was necessary for the Asian and Pacific Islander community, as illustrated by the findings in Table 6.1. Although the findings show that a slight majority (50.7 percent) of Asian Americans tweeted "Against AB 1726" compared to 49.3 percent who tweeted "For AB 1726," the key difference in framing the main narrative on Twitter was due in part to the overwhelming majority (93.3 percent) of Asian American organizations and media outlets that articulated the benefits of AB 1726 under #AllCACount. Ultimately, it was this coalition of Asian American progressives and community leaders, combined with Asian American organizations/media outlets, that was able to defeat the connective action mobilization of conservative Chinese American immigrants.

It must be noted that there is a difference between being able to frame the message of an issue on social media and voting on an issue. Many of those conservative Chinese American immigrants who protested against SCA 5 and AB 1726 cannot vote in U.S. elections because many are not naturalized U.S. citizens or are too young, though recent studies have shown that naturalization and voting are slowly but surely occurring within the Chinese and Asian immigrant community in the United States (Chen et al. 2016). As a result of such studies, a common perception is that the Chinese American immigrant community has not yet arrived politically because of relatively low voter turnout percentages. According to California State Assemblyman Evan Low:

> The Chinese American community can protest state representatives like me, but they don't have the voting numbers to make the difference or to make me change my mind on the issue. They are politically unsophisticated in that they don't understand the complexities of the issue.[2]

Despite the fact that Chinese and other Asian immigrants have low voter turnout due to factors such as low U.S. naturalization rates and a relatively young population, one would be remiss to ignore the impact that they will likely have in future U.S. politics. Such groups will find ways to influence the U.S. political process via other means. In the past, Asian immigrants have flexed their political muscles in other ways aside from voting, such as through campaign contributions, which is still the case today. As discussed earlier, one of the intermediate impacts that connective action affords Asian American immigrants and those who are unable to vote is providing them a platform to express their dissent or approval of policies and/or social issues when they cannot otherwise do so on election day.

The AB 1726 case study illustrates how social media provides a critical platform that allows voices of politically disenfranchised groups, such as immigrants and youth, to be heard on critical issues that are being debated in the civic arena. While discussions on online forums are not enough to make policy and social changes, it is an important first step to achieving these goals. For example, people are not going to attend rallies for or against AB 1726 if they don't know others who support their stance will also be there. Thus, social media platforms create both solidarity among like-minded individuals (i.e., echo chambers) and the online organization infrastructure to mobilize. However, one challenge that is emerging from the echo chamber effect is that groups may be led by misinformation and self-interest in social media networks and forums that have been created around a particular volatile issue. A recent study of WeChat chat groups found that misinformation was a driving force for political polarization among the immigrant Chinese community, particularly among those who are more conservative (Zhang 2018). Mitigating the echo chamber effect is critical to ensuring constructive dialogues take place between proponents and opponents within the Asian American community and help to prevent "fake news" or misinformation from determining the main narrative of an issue.

Case Study 4

The 18 Million Rising Website and Its Role as an Online Conduit for Progressive Asian American Activism

We are interested in organizing people with their power to effect social change. I am working to make my organization obsolete.
—CAYDEN MAK, former executive director of 18 Million Rising

My role, as well as my other team members, is to serve as educators and teach young Asian Americans in particular their invisible histories and activate their cultural and political identities. The values of our organization are grounded in the understanding that our diverse community is not a monolith, and that as Asian Americans we must strive to reject the model minority and racial wedge narratives assigned to us.
—LAURA LI, campaigner for 18 Million Rising

Activating Progressive Asian America through Websites and Online Campaigns

The previous case studies have demonstrated the challenges of the echo chamber effect among Chinese American immigrants with regard to social media networks that promote and amplify one-sided forums on social issues as a cost of personalized politics. This chapter examines how social media networks might be used effectively among progressive Asian American activists to promote civic engagement through social media and internet platforms on a variety of public policy issues affecting Asian Americans. The 18 Million Rising (18MR) website, which was named after the critical demographic marking point when Asian Americans reached the milestone of comprising 18 million in total population in 2012, represents an ideal example of how a website can work in lieu of a formal organization to disseminate vital information and to consolidate various progressive Asian American projects.

The former executive director of 18MR Cayden Mak reiterated these goals: "We think of ourselves as a laser collectively dispersing light and refocusing it for change in the Asian American community."[1]

An increasing number of websites that are focused on Asian American civic issues and activism can be found online. For example, Angry Asian Man is a website that focuses on news feeds that relate to Asian Americans on a broad range of contemporary issues related to racism, politics, and popular culture. Such websites are critical to helping build a sense of online group consciousness among progressive Asian Americans, and thus eventually serving as a building block for Asian American activism through awareness. What makes the 18MR website so unique is that it does this critical group-consciousness building through the process of articulating and connecting civic and political action issues to Asian Americans through various digital projects and online campaigns. In effect, the 18MR website serves the Asian American community in a critical triumvirate way as part campaign strategist, part online portal for campaign issues, and part political mobilizer. For this reason, it is a website like no other in Asian America.

While the 18MR website is certainly not the only one that shares these ideals, it speaks to the digital power shifts that social media technologies can have in twenty-first-century political action, specifically within the Asian American community. The listed staff, all dispersed throughout the United States, consists of about a dozen committed individuals. All of the business is conducted online. The office address has been replaced by a URL.

On the 18MR website, one can find various tabs at the top of the home page such as Ideas, Culture, Identities, Communities, Action, and About. After clicking on the Action tab, one is taken to several pages with individual descriptions of various 18MR-led campaigns, each with their respective Twitter hashtags and a red button below labeled "Take Action." There two primary types of campaigns that the 18MR staff work on, ranging from long-term campaigns (e.g., Release the Minnesota 8) to rapid-response campaigns (e.g., Save Tule Lake). As of September 2018, fifty-three civic engagement projects were listed on the website, covering diverse topics such as "Tell the NYPD: End Vertical Patrols" (related to the Akai Gurley shooting by former NYPD Officer Peter Liang) to "Challenge [Indian prime minister] Modi to Take a Stand for LGBT Indians (#ChallengeModi)." When the user clicks on the "Take Action" button, a project description page comes up with a signable petition complete with signature and goal totals. The "Tell the NYPD" project had a total of 103 signatures collected for its 200 signature goal while the "Challenge Modi" project had a total of 252 signatures collected toward its 400 signature goal.

The 18MR website's action pages demonstrate what previous studies on connective action have found: that websites become necessary to allow for civic engagement projects to continue and become self-sustaining in the absence of traditional formal organizations (Jost et al. 2018). In one sense, as political information becomes decentralized on the internet, these websites have replaced traditional civic organizations, as discussed in the collective action model. In another sense, websites like 18MR become part of the infrastructure that sustains and extends civic engagement projects. Several of the projects listed on the 18MR website are past and continuing projects. For example, "Tell the NYPD: End Vertical Patrols" is an extension of the "Justice for Akai Gurley" project that was previously listed on the 18MR website but has since been resolved, as discussed in Chapter 4. Visitors can fill out an online questionnaire and then be contacted by email later to participate in the respective affinity groups through social media platforms. By extension, the website link serves as a virtual formal organization by both providing the relevant information and bringing together those who share common interests and concerns about the issue. The significance of this is that it allows the entry point into civic engagement to be lower for outsiders, including youth and immigrants, by removing institutional barriers such as voting age restrictions, language assistance materials, and the need to join formal organizations to gain access to information; it is also less costly with regard to time.

Asian American Connective Action: Organization-Led and Brokered Networks

18MR represents the sole case study in this book of Asian American connective action via organization-led and brokered networks. Online organizations such as 18MR can shape the action frames around either a single or multiple social justice issues and political campaigns through various social media platforms (e.g., Twitter, organization websites). Part of the logic of connective action is that social technologies not only have replaced the necessity for high-level organizations to communicate and organize for collective action but are becoming part of the principal organizational structure itself (Bennett and Segerberg 2013). This belief is particularly evident with the 18MR website. As a result, having a large brick-and-mortar office is becoming less prevalent for similar online organizations in comparison to having a vibrant online website. This has essentially leveled the playing field for all groups when it comes to one of the most important issues for the survival of any nonprofit organization: public funding.

When it comes to underrepresented groups, particularly racial minorities, this difference can be even more salient and crucial in two ways, especially when mobilizing social justice movements. First, many minority organizations rely on federal funding to help subsidize costs, and thus they became vulnerable to ideological shifts that are antithetical and antagonistic to progressive issues and concerns of minority communities. For example, during the 1980s, President Ronald Reagan's administration began to reduce federal funding of local programs of minority organizations such as the NAACP, a period that has been referred to as the "Winter of Civil Rights" (Omatsu 1993, p. 144). Second, operational costs are less for online affinity groups than for formal organizations in that the former no longer have to rely on obtaining local and state funding as well as grants to fund projects and other organizational activities. In short, online affinity group and organization websites no longer need the same amount of economic or political resources to operate and recruit members, as they often require few staff members beyond a webmaster and a virtual board of directors.

For 18MR, there are three full-time (executive director, campaign strategist, and campaigner) and one part-time (social media manager) staff members. In addition, back-office support around fundraising and leadership coaching is provided by other social media incubator organizations. All 18MR weekly staff meetings are conducted online.

Campaign One—The 2017 Asian American Pacific Islander (AAPI) Immigrant Rights Organizing Table

The AAPI Immigrant Rights Organizing Table was launched in the last quarter of 2017 in order to pass a clean DREAM Act.[2] It was a concerted online effort led by 18MR and other members of the coalition to raise the visibility of Deferred Action for Childhood Arrivals (DACA) recipients and the failure of Congress to pass a clean DREAM Act, culminating in two weeks of actions and Capitol Hill visits in November and December 2017. In the latter, 18MR worked with the Undocublack Network to bring over one hundred Black and AAPI immigrants to Washington, DC, to demand a clean DREAM Act and a permanent solution for temporary protected status (TPS) holders who are at risk of losing their status.

One of the most controversial issues in Washington, DC, has been what to do policy-wise with regard to DREAMers, the estimated thirteen million undocumented youth who came to the United States along with their parents. Despite the fact that this issue has been primarily framed as a Latinx issue given the geopolitics of Mexico and other Central American countries along the United States' southern border, the salience of this issue is not lost when discussing Asian American undocumented immigrants. In 2017, an estimated 1.7 million undocumented Asian Americans currently reside in anonymity throughout the United States, which accounts for one out of every seven Asian immigrants and approximately 16 percent of all undocumented in the United States (Ramakrishnan and Shah 2017).

On September 15, 2017, the Trump administration announced their decision to end the DACA policy. As a result, over 800,000 minority students who relied on the DACA program became subject to deportation and loss of jobs. About 30,000 of these affected immigrants were Asian Americans. According to a study by Loan Thi Dao, associate professor of Asian American studies and transnational cultural and community studies, "AAPI un-docu/DACAmented young people, 18–26 years old, negotiate dual liminal identities that lead to their political participation in as AAPI immigrant rights activists" (Dao 2017, p. 2). Another study in 2015 by the Center of Migration Studies study found that the top three largest groups of undocumented Asian American immigrants are from India (485,663), China (387,369), and the Philippines (247,304) (Wong 2015).

The AAPI Immigrant Rights Organizing Table formed as a collective organization in order to demand change and push for a "clean" DREAM Act, passed without the attachment of any other provisions that would further negatively impact our immigration system. Their mission is deeply rooted in the opposition of provisions that would enhance enforcement measures such as increasing the number of immigration agents, expanding the grounds of deportability or inadmissibility, persecuting jurisdictions with policies that limit entanglement with ICE, adding restrictive changes to the visa system, and further limiting immigrants' access to public benefits. They believe in the utmost importance that immigrants receive a pathway to citizenship. The DREAM Act, with its current provisions, makes this difficult as the pathway takes up to thirteen years, with many additional measures that must be met.

The ultimate goal of the AAPI Immigrant Rights Organizing Table is to make sure that undocumented Asian Americans' voices are heard and that there is unity among the Asian American community no matter the ethnicity, language, or gender. Advocacy through social media has allowed this collective organization to gain followers and support.

Asian Americans also have an important stake in the undocumented immigrant debate that surrounds DACA, because of the number of undocumented Asians who reside in the United States. Indeed, many Asian American progressive activists have taken to political action to make their case. For example, On November 17, 2017, nineteen Asian Americans were arrested by while peacefully protesting outside of U.S. Congressman and House Speaker Paul Ryan's office.

Connective action has further intensified and mobilized the progressive Asian American organizations around DACA and to build sustainable multiracial coalitions on this issue. With the rescindment of DACA and tempo-

Figure 7.1 #BlackAAPIaction: Building and Sustaining a Biracial Progressive Coalition around Immigration Reform (Source: Shauna Siggelkow.)

rary protected status (TPS) under the Trump administration, political action had to emerge so African American and Asian American undocumented voices can be heard. The African American and Asian American undocumented communities knew that the time for action was now, which is why the UndocuBlack Network and the National AAPI immigrant Rights Organizing Table, with the help of ally organizations, planned a joint action day to take place on December 5, 2017 in Washington, DC (UndocuBlack Network 2017a). The action would become an important day for solidarity among the Asian American and Pacific Islander community centered on immigration justice. There would be opportunities for coalition building along multiracial lines where various organizations and activists from all backgrounds would come together.

Over one hundred African American and Asian American immigrants came to Washington, DC, for the joint action day on December 5, 2017 (UndocuBlack Network 2017c). An estimated 150 protesters, led by the UndocuBlack Network and the AAPI Immigrant Rights Organizing Table, demanded Congress pass a clean Dream Act, along with a permanent solution for TPS and DACA recipients. The UndocuBlack Network and AAPI Immigrant Rights Organizing Table organized these recipients along with community leaders and other undocumented folks to lead a demonstration that would demand the reinstatement of DACA as well. At the beginning of 2018, President Trump removed the TPS of more than 300,000 people, many of them racial minorities. Along with the help of allies, 18MR was able to uplift their voices and advocate for were those who are undocumented.

Activists showed their unity and strength on social media with tweets such as "drumming to chanting, and marching in solidarity with . . . so many other organizations and allies for a #cleanDREAMact" (UndocuBlack Network 2017b). Social media was a major tool for getting the message out, and the hashtag #BlackAAPIAction was highly utilized on Twitter.

Online Connective Action Findings

1. Analysis of Twitter Hashtag #BlackAAPIAction

Among the total 124 tweets that included #BlackAAPIAction from December 4 to December 21, 2017, Asian Americans and non-Asians equally accounted for 14 tweets for 11.3 percent of the grand total, respectively. Since this was an organization-driven campaign, organizations accounted for 96 tweets for 77.4 percent of the grand total. African American organizations represented the greatest percentage with 63 tweets for 50.1 percent of the grand total. Asian American organizations, led by 18MR, were the second largest at 21 tweets for 16.9 percent of the grand total. Organizations where race was not determinable accounted for 12 tweets for 9.7 percent of the grand total.

A coalition of panethnic Asian American organizations mobilized online around the #BlackAAPIAction campaign. 18MR had 9 tweets with #BlackAAPIAction for 42.8 percent of the total Asian American organization tweets, followed by Asian Americans Advancing Justice and the National Asian Pacific American Women's Forum (NAPAWF) with 3 tweets for 14.3 percent, respectively; the Asian Pacific American Labor Alliance with 2 tweets for 9.5 percent; and the National Korean American Service & Education Consortium with one tweet for 5 percent.

A majority (10 for non-Asians and 13 for Asian Americans) of the grand total of 28 individual tweets that included #BlackAAPIAction were from locations that were not determinable, followed by Washington, DC (1 Korean American and 3 non-Asians), and Michigan (with 1 non-Asian). The low number of total tweets by individuals is due to the fact that #BlackAAPIAction was an online campaign that was predominantly organization-driven.

2. Geocode Analysis of #BlackAAPIAction

The geocode findings illustrate that #BlackAAPIAction was an online campaign driven by several national African American and Asian American organizations, such as Black Alliance for Just Immigration (BAJI) and 18MR. Among the 20 total Asian American organization tweets with #BlackAA-PIaction, 13 were from locations that were not determinable, followed by 7 from Washington, DC, and 1 from Chicago. 18MR accounted for 9 of these tweets, the largest of the 5 national Asian American organizations that participated. African American organizations accounted for 63 total tweets with #BlackAAPIAction, with 61 tweets from locations not determinable and 2 tweets from Washington, DC. BAJI accounted for the largest number of African American organization tweets with 23, followed by UndocuBlack with 10 tweets.

Allyship in Organizing

Organizers understood the need for intersectionality during the demonstrations. An example of this intersectionality is the issue of how increased enforcement at the hands of ICE meant more potential violations of human rights and police brutality for all undocumented folks, including African immigrants, who face a greater amount of brutality at the hands of law enforcement due to criminalization of African Americans and other minorities. On top of the use of excessive force among ICE agents, there have been reports of sexual assault in detention centers against undocumented women and minority children (Kassie 2018).

The significance of the coming together of the African American and Asian American communities for a clean DREAM Act is important because of the previous history of cultural tensions between the two racial groups in inner cities, as seen during the 1992 Los Angeles and the 2015 Baltimore riots between Asian American small-business owners and their largely African American patrons. On December 5, 2017, the day of joint action, there were several displays of unity between African American and Asian American protesters who spoke out not only for pro-immigrant legislation but also against anti-blackness, mass incarceration of predominantly people of color, and police brutality that happens throughout their communities (HANA Center 2017).

Both African American and Asian American leadership by progressive organizations like 18MR understood that immigration affects both communities, especially since under the Trump presidential administration non-White undocumented immigrants were targeted by the Department of Homeland Security and all the immigration law enforcement that falls below it. For all of these reasons, #BlackAAPIAction was crucial to coalition building and solidarity that needs to take place. This will open the doors for these individuals to advocate and fight for other issues that affect them with more security (i.e., getting involved more politically, such as a chance to vote, etc.).

At the end of the day, this action can be the beginning of a long-lasting, powerful unity between both minority communities.

On October 4, 2017, the day before the #BlackAAPIAction campaign was launched, a Twitter town hall took place that was facilitated by Color of Change, an organization that fights African American injustice, which posed a series of online questions for the African American and Asian American communities to answer. There were over 100 tweets in the Twitter town hall, with about 80 tweets that included #BlackAAPIAction. The answers and discussion featured multiple people from several organizations that gave detailed answers with factual data to address immigration reform questions.

18MR participated in the Twitter town hall. In one instance, 18MR responded to an online question about how they can help if they cannot attend the December 5, 2017, joint action day with the following: "Call, call, call your members of Congress (all 3 of them). Jam their phone lines to demand that they don't go home without a #cleanDreamAct. #BlackAAPIAction #DreamActNow" (18MillionRising.org 2017b). In other responses, 18MR articulated that xenophobia was at the root of U.S. immigration legislation that had targeted non-White immigrants negatively throughout U.S. history. They also highlighted that "there is no singular, monolithic 'AAPI experience,' our communities interfaced immigration in all different ways" (18MillionRising.org 2017d).

On 18MR's Twitter page, they answered a series of questions throughout the few days of the solidarity actions among the Black and AAPI organizations that came together. 18MR tweeted #BlackAAPIAction a total of 9 times throughout the Twitter Town Hall on December 4 as they were spreading awareness to the multiracial action through their social media platforms (18MillionRising.org 2017a). The 18MR Twitter page made an important point that the #cleanDREAMAct "does not further bolster law enforcement or grant additional powers to abuse our communities" (18MillionRising.org 2017c). This tweet in particular illustrates how there is an understanding of ICE and other law enforcement targeting, disrupting, and separating predominantly Latinx families throughout the United States.

The significance of the Twitter town hall is how organizations like 18MR have effectively utilized social media to educate the larger public about their various campaigns. In this case, it was about passing a clean DREAM Act and how this issue extended beyond the Asian American community to work with African American and Latinx organizations. This is arguably one of the most important aspects of social media, as it can be an effective medium for sharing political information with a large number of people. One of the criticisms of hashtag movements has been that they take place because of weak social networks that make it convenient to broadcast perspectives rather than take part in actual protests. This one-to-one comparison of hashtag activism and political protests is unfair; the former can facilitate the latter, as seen on the day following the Twitter town hall, when a large, multiracial contingent gathered in front of the U.S. Congress to demand the passage of a clean DREAM Act.

The emphasis of the progressive mobilization by 18MR is to build a broader, more inclusive coalition with Latinxs and African Americans that incorporates Asian Americans into the DREAM Act movement and its multiracial coalitions. According to Laura Li, campaigner for 18MR:

> The AAPI Immigrant Rights Organizing Table was launched in the last quarter of 2017 in order to pass a clean DREAM Act. The concerted work by 18MR and other members of the coalition to raise the visibility of DACA recipients and the failure of Congress in passing a clean DREAM Act online helped us to organize two weeks of actions and Hill visits in November and December 2017. In our December 2017 week of action, our coalition worked with the Undocublack Network to bring over 100 Black and AAPI immigrants to Washington, DC, to demand a clean DREAM Act and a permanent solution to TPS holders who are still at risk of losing their status in the U.S. Additionally, because we cannot count on mainstream media to cover these actions and acts of solidarity, using "hashtag" and online activism is doubly important to document this online civil rights movement. This is why 18MR invests time and energy in cultivating our social media accounts and followings.[3]

While the goal of a clean DREAM Act has yet to be realized, the 2017 online national Asian American/Pacific Islander Immigrant Rights Organizing Table campaign demonstrates how minorities (particularly Asian American youth and young adults) can lead effective campaigns through social media platforms to educate and mobilize African Americans and Asian Americans around the issue of immigration in coalition with Latinx immigration activists. Connective action is facilitating this new multiracial group consciousness that is surfacing and one that is necessary to make change on immigration reform.

Campaign Two—The Release the Minnesota 8 (#ReleaseMN8) Movement

While national debate centers on the U.S. ICE detainment of thousands of undocumented immigrants of Mexican and Latin American descent and

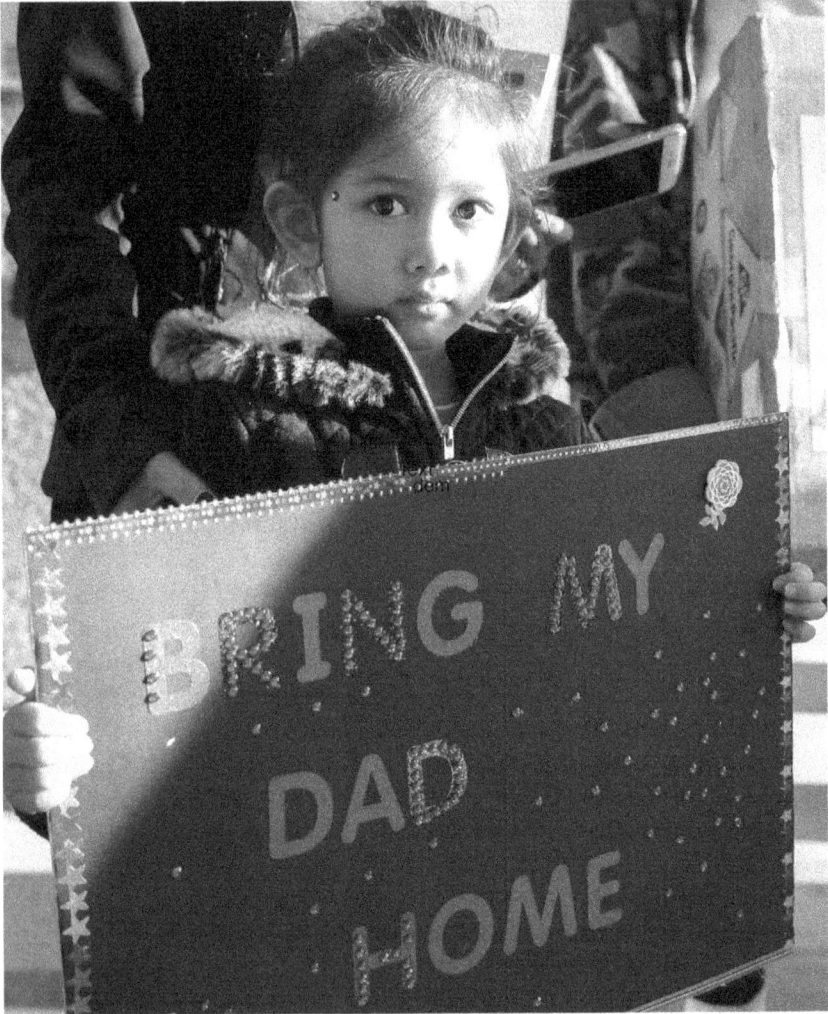

Figure 7.2 Bring My Daddy Home. "Demand That Ramsey County Attorney John Choi Bring Chamroeun Phan Home to His Family Today, #ReleaseMN8."—18MR.org
(Source: Thai Phan-Quang.)

their deportation back to their native homelands, this issue is also salient for Cambodian Americans. Minnesota is home to one of the nation's largest Cambodian American communities. In August 2016, the following eight Cambodian Americans from Minnesota were detained by ICE: Chamrouen Phan, Sameth Nhean, Ched Nin, Soeun "Posy" Chheng, Ron An, Phueoy Chuon, Chan Ouch, and Chan Om. These men were known afterwards as the Minnesota 8.

All of the Minnesota 8 men are in their thirties and forties and legally immigrated as refugees to the United States during the 1980s (Blitzer 2017). Under U.S. law, legal permanent residents are automatically deported if they are convicted of an aggravated felony. However, a diplomatic dispute between the United States and Cambodia resulted in these men being released after serving their respective prison sentences rather than being deported (Blitzer 2017). Part of their release conditions required each of the men to check in twice a year with their ICE office in St. Paul, Minnesota. But something changed in the summer of 2018 when they showed up for their appointments with ICE. All eight men were abruptly rearrested and told that they would be deported (Blitzer 2017).

Many of the Minnesota 8 have no family in Cambodia and have never even been there before. The majority were born and raised in the United States. The men do not speak Khmer, the main language in Cambodia. Only two were even born in Cambodia, with the remaining six born in refugee camps, in either Thailand or the Philippines, before coming to the United States with their families. In short, the United States is the only country that they have ever truly known.

The Minnesota 8 were held until the spring of 2017. A reason for ICE's detainment of the Cambodian Americans is that they each had a past felony conviction. For example, one served ten years in prison in the '90s for attempted murder. Another broke three windows at a bar in 2009 and served forty days in jail after paying a fine. A third pleaded guilty to second-degree assault in 2010 (Chhuon 2017). All of the Minnesota 8 had served their respective times for their respective crimes. They had rehabilitated and were leading reformed lives with families and young children.

During the Minnesota 8's detainment, Ched Nin was released back to his family in February 2017 because he convinced the court that his deportation would cause extreme hardship for his U.S. citizen wife and son (Chhuon 2017). Two others—Sameth Nhean and Chamroeun "Shorty" Phan—would also be released in 2017. Five—Soeun "Posy" Chheng, Phoeuy Chuon, Chan Ouch, Chan Om, and Ron An—were deported to Cambodia in 2017.

With time being essential, the families of these individuals came together to get the community involved in order to start bringing attention to the Minnesota 8. According to Nicki Chhoeurng, the niece of one of the Minnesota 8, "In the Cambodian community, we usually don't like to talk about this—people are embarrassed. In Minnesota, it's the younger generation that's standing up, because this makes no sense" (Blitzer 2017, par. 2). Jenny Srey, wife of Ched Nin, did everything in her power to get him back, and that included a public campaign with the support of a group of community organizers that would lead to the founding of a 501(c)(3) organization called Release MN8 (Potter 2017).

In addition to the families who mobilized, a national coalition was developing that included Cambodian American community-based organizations such as the Southeast Asia Resource Action Center (SEARAC), a Sacramento, California, based organization that was created in 1979 by a group of Americans concerned with genocide in Cambodia; the Southeast Asian Coalition in Charlotte, North Carolina; local Minnesota community-based groups such as the Minnesota Immigrant Rights Action Committee (MIRAC); and online organizations like 18MR. They all worked together to bring attention to and create political action around this issue.

18MR's specific role was to collaborate with the existing Minnesota 8 coalition on various efforts to get these eight Cambodian Americans back to their families. The first step was to disseminate background information on various social media platforms including Facebook and Twitter. Below is an example of a background summary of the Minnesota 8 that was written and distributed by 18MR on Facebook, which illustrated organization-led connective action:

> **Background on the MN8 and Cambodian deportations nation-wide**
> This past summer, 8 Cambodian Americans in Minnesota ("MN 8") were detained by Immigration and Customs Enforcement (ICE) for unjust deportation. Families, friends, and neighbors have banded together by launching the #ReleaseMN8 campaign. These deportations show how unfair the "felons, not families" policy is—despite their old records, all of the men are devoted and beloved fathers and sons. Unjust deportation is an important Asian American issue and families are fighting to stay together (e.g., the Adam Crasper Korean Adoptee case). Now this administration may escalate attacks on Asian American families, even though we understand that deporting people who contribute to society is a waste of time and money. . . . Why is unjust deportation of the MN 8 a moral issue? It is morally wrong to throw away survivors of war and genocide. Southeast Asian American refugee families from Cambodia, Laos, and Vietnam escaped war and genocide, only to be resettled in poverty-stricken neighborhoods plagued by violence and crime. Many Southeast Asian American (SEA) children and young adults were funneled into the school-prison-deportation pipeline. Since 1998, around 16,000 SEAs have received final deportation orders—78 percent of them based on past criminal records for time served already. (18Mil lionRising.org 2016b)

The significance of the above Facebook post is that it shows how an organization like 18MR generates inclusive personal action frames for the members of its network to be mobilized later on both web-based and smartphone platforms.

The second role of 18MR was to help facilitate political action through various social media platforms including email. In August 2017, 18MR worked with the MN8 coalition to launch a call-in campaign to Ramsey County Attorney John Choi, asking him to release Chamroeun Phan to his family in September 2017, after 387 days of detention, and to stop his deportation to Cambodia. The 18MR staff drove over 130 calls to Choi's office and, together with other partners, was able to secure Phan's release. As Laura Li stated:

> The actual organizing of the call-in campaign was done over the phone with the other members of the MN8 coalition. . . . When we launched the campaign, I sent an email to our members in Minnesota and those who had already taken previous action on MN8 campaigns, and 18MR posted it on our Facebook account. The MN8 Coalition also posted it on their Facebook account. We fielded a number of questions emailed to us and sent to us via the Facebook post about the office of John Choi giving our members the runaround, directing us to call ICE, claiming that the office doesn't have the power to decide Chamroeun's fate. I remember having a handful of other phone calls that day with Montha and emails with the group about instructing our members on how to respond if Choi's office refuses to listen or take a message.[4]

The influence of 18MR and the Minnesota 8 coalition was not lost on Phan's family. Montha Chum, Phan's sister and the lead organizer of the coalition, stated, "We are so thankful and relieved to have Shorty back home with us. Chamroeun's release, only by the grace of God, shows the power of community organizing and effective advocacy. The #ReleaseMN8 community . . . stood by us every step of the way, and refused to let Chamroeun be deported without a fight" (Southeast Asian Resource Center 2017).

Online Connective Action Findings: Analysis of Twitter Hashtag #ReleaseMN8

Table 7.1 shows the ethno-racial breakdown of the individuals and organizations from October 20, 2016, to November 24, 2018, that utilized #ReleaseMN8 in their tweets. Asian Americans accounted for 46 tweets for 33.8 percent of the grand total, the largest among all racial groups. Cambodian Americans, not surprisingly, accounted for 16 tweets for 11.8 percent of the grand total. Not Determinable also accounted for 16 tweets for 11.8 percent,

TABLE 7.1 RACIAL BREAKDOWN FOR #RELEASEMN8 TWEETS (10/20/16 TO 11/24/18)	
Racial and Ethnic Group	Total Number of Tweets (Percent of Grand Total)
Asian Americans	**46 (33.8)**
Cambodian American	16 (11.8)
Vietnamese American	1 (0.7)
Filipina/o American	1 (0.7)
Other Asian	12 (8.8)
Not Determinable	16 (11.8)
Asian American Organizations	**62 (45.6)**
18MillionRising.org	6 (4.4)
Asian Prisoner Support Committee (APSC)	5 (3.7)
National Council of Asian Pacific Americans (NCAPA)	2 (1.5)
Southeast Asian Resource Action Center (SEARAC)	25 (18.4)
National Immigration Project of National Lawyers Guild (NIPNLG)	6 (4.4)
National APA Women's Forum (NAPAWF)	2 (1.5)
Not Determinable	16 (11.8)
Non-Asians	**12 (8.8)**
Non-Asian Organizations	**16 (11.8)**
Grand Total	**136 (100)**

followed by Vietnamese Americans and Filipina/o Americans with 1 tweet each for 0.7 percent, respectively. In comparison, non-Asians accounted for 12 tweets for 8.8 percent of the grand total.

Asian American organizations accounted for the largest number of #ReleaseMN8 tweets of all categories with 62 tweets for 45.6 percent of the grand total. Among those Asian American organizations that were identifiable, SEARAC had the most tweets with 25 for 18.4 percent of the grand total, followed by 18MR and the National Immigration Project of National Lawyers Guild (NIPNLG) with 6 tweets each for 4.4 percent. The Asian Prisoner Support Committee (APSC) had 5 tweets for 3.7 percent, and the National Council of Asian Pacific Americans (NCAPA) and NAPAWF each had 2 tweets for 3.8 percent, respectively.

The significance of the above Asian American organizations findings is threefold. First, it demonstrates how these national organizations were central players in bringing public awareness and working with other non-Asian organizations and key political actors to overturn the deportation of the Minnesota 8. For example, Asian American organizations from Sacramento, California (SEARAC), Washington, DC (NCAPA), and Boston, Massachusetts (NIPNLG) were part of this national online campaign to support Minnesota organizations like the APSC, whose mission is to provide direct support to API prisoners and to raise awareness about the growing number of APIs being imprisoned, detained, and deported. Second, the findings clearly demonstrate Asian American connective action through the organization-led process. For example, 18MR utilized its website, Facebook, Twitter, and their organization email list to bring attention and awareness to the Minnesota 8. In addition, 18MR attempted to coordinate their online efforts with local efforts led by APSC and other Cambodian American groups and individuals. Third, the efforts by these Asian American organizations illustrate a panethnic Asian American coalition to bring attention to the search for justice for the Minnesota 8. The legal battles still continue to return the five who were deported to Cambodia so that they can be with their families in the United States.

An Online Conduit for Progressive Asian American Activism

Progressive Asian American online organizations like 18MR demonstrate how connective action can be equally effective and creative in mobilizing like-minded progressive Asian American activists with other progressive minority activists along a wide range of social justice campaigns through social media and internet platforms, as vividly captured during the #BlackAAPIAction and #ReleaseMN8 campaigns. At the heart of 18MR's mission is its ability to serve as an online conduit for Asian American activism by providing Asian Americans activists and supporters a collective voice in the public arena. One important way that 18MR's pan-Asian American staff achieves this end goal is by bringing the various campaigns to their online community members, whether it be their website visitors, Facebook friends, and/or Twitter followers. This online strategy is critical. According to 18MR campaigner Laura Li:

> Asian Americans and Pacific Islanders live in scattered communities across the U.S. and our communities face unique challenges in organizing, whether those are cultural and language barriers, distrust of the state, or lack of access to courses like Asian American history and political education, and so online activism is an entry point for young Asian Americans to find their place in our movement, voice their thoughts, and become more engaged so that they participate in actions that lead to changes in communities on the ground.[5]

In addition to the above points, 18MR inherently understands that Asian American activists cannot and do not live in a vacuum, that they must forge multiracial coalitions with other progressive minorities and organizations if any significant movements are to transpire. This outward thinking was evident with #BlackAAPIAction campaign, as a viable African American and Asian American multiracial coalition formed to support the DREAMers, who are predominantly Mexican American youth. This strategy may hold how the future of Asian American progressive activism will look as similar multiracial coalitions continue to learn from the opportunities and challenges of connective action.

Case Study 5

The 2016 California Textbook
Controversy—South Asian Americans
and the #DontEraseIndia Campaign

#DontEraseIndia is nothing but Hindu Nationalist propaganda
infecting America. I hope CA schools don't succumb to their
campaign.
—SEPIA MUTINY, Twitter post, May 5, 2016

I am Pakistani but I think [the] *name India has strong roots to*
the history of that region so #DontEraseIndia.
—SYED AKIF ABBAS, Twitter post, May 4, 2016

The Diverse and Intersectional Identities
among South Asian Americans

The 2005 and 2016 California textbook controversies reflect the deep ideological fissures within the transnational and multinational South Asian communities. Two sides existed during both controversies: on one side, Hindu organizations such as the Vedic Foundation (VF), the Hindu Education Foundation USA (HEF-USA), and the Hindu American Foundation (HAF) worked in collaboration with concerned Asian Indians in suburbs of Northern and Southern California to focus on the history of India and Hinduism, the largest religion in India, to represent the larger South Asian region. These organizations are ideologically aligned with the Hindu nationalist movement in India, which is associated with the right wing of the Hindu Nationalist Party, led by the prime minister of India, Narendra Modi. HAF provided the finances for the textbook legal challenges (Bose 2008). The arguments made by these Asian Indian organizations in the California textbook controversies mirror what is taking place in India as Hindu Nationalist governments have sought to overhaul textbooks in certain states (Medina 2016). On other side, secular Hindus, a panethnic coalition of South

Asian progressives and academics, attempted to reframe the representations of South Asian history in required California textbooks to be more inclusive of other South Asian countries besides India (Bose 2008). Given the limited space in required California textbooks on world history, accurate and fair representation were critical issues for both sides, but the controversies also demonstrated larger hegemonic and geopolitical divisions within the larger South Asian communities that have existed for many centuries.

The term *South Asian* has been a long-standing debate among South Asian American scholars and community members along three fronts (Sriram 2016a; Mishra 2016). First, there are those who believe this term captures all of those who are from this region or have ancestral roots in this area. This belief is captured by the term *Desi*, which means "in Sanskrit land or country" and refers to South Asian people and culture from countries such as India, Pakistan, and Bangladesh (Oxford Dictionary 2018b). Second, critics argue that there exists a hegemonic Indian perspective that underlies the first belief, which often does not take into account the diversity and intersectionality of other nationalities within this region. This debate also includes Hinduism, the majority religion in India but not in the other South Asian countries. Third, a recent group of South Asian scholars have used the terms *South Asians* and *South Asian Americans* to create new knowledge about the experiences of more than just those of Indian descent (Purkayastha 2005; Maira 2008; Sriram 2016b; Mishra 2016). A recent example of this third front is Sangay Mishra's *Desis Divided: The Political Lives of South Asian Americans*, which focuses primarily on Indians, Pakistanis, and Bangladeshi to examine how South Asian American political incorporation and mobilization work by using surveys and case studies "as a manner in which it intersects with internal distinctions along multiple lines" (Mishra 2016, p. 10). Mishra is one of the first scholars to create and use an intersectional framework for understanding South Asian American politics to explain retroactively past and current political phenomena (Sriram 2016a). Another example is Sunaina Maira, who examines how intersections within identities emerge into a "flexible citizenship" among South Asian American Muslim youth as they situate themselves in post-9/11 America (Maira 2008).

The 2005 California Textbook Battle: Pre-connective Action Battle over Religion, History, and Politics in the South Asian American Community

The beginning of the California textbook controversies was in 2005, when the state's required sixth- and seventh-grade history textbook's portrayals of Hinduism came under review for the first time, as California requires the state's textbooks and teaching guidelines be reviewed every six years. It was also a period prior to the popular use of smartphones and social media platform apps, which explains why Asian Indian nationalist organizations took the sole lead in voicing their dissent. The Texas-based VF and the New Jersey–based HEF-USA filed a joint complaint with the California Curriculum Commission that claimed the history textbooks' portrayals of Indian history were done in a poor light and Hinduism was being singled out for "bias, distortions and prejudicial treatment" (Vashisht 2006, par. 2). The claim by VF and HEF-USA referenced the *California Standards for Evaluating Instructional Materials for Social Content*, which contains the following methods to be considered for textbooks: "The standards will be achieved by depicting, when appropriate, the diversity of religious beliefs held in the United States and California, as well as in other societies, without displaying bias toward or prejudice against any of those beliefs or religious beliefs in general" (California Board of Education 2013, p. 10).

Topics such as the portrayal of the caste system and the status of women in Indian society were singled out in the complaint. HEF-USA argued a minority perspective that both inequalities were a product of the geographic region rather than Hinduism. In response, the California Department of Education hoped to resolve the controversy by appointing a one-person committee, consisting of Shiva Bajpai, professor emeritus at the California State University at Northridge, to review the revisions proposed by VF and HEF-USA. Bajpai approved most of VF's suggested changes to the textbooks, but it was later revealed that he had a conflict of interest due to a close connection to organization affiliated with VF (Guichard 2010). After learning of this controversy, Michael Witzel, a professor of Sanskrit at Harvard University, organized a letter signature campaign of a rival group of fifty Indian historians to protest VF's proposed changes. According to Witzel's 2005 letter, addressed to the California State Board of Education:

> I write on behalf of a long list of world specialists on ancient India—reflecting mainstream academic opinion in India, Pakistan, the United States, Europe, Australia, Taiwan, and Japan—to urge you to reject the demands by nationalist Hindu ["Hindutva"] groups that California textbooks be altered to conform to their religious-political views. (Witzel 2005, p. 1)

Witzel and two other Indologists were asked by the California State Board of Education to revisit the proposed changes and eventually came to an agreement among them to revert some of the approved changes initially done by Bajpai (Mozumder 2006). A week later, on March 15, 2006, HEF-USA sued the California State Board of Education based on the complaint that the board violated the law when it approved the textbook edits that tended to "demean, stereotype, and reflect adversity" upon Hindus (Mozumder 2006, par. 2).

In 2009, the court ruled that the challenged texts complied with the applicable legal standards and that the portrayals of the Aryan migration were not grossly inaccurate, and that the treatment of Hinduism in the textbooks did not violate the standard set by the state. On the issue of the caste system, the court ruled that the topic had to be discussed even if it resulted in a negative reaction in students. Following this ruling, HEF and the board of education reached a settlement in which the board agreed to pay for part of HEF's legal expenses (Jha 2009).

The reverberations of the 2005 case and subsequent legal battles captured the attention of the California State Legislature. In 2014, California State Senate majority leader Ellen Corbett authored Senate Bill 1057, which called for a complete overhaul of the state's history and social studies curriculum to portray Hinduism and other religions in an accurate light. The bill passed unanimously in both state houses but was vetoed by Governor Jerry Brown because it would slow down the curriculum process that was underway at the time (California Legislative Information 2014). While both sides viewed the settlement as a victory, it would set the stage for the 2016 California textbook controversy and their respective campaigns that centered around connective action on both sides at both the state and national levels.

The 2016 California Textbook Controversy—the Battle Goes Viral with the Emergence of the #DontEraseIndia Movement through Connective Action

One clear difference between the 2005 and 2016 California textbook controversies was the presence of connective action during the latter in which social media served as the primary vehicle for helping to shape public opinion and for political mobilization on both sides. According to Samir Kalra, who is based in the Silicon Valley in California and is the current executive director of HAF, which created the #DontEraseIndia campaign:

> One of the primary goals of #DontEraseIndia was to educate the broader American public about the California textbook edits that we were fighting against. The issue was one community being treated unfairly in a historical manner. The hashtag allowed for a lot more media coverage about our stance on the issue on television, print, and online stories.[1]

TABLE 8.1 SELECTED EXAMPLES OF CONTROVERSIAL EDITS, 2015		
Edit Number	Original Framework Language	South Asia Faculty Group's Edited Language
2454	"A flourishing urban civilization developed in ~~India~~ from as early as 3300 BCE along the Indus River."	"A flourishing urban civilization developed in **South Asia** from as early as 3300 BCE along the Indus River."
2730	"Enduring contributions of ~~ancient Indian~~ civilization to other areas of Afroeurasia."	"Enduring contributions of **South Asian culture** and civilization to other areas of Afroeurasia."
2439	"How did the ~~religion of Hinduism~~ support individuals, rulers and societies."	"How did the **religion of Ancient India** support individuals, rulers and societies."
2480	"Teachers focus students on the question: How did the ~~religion of Hinduism~~ support individuals, rulers, and societies?"	"Teachers focus students on the question: How did the **religion of Ancient India** support individuals, rulers, and societies?"
Source: Hindu American Foundation website.		

In 2016, the California Board of Education and the independent Instructional Quality Commission (IQC) began the process of enacting a state law that required the state agency to review existing state curriculum and teaching standards every six years with regard to California required textbooks and teaching guidelines for sixth and seventh graders. During this review process, a division occurred between two South Asian American groups: on one side was HAF, the nonprofit Washington, DC, organization founded in 2003 that seeks to address contemporary issues and policies by applying the Hindu philosophy, and on the other side was the South Asian Faculty Group (SAFG), an inter-caste and multifaith group of South Asian scholars in various interdisciplinary fields related to South Asian studies.

Table 8.1 provides four selected examples of edits among several hundred that were proposed by SAFG. The focus of these edits was primarily on replacing *India* with the broader term *South Asia*. At issue was the possibility these changes to the language would confuse California's sixth- and seventh-grade students with regard to the accurate portrayal of Indian history. SAFG argued that to change specific references of *India* to *South Asia* was to be more inclusive of the shared history among other countries (Nepal, Bangladesh, Sri Lanka, Bhutan, and Pakistan) that make up the shared region (Yap 2016). In addition, SAFG argued that HAF was attempting to sanitize history by removing any link between Hinduism and castes (Medina 2016). These responses led to those who supported SAFG creating two Twitter hashtags: #SouthAsianHistoryForAll and #DontEraseDalit. The term *Dalit* refers to the "untouchables," or members of the lowest caste in a traditional Indian caste system (Oxford Dictionary 2018a). SAFG argued for the inclusion of *Dalit* in order to retain the history of the caste system in the textbooks (Thaker 2018).

On the opposing side, Suhag Shukla, the former executive director of HAF, stated "Columbus didn't come to the Americas looking for South Asia. Columbus came looking for India. To deny the existence of this term is a little bit nitpicking on semantics for something that is very modern" (Yap 2016, par. 4). HAF also advocated for the portrayal of the caste system in California textbooks as a phenomenon of the South Asian region, not as a Hindu practice, a belief that is not universally accepted in India (Medina 2016).

The mobilization by Asian Indians took shape through both individual-led and organization-led connective action. First, small to medium-size suburbs were the primary geographic sites of individual-led connective action among Asian Indians who were against SAFG's proposed edits. This grassroots campaign was led by community leaders throughout California related to and those who are members of Hindu temples and Asian Indian community organizations to bring awareness on the issue and to take action. Second, in regard to organization-led connective action, HAF took the lead on being one of the key national Asian Indian organizations to help coordinate the information campaign that focused on educating the broader community about the issue through #DontEraseIndia, as well as helping to coordinate with California's Asian Indian communities' various campaigns to influence state elected leaders. For example, HAF created an online signature campaign through a website portal and helped to verify those who were California residents and voters. Once the signatures and emails were verified, the individuals and organization names were then presented by HAF to the California Board of Education, the California Teachers Association, and various California elected officials as far up as Lieutenant Governor Gavin Newsom. As stated by HAF executive director Samir Kalra, "When we engaged various stakeholders, we engaged teachers and elected officials."[2]

HAF's perspective that it needed to educate the broader community, not just the Asian Indian community in California, would lead to the creation of the Twitter hashtag #DontEraseIndia. In April 2016, HAF launched the major social media campaign, which became a rallying cry online. According to the HAF website:

> The #DontEraseIndia campaign is aimed at ensuring that the CA K-12 Historical-Social Science Framework depicts the history, culture, and traditions of India and Hindu Americans accurately and

[in a] culturally competent manner, in order to better educate students and prepare them for an increasingly globalized society. . . . Launched on April 6, 2016 to coincide with the 86th anniversary of Mahatma Ghandi's Dandi March, the campaign is a broad-based initiative supported by community groups, scholars, interfaith organizations, and elected officials to raise awareness about the attempts to minimize the history and contributions of Hindus and Indians from the framework. (Hindu American Foundation 2016, pars. 6 and 7)

In addition to Twitter, Facebook accounts such as "Dignity4Hinduism" and "Save Hinduism" (made by an organization in Mumbai) featured related news stories and photos. YouTube channels with content videos further educated and framed their concerns with the recent textbook edits.

The 2016 textbook controversy, unlike in 2005, effectively used websites such as Change.org to mobilize a signature campaign against the latest edits that could be signed by the large Asian Indian population in California and those living in the continental United States. For example, one petition entitled "Don't Replace 'India' with 'South Asia' in California History Social Sciences Frameworks" on Change.org took the #DontEraseIndia side by asking supporters to endorse a letter written and signed by the "Scholars for People" to the California Board of Education, calling on them "to reject all the changes pushed by the South Asia faculty group that attempt to erase India and Hinduism from California's schools. Let 'India' remain 'India' and 'Hinduism' remain 'Hinduism,' and respect reality at least that much" (Scholars for People 2016, par. 8). This petition received 25,779 supporters' signatures before being closed.

Activating the Nodes: Connective Action Begins in Asian Indian Influenced Suburbs of the Silicon Valley

As discussed in Chapter 3, connective action takes shape with the interaction of three critical areas: goals, medium, and site. All three were clearly evident during the 2016 California textbook controversy among the Asian Indian communities within suburban cities located throughout Santa Clara County, a site known internationally as Silicon Valley. Two major suburbs in Santa Clara County with large Asian Indian populations are Santa Clara and Cupertino, where nearly 1,000 parents signed a petition to protest against SAFG's proposed edits (Harrington 2017).

The Asian Indian population did not begin to flourish in the suburbs of Silicon Valley, as well as other U.S. regions, until the Immigration Act of

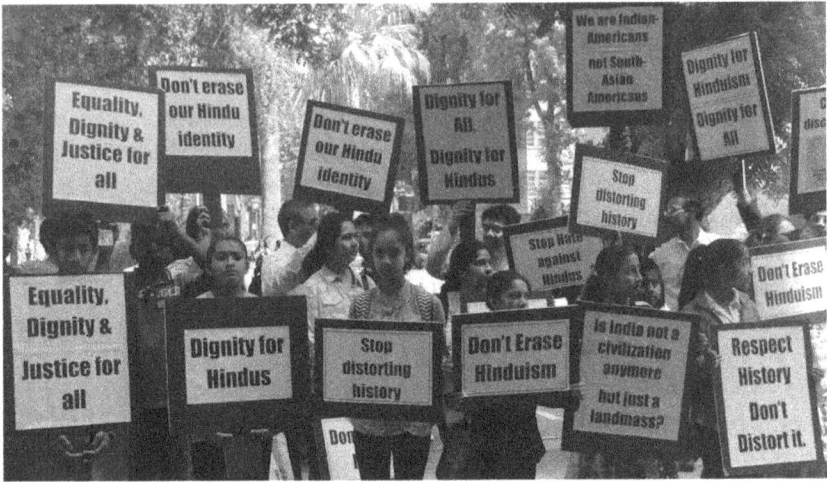

Figure 8.1 Don't Erase Hinduism. Hindu American youth protest proposed changes to California required textbooks during a California Curriculum Commission hearing in Sacramento. (Source: Sonia Paul.)

1965 (Hart-Celler Act) opened up a floodgate of highly trained professional immigrants who arrived with student and working visas. In the early 1990s, when the dot-com era began, Asian Indian immigration simultaneously took shape as a result of the passage of the visa bill in 2000, which raised the H-1B visa quota from 115,000 to 195,000 annually for three years (Bhattacharyya 2017). As a result of this influx of Asian Indian immigrants, this community is highly connected to their diasporic culture, as seen today through activities such as *tabla* classes, *bharatnatyam* dance companies, and cricket academies. These cultural factors are embedded within the Asian Indian community in Silicon Valley and would shape their views in the 2016 California textbook controversy.

Asian Indians made up 24.8 percent of the total population in Santa Clara County, the region that comprises most of what is considered to be Silicon Valley, according to the 2017–2019 American Community Survey (Ruggles et al. 2021). The presence of Asian Indians and members of the Indian diaspora is clearly evident in several of the fifteen cities that make up Santa Clara County as seen with Cupertino where Asian Indians represent 22.6 percent of the total population in comparison with Fremont (18 percent), Sunnyvale (16 percent), and Santa Clara (14 percent) (Rodriguez and Fernandez 2011).

The rapid regional growth of the Asian Indian population has mirrored their impressive socioeconomic characteristics, which are shaped by United States immigration policies. At the national level, according to the 2017–2019

American Community Survey, 32 percent of all Asian Indians (twenty-five years of age and older) have a bachelor's degree and 43 percent have a post-graduate degree (Budiman 2021a). In comparison, 30 percent of all Asian Americans (twenty-five years of age and older) have a bachelor's degree and 24 percent have a post-graduate degree. Income-wise, Asian Indians were found to have the highest reported median household income ($119,000) for any ethnic group in 2019 (Budiman 2021).

Despite the relatively high socioeconomic characteristics and their rapid population growth in the Silicon Valley, elected representation and political power have been largely missing from the Asian Indian community in the region. While Asian Indians have achieved elected representation in the Silicon Valley suburbs, such as current Fremont City Council member Anu Natarajan, who was first elected in 2006 after being appointed in 2004, arguably the most high-profile Asian Indian in Silicon Valley is San Jose City Council member Ash Kalra, who has represented Council District 2 since 2008. Kalra has played an important role in giving Asian Indians a face on the city council of the nation's tenth-largest city and the central city of Silicon Valley.

With the exception of the historic 2016 election of U.S. Representative Ro Khanna from District 17, which contains all of Silicon Valley and the nation's only majority Asian American congressional district on the continental United States, several reasons for the delay of Asian Indian political incorporation in Silicon Valley are reflected in the recent development of this community. These factors may also point to ethnic divisions both among South Asians and among the larger Asian American population in the Silicon Valley and other similar suburbs with large South Asian populations.

Racial lumping and a dramatic increase in bullying and hate crimes against Asian Indians and, more broadly, South Asian Americans during the post-9/11 era impacted the diaspora greatly and led to a rise in cultural solidarity as well as increased political action. During the 2016 California textbook controversy, one of the arguments made by the #DontEraseIndia movement was that the proposed textbook edits that would portray India and the caste system in a poor light could lead to increased bullying against Asian Indians in middle schools (Hindu American Foundation 2016).

Nonprofit community organizations (e.g., India Community Center and the Hindu American Foundation), as well as many professional organizations, were developed to create and cement the Asian Indian group identity in the San Francisco Bay Area. The India Community Center, founded in 2003 by prominent tech executives and businesspeople, was established as the first nonprofit community center of its kind for the South Asian population in North America. Today, the 38,000-square-foot facility serves the San Francisco Bay Area's Asian Indian population through classes, community service programs, and clinics for legal and medical services.

The combination of low Asian Indian political incorporation in suburbs throughout Silicon Valley and the racial "othering" that they have faced in the post-9/11 era set the stage for the California textbook controversy and the role that connective action would play in this community. For example, as the transnational Asian Indian and South Asian community took shape, this community formation served as nodes in the larger process of connective action during the California textbook controversy. In the specific case of Silicon Valley, this region represented one of the key nodes for the communication and sharing of information on social media platforms as well as one of the primary sites where political action would materialize, as seen with this region, where #DontEraseIndia began. Through interconnected digital networks within the Asian Indian community, this hashtag would become a statewide mantra that would coalesce with other Asian Indians in other cities, allowing them to converge on Sacramento to testify and protest against the proposed textbook changes.

The ethnic networks of Asian Indian community-based organizations and Hindu temples in the Silicon Valley, as well as other large Asian Indian–populated cities throughout Northern and Southern California, provided the important infrastructure for heightened connective action during the 2016 California textbook controversy. The first visible outcome of this Asian Indian statewide connective action network occurred in November 2015, when over two hundred protesters descended upon a California Instructional Quality Commission preliminary meeting where over a dozen Asian Indian students testified to express their concern for the portrayals of Hinduism in textbooks. Most of these students were brought to Sacramento via car caravans that had been organized through personal networks facilitated by emails and WhatsApp. According to Mat McDermott, director of communications of HAF, "HAF did offer to help coordinate transportation, but people were taking it upon themselves to figure out their carpools. We [HAF] would send out notifications of hearing times, but it is important to note that HAF did not coordinate any of the grassroots mobilization."[3]

Young Asian Indians in middle school, high school, and college converged onto Sacramento and took turns speaking at the podium and expressing how the proposed edits would affect or erase their identities as Asian Indians and/or Hindu Americans. Many of them had never previously attended or participated at a political rally. HAF leadership was present at the same public hearing, where they collected and presented over seven hundred public comments from an online petition campaign. In addition, HAF and other organizations coordinated over ten thousand emails sent to the California Department of Education that offered suggested edits and counter-edits to the proposed changes (Wang 2016). On November 9, 2017, hundreds of Asian Indian protesters from all over California, holding yellow signs that read "Don't Erase Our Hindu Identity" and "Respect History Don't Distort It," stood outside of the California Department of Education headquarters in Sacramento to protest and to testify to the members of the state board of education on the day that they were to vote (Harrington 2017).

Online Connective Action Findings

1. Analysis of Twitter Hashtag #DontEraseIndia

A grand total of 133 #DontEraseIndia tweets were identified and coded that covered the period from April 6, 2016, to July 15, 2016. The racial breakdown was the following: Asian with 99 tweets for 74.4 percent; Organizations with 27 tweets for 20.3 percent; Non-Asians with 5 tweets for 3.8 percent; and Not Determinable with 2 tweets for 1.5 percent.

Among Asians who tweeted #DontEraseIndia, the following was the breakdown: Asian Indians with 69 tweets for 52 percent; South Asian with 28 tweets for 21.1 percent; Not Determinable with 5 tweets for 3.8 percent; Other Asian with 2 tweets for 1.5 percent; and Korean and Chinese/Taiwanese with 1 tweet for 0.8 percent each. The finding that 97 tweets (73.1 percent) were from Asian Indians and other South Asian Americans is understandable given the topic of this issue.

With regard to issue stance, the largest number and percentage of Asian Indian tweets—38 tweets (55 percent of the Asian Indian total)—were against #DontEraseIndia, 29 tweets (42 percent) were for #DontEraseIndia, and 2 tweets (2.9 percent) were neutral. In comparison, the largest number and percentage of South Asian tweets—25 tweets (89.3 percent of the South Asian total—were against #DontEraseIndia, 2 tweets (7.1 percent) were for #DontEraseIndia, and 1 tweet (3.6 percent) was neutral. The findings demonstrate that the #DontEraseIndia issue was divisive within the Asian Indian community: the majority (55 percent) who tweeted the hashtag were against the hashtag or in favor of the proposed edits, and an overwhelming majority of South Asians tweeters (89.3 percent) were against the hashtag or in favor of the proposed edits.

2. Geocode Analysis of #DontEraseIndia

Of the 133 total tweets with #DontEraseIndia, the largest groups were the following: Asian Indians with 72 tweets (54 percent of the total), South Asian with 28 tweets (21.1 percent), Organizations with 27 tweets (20.3 percent), Not Determinable and Non-Asian with 2 tweets each (1.5 percent), and Chinese and Korean with 1 tweet each (0.8 percent).

Location	Asian Indian	South Asian	Chinese	Korean	Non-Asian	N/D	Org.	GRAND TOTAL
United Kingdom							2	2
California	5	4	1					10
Maryland							2	2
Not Determinable	66	22		1	2	2	18	111
New York		2						2
Washington, D.C.							5	5
GRAND TOTAL	72	28	1	1	2	2	27	133

TABLE 8.2 TWEET LOCATIONS BY ETHNICITY/RACE

The largest geographic locations were the following: Not Determinable with 111 tweets for 84.1 percent (with Asian Indians and South Asians accounting for 66 tweets and 22 tweets, respectively), California with 10 tweets for 7.6 percent (with Asian Indians and South Asians accounting for 5 and 4 tweets, respectively), Washington, DC, with 5 tweets for 3.8 percent, and the United Kingdom, New York, and Maryland with 2 each for 1.5 percent. As discussed earlier, an overwhelming majority of South Asians tweeters were geocoded as Not Determinable and thus likely to represent a significant portion of the Not Determinable locations mostly likely from California. All of the 5 Washington, DC, tweets from an organization came from HAF.

Among gender groups, males were responsible for 66 tweets (49.6 percent of total) compared to females with 40 tweets (30.1 percent) and Not Determinable with 27 tweets (20.3 percent).

Overall, the #DontEraseIndia findings illustrate that connective action played a secondary role to traditional forms of collective action, as exemplified by the 133 total tweets around #DontEraseIndia during the 2016 California textbook controversy time period. In the end, the eventual success of those who supported the campaign was a result of the mobilization that occurred at the grassroots level through personal networks and the use of emails and personal networks through community institutions such as local Hindu temples.

Outcome of the 2016 California Textbook Controversy

The traditional grassroots mobilization by Asian Indians at local levels combined with the efforts by HAF through social media platforms shaped the outcome of the 2016 California textbook controversy along two fronts. With regard to the first front (replacing *India* with *South Asia*), the California Department of Education's Instructional Quality Commission decided to use the word *India* in every instance within the curriculum framework

(*IndiaWest* 2016). This was a major victory for HAF, which advocated this issue effectively through their #DontEraseIndia campaign.

On the second front, concerning Hinduism and the caste system, the Instructional Quality Commission rejected HAF's recommendation to rename (Thaker 2018). Dalit was incorporated into the Instructional Quality Commission's curriculum framework or guidelines (Thaker 2018).

Overall, the California textbook controversy illustrates that ethno-regional identities among Asian Indians are not fixed, nor can they reach a point of stability or stagnation. The Asian Indian community is not homogenous and was not completely reflected by the organizations that sought to represent their interests. In this case study, Hindu advocacy organizations participated in the California textbook adoption process and partially attained their goal of modifying the text in accordance with their agendas. While they attempted to establish a particular image of Hindus in California education based on their ideological alignment with Hindu Nationalism, the fate of their edits ultimately remained under the power of the state board of education. As a result, the 2016 California textbook controversy demonstrated how traditional forms of political action, such as grassroots mobilization and contacting elected representatives, can be effective when combined with connective action in determining a desired political outcome. This will likely be the blueprint in future iterations of California's textbook controversies for the diverse and ideologically divided South Asian American communities as both sides of this debate continue to mobilize across ethnic networks via social media.

Case Study 6

*Establishing World War II Korean Comfort
Women Memorials in U.S. Cities and
the Online Mobilization against Them*

*First person narrative is most powerful. We need to help
#ComfortWomen get justice. They've carried struggles of their
own too long.*
—Kristyn Wong-Tam, Twitter, October 7, 2017

*You should know what #ComfortWomen issue is. It's not about
stories of pitiful women but fictions created by pro-Pyongyang
activists based on forgeries and propaganda.*
—PeaceWithFairnessBack, Twitter, December 1, 2020

How an Issue in South Korea Brought the Asian American Community Together

The sculptures of three young women from Korea, China, and the Philippines, standing in a circle, holding hands, facing outward with stoic and determined looks, are the focal point of the comfort women memorial in downtown San Francisco, California. In front of the Bergen County Courthouse in Hackensack, New Jersey, an engraved plaque attached to the side of a large stone reads, "In memory of hundreds of thousands of women and girls from Korea, China, Taiwan, the Philippines, the Netherlands, and Indonesia." The U.S. memorials commemorating the wartime atrocities experienced by comfort women from Asian countries that include Korea, China, Taiwan, and the Philippines provide an important case study for understanding how connective action can shape goals of diasporic politics and facilitate panethnic coalitions around gender issues. Indeed, the dynamics of getting comfort women memorials in the United States is a confluence of "diaspora politics, coalition building and the gender rights movement" that would shape a panethnic and multiracial coalition through universalistic messaging of human rights (McCarthy and Hasunuma 2018, p. 411).

TABLE 9.1 KOREAN COMFORT WOMEN MEMORIALS IN U.S. CITIES (SUCCESSES AND FAILURES)		
Location	Year	Status
Palisades Park, New Jersey	2010	Success
Eisenhower Park, New York	2012	Success
Bergen County Courthouse, Hackensack, New Jersey	2013	Success
Glendale, California	2013	Success
Buena Park, California	2013	Failure
Southfield, Michigan	2014	Failure
Union City, New Jersey	2014	Success
Fairfax County, Virginia	2014	Success
San Francisco, California	2017	Success
Center for Civil and Human Rights, Atlanta, Georgia	2017	Failure
Brookhaven, Georgia	2017	Success
Museum of Korean American Heritage, New York City	2017	Success

Perhaps the fact that several Asian countries experienced the comfort women atrocities at the hands of the Japanese Imperial Army might explain why and how a panethnic coalition of Asian Americans were influential as a key partner with other racial groups in making these overseas memorials a reality, along with the support of Korean American communities throughout the U.S. mainland. Community activists, community-based organizations, and elected officials (local, state, and federal) within the Chinese American, Japanese American, and Filipino/a American communities were key coalition partners with Korean Americans.

Table 9.1 illustrates that as of December 2018, Korean comfort women memorials were erected in the following nine cities/public places throughout the United States: Palisades Park, New Jersey, in 2010; Eisenhower Park, New York, in 2012; Bergen County Courthouse in Hackensack, New Jersey, in 2013; Glendale, California, in 2013; Union City, New Jersey, in 2014; Fairfax County, Virginia, in 2014; San Francisco, California, in 2017; Brookhaven, Georgia, in 2017; and the Museum of Korean American Heritage in New York City in 2017. With each success, more memorials are likely to follow in other U.S. cities. Harvard University professor of public policy Dara Kay Cohen described these memorials as unprecedented: "I think it is extraordinary. . . . Public memorializing the rape of women is rare" (McGrane 2017, par. 3).

While the comfort women issue in Korea is a national movement led by Korean civil rights groups, the U.S. memorials resemble a decentered movement led by Korean American civic organizations in coalition with White and Asian American community activists and elected leaders. For example, civic Korean American organizations such as Korean American Civic Empowerment (KACE) in Hackensack, New Jersey, and the Korean American Forum of California (KAFC) in Los Angeles played critical roles in establishing the memorials in Bergen County, New Jersey, and Glendale, California, respectively.

Historical Background on the Japanese and the Korean Comfort Women WWII Controversy

In a candid statement on August 4, 1993, by then chief cabinet secretary Kono Yohei declared the following about the findings of a December 1991 government report on the comfort women issue, which is referred to as the Kono Statement:

> It is apparent that there existed a great number of comfort women. Comfort stations were operated in response to the request of the military authorities of the day. The then Japanese military was, directly or indirectly, involved in the establishment and management of the comfort stations and the transfer of comfort women. The recruitment of the comfort women was conducted mainly by private recruiters who acted in response to the request of the military. The Government study has revealed that in many cases they were recruited against their own will, through coaxing, coercion, etc., and that, at times, administrative/military personnel directly took part in the recruitments. They lived in misery at comfort stations under a coercive atmosphere. (Ministry of Foreign Affairs of Japan 1993, par. 2)

Two years later, during the fiftieth anniversary of the end of WWII on August 15, 1995, then prime minister Murayama Tomiichi issued the following statement, which is known as the Murayama Statement:

> Through its [Japan's] colonial rule and aggression, [it had] caused tremendous damage and suffering to the people of many countries, particularly to those of Asian nations. (Ministry of Foreign Affairs of Japan 1995, par. 5)

The Kono and Murayama statements were significant because they illustrated the formal recognition and contrition by the Japanese government regarding the WWII comfort women atrocities that it inflicted on its neighboring Asian countries (Higashi et al. 2015). Both statements would begin the challenging process for the remaining surviving comfort women of gaining recognition and redress from the Japanese government, as marked by the historical political mobilization in South Korea to bring attention to the comfort women issue and to seek redress.

In South Korea, in a tradition that began on Wednesday, January 8, 1992, surviving comfort women, women's organizations, religious groups, and individuals protested in front of the Japanese embassy in Seoul, South Korea. This was known as the Wednesday Demonstrations to demand redress from the Japanese government for comfort women's problems. According to the Korean Council, "Wednesday Demonstrations have turned into a place for solidarity between citizens and the victims, a living site for history education, a platform for peace and women's human rights, bringing people together in solidarity beyond gender, age, borders, and ideologies" (The Korean Council 2011, par. 6).

A seeming breakthrough happened on April 29, 2015, when Japanese prime minister Shinzo Abe made history by being the first in his position to address a joint session of the U.S. Congress in a speech entitled "Toward an Alliance of Hope." The myriad of topics discussed ranged from the relationship between the United States and postwar Japan to the Trans-Pacific Partnership (TPP). One issue that Prime Minister Abe commented on that garnered him great condemnation from progressive Asian Americans (Korean American, Japanese American, and Chinese American) as well as South Koreans was Japan's wartime atrocities in relation to comfort women or sex slaves:

> Our actions brought suffering to the peoples in Asian countries. We must not avert our eyes from that. . . . Armed conflicts have always made women suffer the most. In our age, we must realize the kind of world where finally women are free from human rights abuses. (Abe 2015, pars. 42 and 109)

What Prime Minister Abe's critics deemed ingenious about his above comments was his failure to admit that approximately two hundred thousand girls and women, a majority of them Korean, were abducted from their villages and forced into sexual slavery under Japan's military sexual slavery program during World War II (Hu 2017). The comfort women issue is a microcosm of the historic tensions between Japan and South Korea, as both countries share a bitter history as a result of Japan's colonization and occupation of the Korean peninsula from 1910 to 1945.

U.S. Representative Mike Honda (D-California), a Japanese American, was the author of the July 30, 2007, House Resolution 121, which called for the Japanese government to "acknowledge, apologize, and accept historical responsibility in a clear and unequivocal manner for its Imperial Armed Forces' coercion of young women into sexual slavery, known to the world as comfort women, during its colonial and wartime occupation of Asia and the Pacific Islands from the 1930s through the duration of World War II" (Honda 2007, par. 12). The resolution passed in the House. The significance of Honda's resolution is the role that a panethnic coalition of Asian Americans would later play in the establishment of comfort women memorials throughout the continental United States.

In addition to authoring House Resolution 121, Honda was also part of a coalition of 25 U.S. congressional members who had written to Prime Minister Abe asking for an apology for Japan's wartime use of Korean and Chinese sex slaves as comfort women. Honda stated that Abe's historic joint session speech was "shocking and shameful" for not directly mentioning the issue (Dorell 2015, par. 9). Representative Honda invited a former comfort woman, Yong-Soo Lee, who was eighty-seven, from South Korea to be his guest in the House gallery during Prime Minister Abe's speech. In a formal statement afterward, Honda declared, "Without acknowledging the sins of the past, history will repeat itself" (Dorell 2015, par. 10).

On December 28, 2015, Japan and South Korea announced that they had reached a formal bilateral agreement in which Japan would provide $9 million in aid for those who served as comfort women as well as a formal apology. In a written statement by Japanese foreign minister Fumio Kishida, he outlined the three key parts of the 2015 agreement:

(1) The issue of comfort women, with an involvement of the Japanese military authorities at that time, was a grave affront to the honor and dignity of large numbers of women, and the Government of Japan is painfully aware of responsibilities from this perspective. As Prime Minister of Japan, Prime Minister Abe expresses anew his most sincere apologies and remorse to all the women who underwent immeasurable and painful experiences and suffered incurable physical and psychological wounds as comfort women.

(2) The Government of Japan has been sincerely dealing with this issue. Building on such experience, the Government of Japan will now take measures to heal psychological wounds of all former comfort women through its budget. To be more specific, it has been decided that the Government of the ROK establish a foundation for the purpose of providing support for the former comfort women, that its funds be contributed by the Government of Japan as a one-time contribution through its budget, and that projects for recovering the honor and dignity and healing the psychological wounds of all former comfort women be carried out under the cooperation between the Government of Japan and the Government of the ROK.

(3) While stating the above, the Government of Japan confirms that *this issue is resolved finally and irreversibly with this announcement*, on the premise that the Government will steadily implement the measures specified in (2) above. (Kishida 2015, pars. 2–4)

While Foreign Minister Kishida stated that the 2015 agreement would resolve "finally" and "irreversibly" the issue of comfort women, the controversy around justice for comfort women continues to flare up. On December 27, 2017, an independent special task force was commissioned by South Korean president Moon Jae-in, which was to look into the 2015 agreement. The task force released its findings that the 2015 agreement failed to meet the victims' needs and called for more steps to be taken. The task force further concluded that the bilateral agreement was flawed, and it criticized the South Korean government for failing to interview Korean comfort women survivors (Tatsumi 2018). President Moon Jae-in acknowledged that the 2015 deal was official but that Japan should offer a "heartfelt" apology (*Kyodo News* 2018, par. 1). Japanese foreign minister Taro Kono issued an immediate statement following the special task force's announcement, in which he sternly warned that any attempts to revise or renegotiate the 2015 agreement would result in an "unmanageable" fallout for Japan-South Korea relations (Kono 2017, par. 3).

As the Japanese and South Korean governments waffled on the bilateral accord and whether it was sufficient, South Korean activists took the matter into their own hands with the Peace Statue in Busan, South Korea, which was erected in December 2011 in front of the Japanese consulate. According to Elizabeth Son in her book *Embodied Reckonings: "Comfort Women," Performance, and Transpacific Redress*, embodying claims for comfort women redress can be found in public spaces, performances, and works dedicated to the memory of South Korea's colonial past (Son 2018). The symbolism of the Peace Statue in Busan and the subsequent U.S. remembrance statues illustrate Son's embodiment perspective and the belief that memorials can reflect and shape collective memories.

The bronze Peace Statue depicts a Korean girl with a determined frontward gaze dressed in a traditional Korean dress, or *hanbok*, barefoot, with a clenched fist, sitting next to an empty chair. Approximately fifty parks and public spaces in South Korea, as well as public buses, have replicas of the statue. The Japanese government, led by Conservative Nationalists, has demanded that they be removed (Hu 2017).

Many cities in other countries as far away as Australia have commissioned and erected similar memorials throughout the world, including several U.S. Asian-influenced small to medium-size cities such as Glendale and San Francisco, California, and Fort Lee, New Jersey. Indeed, the ideological battle around comfort women remembrance memorials would shift away from South Korea to the United States as the major battleground, led by the transnational Korean American community that was establishing roots in cities throughout the continental United States and supported by a panethnic coalition of Asian Americans among a multiracial group of key players. In response, a Japanese conservative nationalist group in Japan and the United States would mobilize through a revisionist narrative to "redeem their country's tarnished honor" against the comfort women memorial statues (Field and Yamaguchi 2015, p. 1).

The Battleground around Comfort Women Memorials Shifts to the United States

With the diaspora of Korean immigration moving toward the United States in various cities since the Immigration Act of 1965, so has the battleground for the recognition of comfort women as illustrated by San Francisco's "Column of Strength" memorial in Figure 9.1. One side of the battleground is made up of Korean American communities throughout the United States who are part of the Korean diaspora while the other side comprises the Japanese conservative revisionist movement. The Washington Coalition for Comfort Women Issues (WCCW) was founded in 1992 by Korean American immigrants to "give official apology, provide redress from government sources, and open all government records regarding its involvement" on the comfort women issue (McCarthy and Hasunuma 2018, p. 416). At local levels, in various heavily populated Korean American communities in states like California, Virginia, New York, and New Jersey, Korean American organizations began to work on the comfort women issue and would take the lead on their respective city's campaigns to get a comfort women remembrance statue.

The growth of the Korean American community in cities throughout the United States would facilitate local efforts around comfort women memorials. According to the 2015 American Community Survey, from 2000 to 2015 the growth of the Korean American population in the United States went from 1.3 million to 1.8 million, an increase of 38 percent (Budiman 2021b). California (two memorials), New York (one memorial), and New Jersey (three memorials) also are home to the three largest Korean American populations among all U.S. states. The 2010 U.S. Census estimated that California is home to the nation's largest Korean American population with 452,000 for 1.2 percent of the total population, followed by New York with 141,000 for 0.7 percent and New Jersey with 94,000 for 1.1 percent. The significance of this finding illustrated the importance of identity and place, which are central aspects of Asian American Connective Action model as

Figure 9.1 Column of Strength. The memorial was unveiled in San Francisco on September 22, 2017. The ten-foot-tall bronze statue depicts three teenage girls from Korea, the Philippines, and Mainland China holding hands while a Korean grandmother looks on from afar. (Source: Ethan Francis Lai.)

discussed in Chapter 3. As Asian Americans make these metropolises and suburbs their homes in these states, racial tensions and political shifts within local institutions also follow (Lai 2011; Cheng 2013; Lung-Amam 2017).

The establishment of comfort women memorials on public lands in the heavily populated Korean American cities goes beyond the memorialization of this issue. The movement reflects each respective Korean American community's desire to bring this issue to the attention of their local government, to increase public awareness in the larger community on this issue, and to gain greater recognition for the Korean American communities in these cities (McCarthy and Hasunuma 2018).

A "comfort women denial" movement was materializing in the United States among the Japanese Right, particularly with the revisionist right-wing organization known as the Global Alliance for Historical Truth (GAHT), which is aligned with the domestic goals of the Nippon Kaigi (the Japan Conference), the largest right-wing organization in Japan and a major supporter of Japanese prime minister Abe's administration (Higashi et al. 2015; Yamaguchi 2017). The revisionist movement can trace its roots to Japan's nationalistic issues such as the revision of the Fundamental Education Law in 2006 and the dismantling of the postwar Constitution Article 9's "no war clause" (Field and Yamaguchi 2015).

As the memorial issue took shape in the United States, the revisionist movement began to mobilize conservative Japanese Americans in the United States to raise doubt with regard to the historical knowledge of comfort women to "paralyze international efforts to hold the Japanese government accountable" (Koyama 2015, p. 1). An example of one of these voices is Okamoto Akiko, who was the former head of the Family Values Society of Japan. Okamoto wrote in an essay in the May 2012 issue of *Seiron*, a conservative magazine, that the comfort women issue was a fabrication, and despite the Japanese dominating the political discourse around the comfort women issue, they were losing ground in the United States and the United Nations (Koyama 2015). Okamoto, along with the conservative Japanese media and activists, believed conservatives needed to respond to the criticisms against Japan's history of comfort women by promoting "Japan's side" of the controversy in the United States (Koyama 2015, p. 1).

To counter the Japanese national conservatives' revisionist efforts, a pan-ethnic coalition of Asian American organizations that included local Japanese American groups such as the Nikkei for Civil Rights and Redress; the San Fernando Valley chapter of the Japanese American Citizens League; and the Japanese American Bar Association of California. The coalition also included Korean American and other Asian American communities and sought to support comfort women memorials and oppose the revisionism of this issue (Koyama 2015).

It is important to acknowledge how the complex political process of strategic messaging, political maneuvering with local elected leaders, and coalition building both within the Asian American community as well as with other racial groups helped to achieve each U.S. comfort women memorial (McCarthy and Hasunuma 2018). This belief was evident in cities from Hackensack, New Jersey, to Glendale and San Francisco, California. In each of these cities a common theme took shape as local Korean American community-based organizations took the lead in establishing their respective cities' comfort women memorials with their funding and the majority support of their respective city councils.

Palisades Park, New Jersey, was the initial Korean American influenced suburb to have success in erecting a comfort women memorial, an engraved plaque bolstered from behind by a rock that rests next to a public library, beginning the national movement. The inscription on the plaque reads, "In memory of the 200,000 women and girls who were abducted by the armed forces of the government of Imperial Japan 1930s–1945 known as 'comfort women.' They endured human rights violations that no peoples should leave unrecognized. Let us never forget the horrors of crimes against humanity." The phrases *human rights violations* and *crimes against humanity* emphasize the universalistic human rights that help build a broader coalition that would be instrumental in getting memorials approved. This memorial would not have happened were it not for Korean American activists and organizations working in coalition with city elected leaders. This belief was captured by Palisades Park mayor James Rotundo: "This monument was not for the Korean women. . . . It was for educational purposes so that the world and people knew that during war travesties that happen should never happen" (NJTV News 2012, par. 4).

Another impetus that helped shape local government support in favor of the memorial was the significant population of the Korean American community in Palisades Park. In 2010, the Korean American population in Palisades Park was 51.5 percent of the city's total population (10,115), the highest percentage and density of Korean Americans for any U.S. municipality. With this demographic growth followed potential voting power, with one-quarter of the city's voters being Korean American. Jason Kim became Palisades Park's first Korean American and Asian American city council member when he was elected in 2004. The growing Korean American political presence in Palisades Park, along with the comfort women memorial's framing of the issue as a global human rights injustice, were the key factors in their success in establishing the comfort women memorial.

On the other side of the United States from Palisades Park, the Korean American community in Glendale, California, paid close attention and harbored hopes of having their own comfort women memorial. Phyllis Kim, executive director of the KAFC, the community-based organization that would lead the efforts, expressed the disbelief that other Korean Americans felt about what the Korean American community in Palisades Park was able to accomplish with the nation's first comfort women memorial (McCarthy and Hasunuma 2018). However, this disbelief quickly shifted to optimism given the large Korean American population in Glendale, which in 2010 comprised 5.7 percent of the total population. Similar to Palisades Park, Korean American community-based organizations and activists in Glendale were successful in getting a comfort women statue with a universalistic framing of the issue that garnered the backing of a multiracial coalition of elected leaders. According to Kim, "This is a very important piece of history that a lot of Westerners are not aware of. . . . Everyone needs to work together to eradicate violence. . . . We want to raise awareness about this problem in the world" (Chew 2017, pars. 3 and 9). In addition, the Korean American community worked with Armenian Americans, as Glendale is home to the Armenian Genocide memorial and the city will house the nation's first Armenian American museum dedicated to the cultural and educational center for Armenian Americans and the public.

Tensions between GAHT and the progressive coalition that supported the remembrance statue in Glendale took shape along three fronts. First, through social media, particularly Twitter, right-wing groups took to discrediting the historical facts related to WWII comfort women, as is illustrated later in this chapter. Second, political protests from Japan's side were conducted to bring attention to their disapproval of the Glendale remembrance statue. For example, after the statue was erected, the Japanese city of Higashiosaka decided not to send their students in an exchange program to Glendale as a form of political protest. Third, GAHT took to legal pressure, with the endorsement of the Japanese government, to thwart the Glendale statue by making the argument that it violated the U.S. Constitution by disrupting U.S. foreign policy and the nation's relationship with Japan (Zhu 2017).

In 2014, the Pasadena-based DeClercq law firm filed a lawsuit to remove the Glendale remembrance statue on behalf of GAHT and with the support of the Japanese government against the City of Glendale for adopting "its own foreign policy which favors the view more favorable to Korea," with the argument that "the monument remains along with its permanent words that accuse Japan of wrongdoing on a basis that it strongly denies" (Zhu 2017, par. 15). A U.S. District Court dismissed this lawsuit, and the Ninth Circuit Court of Appeals upheld the ruling in August 2016. In March 2017, the three-year legal battle ended when the U.S. Supreme Court denied hearing the case, thereby allowing the Glendale and other comfort women remembrance statues and memorials to stand (Constante 2017).

San Francisco was another medium-size city with a substantial and diverse Asian American population containing established, progressive Asian American community organizations and leaders who mobilized together to form a broad pan-Asian and multiracial coalition of community activists known as the Comfort Women Coalition (CWC) to achieve a remembrance statue. While Phyllis Kim of KACE visited San Francisco a dozen times to help consult and strategize, unlike the other cities previously discussed, San Francisco was unique in that the efforts were led by two female Chinese American retired judges, Lilian Sing and Julie Tang (Garchik 2017). Both would eventually help found and currently cochair the "Comfort Women" Justice Coalition (CWJC). According to the CWJC website, it is a "grassroots, multiethnic and multi-national group of individuals and organizations that are part of the global 'Comfort Women' Justice Movement" ("Comfort Women" Justice Coalition 2018, par. 1). Thirty-four organizations (e.g., Asian Americans for Peace & Justice, Chinese American Association of Commerce, Filipina Women's Network, Japan-U.S. Feminist Network for Decolonization, and the Korean American Forum of California) currently serve as partner organizations.

Prior to getting involved with the San Francisco remembrance statue and CWJC, both Sing and Tang were long-time human rights activists, as both cochaired the Rape of Nanking Coalition, which was a panethnic coalition of Chinese, Japanese, Korean, and Filipino American activists (McCarthy and Hasunuma 2018). According to Julie Tang, as a judge for twenty-six years, her goal was to "make sure in each case that if somebody committed a crime, the person would be held accountable . . . [but in the instance of comfort women, the criminals] went away and got free, there was no justice for the comfort women" (*Xinhua* 2017).

Similar to the other cities, a coalition of local San Francisco elected officials proved to be key allies. Former Supervisor Eric Mar (District 1), a Chinese American, took the lead in the Board of Supervisors to urge his fellow supervisors to endorse the comfort women remembrance statue. At the public unveiling ceremony, Supervisor Mar choked back tears when he introduced Grandma Yong-Soo Lee, a comfort woman survivor, and shared the story of how he taught his seventeen-year-old daughter about Lee's inspiration for future generations to stand up against sexual violence and historical crimes (*Xinhua* 2017).

GEHT and the Japanese government would once again mobilize against San Francisco and its attempt to memorialize comfort women. In 2018, Hirofumi Yoshimura, the mayor of Osaka, Japan, ended its sixty-year sister-city relationship with San Francisco in protest of the city's remembrance statue (McCurry 2018). In a ten-page letter dated October 2, 2018, addressed to San Francisco mayor London Breed, Yoshimura wrote the following:

> In spite of the prosperous relationship, I am afraid to announce that the City of Osaka must hereby terminate its sister city relationship with the City and County of San Francisco. The grounds to termination shall be detailed as follows. I must sternly emphasize that the Japanese Government holds a distinctive standpoint on perceiving history, and there is also disagreement among historians when regarding the historical facts such as the number of "comfort women," the degree to which the former Japanese Army was involved, and the extent of the wartime harm. Granted the aforementioned, it was solemnly disappointing when the previous Mayor of San Francisco personally finalized the resolution on November 22, 2017, to accept the Comfort Women Memorial and plaque as a gift with provision of artwork maintenance on public property as an expression of the

will of the City and County of San Francisco; a memorial containing inscriptions that present uncertain and one-sided claims as historical facts. (Yoshimura 2018, pars. 1 and 2)

Online Connective Action Findings

1. Analysis of Tweets for #ComfortWomen

The overall findings show that of the 398 total tweets during July 1, 2009, to January 31, 2019, that included #ComfortWomen, those identified as Asians and Organizations accounted for the most with 131 tweets for 32.9 percent, respectively followed by Non-Asians with 70 tweets (17.6 percent) and Not Available with 66 tweets (16.6 percent).

Among the Asian-identified tweets, Japanese were the largest with 70 tweets (17.6 percent), followed by Korean with 32 tweets (8 percent), Chinese/Taiwanese with 16 tweets (4 percent), Filipino with 5 tweets (1.3 percent), and Asian Indian with 4 tweets (1 percent).

With regard to gender, those who were unidentifiable accounted for the most with 246 tweets for 61.8 percent, followed by females with 98 tweets (24.6 percent) and males with 54 tweets (13.6 percent).

2. Geocode Findings for #ComfortWomen

Figure 9.2 illustrates the top 10 most frequently coded locations for tweets containing #ComfortWomen from July 1, 2009, to January 31, 2019. The most frequent location was Not Available with 155 tweets for 38.9 percent of the total, followed by Mainland China/Taiwan with 48 tweets (12.1 percent), Japan with 40 tweets (10.1 percent), Europe with 33 tweets (8.3 percent), California with 24 tweets (6 percent), Other States (America) with 22 tweets (5.5 percent), New Jersey/New York with 18 tweets (4.5 percent), Korea with 16 tweets (4 percent), Canada with 13 tweets (3.3 percent), and Australia with 12 tweets (3 percent). The significance of these findings demonstrated the transnational dimensions of the comfort women issue and the international debate that it generated.

Table 9.2 captures the #ComfortWomen tweets by race/ethnicity, location, and issue stance during July 1, 2009, to January 31, 2019. Out of 201 tweets with #ComfortWomen, those whose locations were Not Determinable (N/D) accounted for the most with 71 tweets for 35.3 percent of the grand total.

Among those tweets where location could be identified, the most tweets by Chinese/Taiwanese users were from California (3 tweets) and Canada (3 tweets), followed by China/Taiwan (2 tweets), New York/New Jersey (NY/NJ)

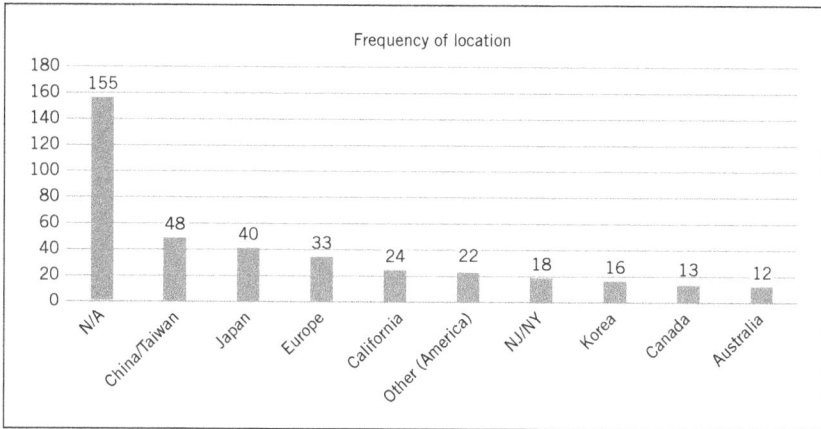

Figure 9.2 Top Ten Frequency of Location for #ComfortWomen

(1 tweet), and U.S. Other Regions (1 tweet). The most tweets from Japanese (JPN) users were from Japan (24 tweets), followed by Europe (2 tweets) and California (1 tweet). The most tweets from Koreans (KOR) were from California (6 tweets), followed by Korea (4 tweets), New York/New Jersey (NY/NJ) (3 tweets), China/Taiwan (2 tweets), U.S. Pacific Northwest (NW) (1 tweet), U.S. South (1 tweet), and Other (Asia) (1 tweet). For Asian Indians (AI), the most tweets were from Europe (3 tweets) and Other (Asia) (1 tweet). For other South Asians, all of the tweets were from locations Not Determinable (N/D) with 2 tweets. For Hawaiians (HI), the most tweets came from the location U.S. Other Regions with 1 tweet. Among Filipinos (Fil), the most frequent tweets were from the Philippines (2 tweets) and New York/New Jersey (NY/NJ) (2 tweets).

Overall, two key findings emerge from the #ComfortWomen coding: one, Twitter was not a driving force in developing a consensus through personal frames around comfort women memorials; and two, the transnational context of this issue reflects the larger characteristics of the Asian American community. In regard to the first trend, unlike this book's other case studies, social media was not a major platform used by both opposing sides, as illustrated by only 201 tweets using #ComfortWomen during the nearly ten-year time frame. However, those Japanese Americans who opposed the comfort women memorials took to Twitter using #ComfortWomen to convey their personal action frames among themselves and in response to the proponents. These personal action frames attempted to delegitimize the historical atrocities that comfort women experienced during World War II.

For those who supported comfort women memorials, Twitter was also the main social media platform utilized to share their thoughts and/or to

TABLE 9.2 #COMFORTWOMEN TWEETS BY RACE/ETHNICITY, LOCATION, AND ISSUE STANCE (7/1/09 TO 1/31/19)

Location	CHN/ROC	JPN	KOR	AI	S. Asian	HI	FIL	N/D	Asian Total	Non-Asian Total	Grand Total
Korea			4						4	3	7
For			1						1	2	3
Neutral			3						3	1	4
Japan		24							24	6	30
For		3							3	1	4
Neutral		4							4	5	9
Against		17							17		17
China/Taiwan	2		2						4	1	5
For	1								1		1
Neutral	1		2						3	1	4
Australia										6	6
For										4	4
Neutral										2	2
Philippines							2		2		2
For							1		1		1
Neutral							1		1		1
Other (Asia)				2					2		2
For				1					1		1
Neutral				1					1		1
Europe	3	2	1	3					9	11	20
For	3		1	3					7	3	10
Neutral										6	6
Against		2							2	2	4

										Total
California	3	1	6					10	6		16
For	2		6					8	2		10
Neutral	1							1	4		5
Against									1		1
U.S. Pacific NW		1						1	1		2
For		1						1	1		2
N.Y./N.J.	1		3		2			6	4		10
For			3		2			5	3		8
Neutral	1							1	1		2
U.S. South		1						1	1		2
For	1							1	1		2
U.S. Other Regions	1	2		1				4	13		17
For	1							1	9		10
Neutral		1		1				2	4		6
Against		1						1			1
Canada	3						1	4	5		9
For	3						1	4	2		6
Neutral									3		3
Africa									2		2
Neutral									2		2
N/D	3	43	11		2	1		60	11		71
For	3	4			2	1		7	7		14
Neutral	3	6	7					16	4		20
Against		37						37			37
Grand Total	16	70	32	4	2	1	5	131	70	1	201

respond to those who were attacking the legitimacy of comfort women. An example was Twitter user Aya Tasaki, who tweeted on November 29, 2018, "When Japan refuses and continues to deny that sex slavery—cloaked under terms like 'war time' and 'comfort women'—was and is our history and reality, it continues to perpetrate violence and trauma" (Tasaki 2018).

Rise of the Twitter Bots: Efforts to Discredit the Korean Comfort Women Movement

Twitter bots are created from software that controls a Twitter account and may autonomously perform actions such as tweeting, retweeting, liking, following, or direct messaging other accounts. They are relatively simple and easy to create, with various "how-to" websites asserting that users are able to build a bot in under thirty minutes, and some websites even offering up premade code for users to copy and paste to start their own bots. Within the context of tweets that included #ComfortWomen, many of these suspected Twitter bots could be identified fairly easily, as many would have a rotating set of tweets, repeating the same tweet at various intervals.

Figure 9.3 provides three Twitter screen captures taken within the span of a single day. As they show, the same tweets (the first and third from the top) contained the same content but were tweeted at different times—a key characteristic of a Twitter bot account. For example, in the second screen capture, Jet Mallein tweeted the following on November 27, 2018: "#ComfortWomen were recruited by private #sexbrokers NOT coerced by #Japanese government. #Fairfax #VA #Virginia #Glendale" (Mallein 2018). Another Twitter bot account used the guise of former Korean comfort women to regularly rotate the same messages against comfort women memorials, with a focus on discrediting the history of the exploitation and forced sexual slavery of WWII comfort women by the Japanese Imperial Army. The above Twitter screen captures are from the account known as "I Was a Sex Slave of Japanese Army," which consistently included #ComfortWomen with the main narrative of creating the view that this person, who was a former sex slave, profited greatly from the Japanese government.

Why the rise of Twitter bots in this case study and not in the other case studies? Given the transnational and political dimensions of the comfort women movement and issue, it is not surprising to see social media playing a different type of role during connective action among those outside of the United States in an effort to influence local U.S. political outcomes. Public opinion at the local, state, national, and international levels was on the side of comfort women and their efforts to establish local remembrance statues

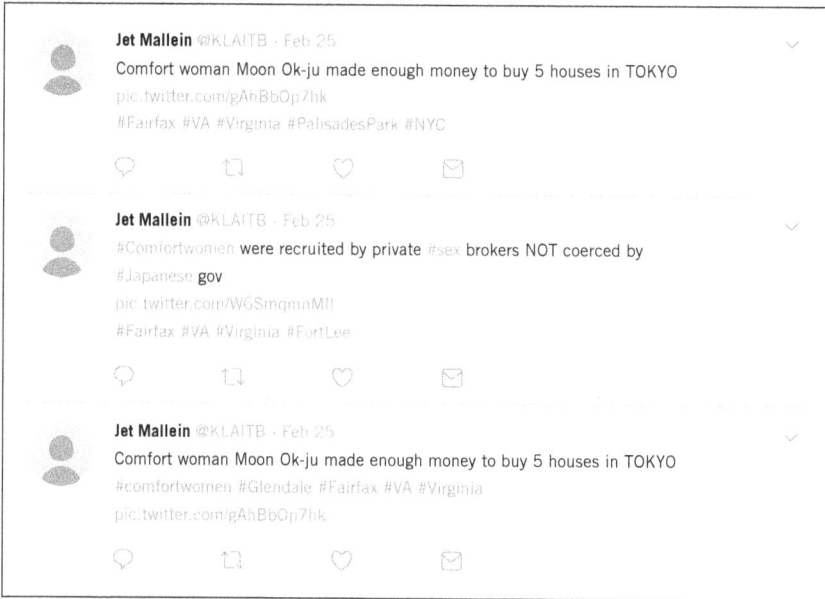

Figure 9.3 Anti-Comfort Women Twitter Bot Example (Source: Twitter.)

and memorials. All of the suspected Twitter bot accounts in this case study were coded as being against comfort women memorial statues, with several geocoded as outside of the United States. As discussed earlier, Korean Americans in various cities created both multiracial and panethnic coalitions that were effective in creating a consensus that allowed for the establishment of these statues and memorials. Twitter bots were likely created by those who sympathized with the Japanese ultra-conservative perspective in an effort to sway public opinion through misrepresentation of the historical facts. This supports other evidence that the Japanese government encouraged Japanese nationalists via email to speak out against the comfort women memorial statues (McCarthy and Hasunuma 2018).

An important tale that emerges from the comfort women memorial movement in the United States is that traditional political action through grassroots mobilization and coalition building still has great significance in regard to political outcomes. In each of the locations where comfort women memorials were successfully established, Korean American community leaders were effective in creating strong coalitions that included other Asian ethnic groups and racial groups despite the efforts of individuals collaborating with an ideological faction of a foreign government through social media platforms to discredit the issue from far away. As mentioned previously, this was the only case study where social media platforms were not the main tool in framing the issue and shaping a consensus, and this demonstrates the salience of collective action. Moreover, it illustrates why connective action cannot be a substitute for collective action but a supplement to it.

On the Virtues and Perils of Asian American Connective Action

Our digital social existence has turned into a huge echo chamber, where we mostly discuss similar views with like-minded peers and miserably fail to penetrate other social bubbles that are often misled by fear and xenophobia.
—MOSTAFA M. EL-BERMAWY, "Your Filter Bubble Is Destroying Democracy" (2016, par. 6)

It's true that echo chambers can obstruct the flow of information, and that's a problem. But those echo chambers can also be a formidable tool for political resistance. Where else do you have such immediate access to hundreds, thousands or even millions of people that agree with you? The key is to use social media for mobilization, not persuasion.
—EMILY PARKER, "In Praise of Echo Chambers" (2017, par. 4)

Asian American connective action embodies both virtues and perils, as illustrated in all of this book's case studies and their respective findings. This final chapter will explore these virtues and perils in addition to critical issues, emerging online political identities and coalitions, and what they portend for the future of Asian American politics. As is argued, the future of Asian American politics is inextricably linked to connective action. However, the latter cannot be the sole driving force among its largely foreign-born community in that it must coexist with traditional forms of political action, including voting and elected representation to allow Asian Americans, both U.S. and foreign born, to achieve a greater presence in influencing policy outcomes and distribution of resources in U.S. politics. This trajectory will likely continue as the Asian American community naturalizes as U.S. citizens, matures in age, and becomes more politically socialized while at the same time remaining one of the most digitally connected racial groups.

Inward vs. Outward Connective Action
Mobilization Networks

The book's case studies reveal two patterns of Asian American connective mobilization—one that is much more rooted in ethnic/community networks, as evident among immigrant Chinese Americans and Asian Indians, and another that is progressive connective mobilization, which tends to be more outward and panethnic in the Asian American community. One of the defining virtues of social media and smartphone app platforms is that they facilitate closing the ranks among those of a particular side by amplifying consensus among them. However, the methods of closing ranks may vary among Asian American national origin groups during online mobilization.

Immigrant Chinese Americans and Asian Indians tend to rely heavily on inward ethnic networks for efficacy around contested issues. One major reason for inward mobilization may be tied to the ethnic group's concerns about being targeted regarding the respective issues. For example, the protests for Peter Liang (Chapter 4) were a Chinese American immigrant social movement that relied exclusively on ethnic networks to facilitate offline political mobilization, as illustrated in the national protests. In the California SCA 5 case study (Chapter 5), immigrant Chinese American voters, activists, and community members all converged online and offline in Northern and Southern California to protest or support the controversial California Senate amendment that would bring affirmative action back into the state's University of California system as one of hundreds of criteria in its admission process. Asian Indians heavily utilized internal ethnic online networks to mobilize both locally and statewide during the California textbook controversies (Chapter 8). Neither of two ethnic groups attempted to build external coalitions to achieve efficacy around their contested issues.

The inward ethnic network pattern embodies both opportunities and challenges. On one hand, the inward ethnic mobilization that is arising among immigrant and conservative Chinese Americans and Asian Indians is that they illustrate how effective ethnic networks can be in amplifying their voices, particularly when they feel that they are collectively being targeted by unjust policies or legal decisions. On the other hand, as we discuss later in this chapter, these inward mobilization networks often result in echo chambers, which can limit their ability to see larger issues and other perspectives that are part and parcel of their issue.

In contrast to the inward ethnic networks, progressive Asian American connective action is characterized by outward efforts to build both panethnic and multiracial coalitions. During the California Assembly Bill 1726 case study (Chapter 6), Southeast Asian American refugees, perhaps the most socially disadvantaged group among immigrants, were able to mobilize and work with other Asian American ethnic groups and panethnic Asian American organizations as well as reach out to other racial groups to create a multiracial, panethnic coalition that successfully implemented state policy around data disaggregation for the economically and socially diverse Asian American community. Outward connective action was also evident during the two campaigns of the 18MR website (Chapter 7). In the Release the Minnesota 8 online campaign where local Hmong Americans in Minnesota worked with 18MR as well as other Southeast Asian and panethnic Asian American civil rights organizations in Washington, DC, and California to bring attention and action to this issue. Efforts by 18MR to create a biracial coalition with African American organizations both online and offline were a key characterization in the campaign for a clean DREAM Act.

While both inward and outward faces of Asian American connective action continue to develop, immigrant Asian American–influenced suburbs throughout the continental United States will remain the main battleground sites of future digitized mobilization. It is within this local context that the fastest and greatest demographic growth among Asian Americans has emerged over the past two decades (Lai 2011). Social media is the critical platform that binds and amplifies these Asian American voices over geographic spaces into a larger collective ethnic network, albeit with different challenges and opportunities, as the following sections discuss.

Controlling the Narrative through both Crowd- and Organization-Led Connective Action

A truism of American politics is that controlling the narrative on any issue is crucial to determining public opinion and eventually the outcome of an issue. Such is also the case for Asian Americans in the world of social media, as illustrated in the book's case studies. In the digital world, the key is getting out in front early and controlling the message. Controlling the narrative on social media is an effective tool because it can create a public backlash against any social movement and/or public policy, as we have seen in this book, with one unified goal of defeating the movement and/or policy. The public backlash is facilitated by whichever side can control the narrative that is on social media about the movement and/or policy. The ability to control the narrative in Asian American connective action is through rapid, consistent, and concentrated messaging via social media networks within Asian ethnic communities.

The Chapter 5 SCA 5 case study, for example, demonstrates how the opposition, led predominantly by a segment of highly educated Chinese American immigrants, was able to reframe the main message about SCA 5. The California Legislature's intent with the amendment was to address the growing racial gaps in higher public education in a majority minority state backed by a decade of empirical data on the detrimental effects of the 1996 California Proposition 209 on African American and Latinx enrollment in the University of California system. Instead, the reframed narrative focused on racial targeting and potential discrimination against Asian Americans. The opposition to SCA 5 even evoked Dr. Martin Luther King Jr.'s famous quote about judging one by their character not the color of their skin as the reason they were against affirmative action. The Chinese American immigrant community achieved this through multitiered approaches that involved sharing and discussing the issue to create a consensus on social media platforms, creating online petitions through websites like Change.org, and mass email and letter writing campaigns targeting Asian American state representatives to pressure them to change their support, which would ultimately break up the multiracial legislative coalition behind SCA 5. A social media campaign among the Chinese American opponents of SCA 5 on digital platforms such as WeChat, Facebook, and Twitter was done to create consensus among Chinese Americans who shared similar concerns and interests by articulating their concerns and thus shaping the narrative. According to Jason Xu, a member of the Silicon Valley Chinese Association (SVCA), which was publicly against both SCA 5 and AB 1726:

> With first generation [Chinese] immigrants, WeChat was obviously the first choice for communication and mobilization. Organizing public demonstrations was done via WeChat. It has a group feature with a cap of 500. A roll call WeChat would generate a response from the members. For the AB 1726 State Capitol demonstration, we did it this way. We did have Facebook and Twitter in small scale quantity wide. For SVCA, topic discussion was in WeChat, but consensus was reached by using voting via email.[1]

Former state assemblyman Paul Fong also recounted this effective reframing of SCA 5 on social media networks from his vantage point, which caught the pro-SCA 5 coalition in the State Legislature completely off guard. Their focus had to shift immediately to denying the accusations of racial profiling and discrimination against Asian Americans rather than focusing on the merits of SCA 5.

An example of controlling the narrative from the progressive side of the spectrum is seen in the Chapter 6 California AB 1726 case study, in which the progressive coalition who supported data disaggregation within the Asian American community were able to frame the main debate around the message "All Californians count" on social media platforms like Twitter in hashtag form (#AllCACounts), despite efforts of the Asian American proponents to cast AB 1726 as an extension of SCA 5. Asian American progressives learned from SCA 5 that they needed to get out in front and shape the narrative around AB 1726 with the "All Californians count" campaign if AB 1726 were to have a chance.

The ability of progressive Asian America activists and organizations through both crowd-led and organization-led connective action to get ahead of framing the narrative about AB 1726 was why it eventually passed and was signed into law, unlike SCA 5. The narrative that "All Californians count" was a powerful message about being inclusive while recognizing the ethnic diversity of the Asian American community and the need to disaggregate the data to get at this diversity when it comes to their health care. We know that different diseases afflict different racial minority groups, and without such data, these health care issues cannot be addressed in the diverse Asian American community through effective research funding and outreach strategies.

The online narrative that all Californians count was continuously articulated by Asian American activists and organizations through the prominent inclusion of #AllCACounts during the entire period of the public debate around AB 1726, as discussed in the case study findings. In Table 6.1, "#AB1726 Tweets for Race and Gender by Issue Stance," the prominence of organization-led connective action was captured by the fact that among the 165 total tweets that included #AllCACounts, 154 (93.3 percent of the total) were in favor of AB 1726. These tweets were strategically linked to and shared on Facebook. Progressive Asian American activist websites, through the process of organization-led connective action, frequently and consistently pushed the same narrative. For example, the Reappropriate website, which featured essays such as "All Californians Deserve to be Counted: Why Data Disaggregation Matters for AAPIs (#AllCACounts)," was instrumental in creating public awareness and consensus among progressive Asian Americans (Reappropriate 2016).

Emerging Identities during Asian American Connective Action

Three forms of emerging identities took shape during Asian American connective action along the entire ideological spectrum and were in full view during this book's case studies: a panethnic identity among progressive Asian Americans, a conservative identity among highly educated Chinese American immigrants, and a transnational identity among Asian American immigrants related to homeland politics. This finding illustrates previous studies that found the Asian American community is not an ideological monolith despite the recent Democratic voting trends discussed earlier in Chapter 2. Because no ideological group controls the internet, it would be expected that with the growing influence of social media and its ability to amplify concerns and interests, emerging identities along the entire ideological spectrum would materialize online as public policies, political candidates, and social justice issues are contested or supported through personal action frames during either crowd- or organization-led Asian American connective action.

1. Panethnic Identities among Asian American Progressives

One of the most positive developments that came out of the case studies' findings is the emergence of panethnic coalitions along ideological lines, particularly among Asian American progressives, through the processes of both crowd- and organization-led Asian American connective action (see Figure 3.1 for characteristics of both forms). This trend may mirror larger national trends that include the majority of Asian American voters identifying as Democrats, which has grown exponentially since 1992. The case studies where panethnic coalitions took shape among Asian American progressives and activists were the following: #AAPIs4BlackLives (Chapter 7), Asian American blogs in favor of SCA 5 (Chapter 5), #AllCACounts (Chapter 6), #ReleaseMN8 (Chapter 7), and #ComfortWomen (Chapter 9).

In each of the book's case studies, Asian American progressives worked in coalition with Asian American organizations and their leaders to utilize social media to bring attention to and create consensus around respective social justice issues that involved Asian Americans.

A vivid example of these panethnic progressive coalitions between activists and organizations was evident in the #ReleaseMN8 case study, a movement that involved Southeast Asian American activists and organizations primarily from the Hmong American community in Minnesota combined with the following six national, pan-Asian American organizations: Asian Prisoner Support Committee (APSC) in Oakland, California; the National Council of Asian Pacific Americans (NCAPA) in Washington, DC, the Southeast Asian Resource Action Center (SEARAC) in Sacramento, California; the National Immigration Project of National Lawyers Guild (NIPNLG) in Boston, Massachusetts; and the National APA Women's Forum (NAPAWF) in Washington, DC. National Asian American organizations accounted for 46 percent of the total #ReleaseMN8 tweets, compared to 34 percent by Asian American individuals. Both groups were instrumental in helping bring attention to the Minnesota 8 and to organize political action that would eventually get two released from ICE custody, and the legal battles continue to bring back those who were deported to Cambodia.

Ideological convergences in the form of panethnic coalitions among progressive Asian Americans and panethnic organizations were also emerging during the SCA 5 and AB 1726 controversies. With regard to SCA 5, Asian American progressives and panethnic progressive organizations who were for SCA 5 accounted for the majority with approximately 46 percent and 6.7 percent, respectively, of the total tweets that included #SCA5 (see Table 5.1). A majority of these tweets came from progressive Asian American legal and civil rights organizations such as Asian Legal Defense and Education Fund in Washington, DC; Advancing Justice in Los Angeles, California; and the Asian Law Caucus in San Francisco, California. For AB 1726, Asian American progressives and panethnic progressive organizations who were for AB 1726 accounted for a majority with approximately 31 percent and 29 percent, respectively, of the total tweets that included #AB1726 (see Table 6.1).

2. Emerging Conservative Identities among Well-Educated Chinese American Immigrants and the Role of Digital Chinese Dailies

As Asian American progressives mobilized panethnically during connective action, it is important to note that competing, emerging identities were also developing among conservative Chinese American immigrants. This was evident in the Peter Liang (Chapter 4), SCA 5 (Chapter 5), and AB 1726 (Chapter 6) case studies. While it is true that Asian American moderates and progressives do represent a substantial percentage of the larger Asian American community, one would be remiss to ignore its growing conservative segments. Indeed, one of the hallmark traits of connective action is that it is not confined to one end or section of the political spectrum but includes the entire spectrum. During the Peter Liang trial, as illustrated in the findings from Table 4.1, Asian Americans for Liang accounted for 27 percent of the total tweets that included #PeterLiang, with 88 percent of these tweeters being Chinese American, the largest percentage for any ethnic group. Thus, it is clear that the issue of Peter Liang and his trial would galvanize and mobilize Chinese Americans who clearly felt a connection to Liang around their shared ethnicity and who clearly agreed with the perspective that he was a racial scapegoat.

A critical component within the Chinese American community that allowed for the creation, transmission, and mobilization of conservative Chinese American political culture and identity in favor of Liang are digital platforms such as WeChat and online Chinese dailies. Information in Chinese is often shared in two ways: the ethnic newspaper media tweeting the story and/or an individual sharing these stories with other co-ethnics through social networks.

WeChat has become an important platform for the emerging conservative Chinese American counter-public, which challenges the progressive political culture and ideology within Asian American communities including the larger Chinese American community. WeChat has provided an important oppositional space for conservative Chinese Americans to voice their concerns and to challenge various perspectives within public spheres as well as those within Asian American public spheres. The idea of counterpublics has been examined by scholars of African American politics and involves contesting discrimination within the public sphere and often suppressed internal differences of race, class, gender, and sexual identity (Dawson 1994; Cohen 1999). Dawson argued that the African American counterpublic sphere is "the product of both the historically imposed separation of blacks from whites throughout most of American history and the embracing of the concept of black autonomy as both an institutional principle and an ideological orientation" (Dawson 2001, p. 27). In comparison, conservative Chinese Americans are also effectively contesting notions of a homogenous political identity along ethno-racial lines with the aid of social media.

During the Peter Liang trial and the national protest against Liang's jury conviction that was organized and took place in forty-one U.S. and Canadian cities on February 20, 2016, one of the critical aspects allowing this to develop were the digital Chinese media stories about Peter Liang often shared among those who participated. For example, on February 21, 2016, the day after the national protests, *China Xinhua News* tweeted the following through their own Twitter account: "Legal experts voice serious concern, objections over conviction of former NY cop #PeterLiang" with a link to the story embedded in the tweet (*China Xinhua News* 2016). The story focused on the common perspective that mobilized the Chinese American immigrants who protested in various cities that Peter Liang was a legal and racial scapegoat of the NYPD.

In the cases of SCA 5 and AB 1726, the progressive Asian American media dominated the stories on Twitter, unlike the majority of Asian Americans, mainly Chinese Americans, opposing both issues on Twitter. Among those tweets from the media, as reflected in Table 5.1, a majority were "For SCA 5" with 26 tweets (60.5 percent) compared with those "Against SCA 5" with 10 tweets (23.3 percent) and those "Neutral" with 7 tweets (16.3 percent). During the AB 1726 controversy, as reflected in Table 6.1, an overwhelming majority of those tweets identified as from the media were "For AB 1726" with 154 tweets (93.3 percent) compared with those "Against AB 1726" with 3 tweets (1.8 percent) and those "Neutral" with 8 tweets (4.8 percent). Conservative perspectives were in the minority as expressed by ethnic digital newspapers in both cases. Both of these case studies were primarily crowd-led Asian American connective action efforts among conservative interests, which would explain the outcome of SCA 5 and efforts to reintroduce affirmative action being tabled indefinitely, and in AB 1726 with higher education being left out of the final bill that was passed and signed into law by Governor Brown.

The significance of Asian American connective action is that local issues can become statewide, national, and/or transnational in a matter of hours as information is shared through social networks. All of the case studies demonstrate this belief and why Asian American connective action can alter both in-group and out-group perceptions of this racial group in the traditional U.S. racial hierarchy. Can the perception of Asian Americans as forever foreigners continue if Asian American groups make their voices heard in the public arena when it comes to issues within the United States, whether it is a local policy, a candidate, or a social movement? At the same time, emerging identities that are voiced within the Asian American community demonstrate that it is not a monolithic, political voice even if it is a minority perspective. This has always been a central hallmark and arguable strength of this community when it comes to ethnic and socioeconomic characteristics, so it should not be surprising that these intersections can produce diverse political views and ideologies.

3. Transnational Identities, Homeland Politics, and Connective Action

Another form of emerging identity during Asian American connective action that the case studies reveal is one that reflects the intersections and complexities of transnational identities and regional geopolitics that are transplanted through the South Asian and East Asian diasporas. The South Asian identity is not monolithic but consists of differences around factors such as class, religion, language, caste, and national origins, which challenge a unified identity (Mishra 2016). These characteristics are part and parcel of majority foreign-born communities. As the late Asian American politics scholar Don T. Nakanishi wrote:

> Asian Americans have engaged in and been affected by political activities, process, relationships, and actors that are non-domestic or international in nature, particularly as they relate to their ancestral homelands, to other communities globally in their diasporic networks, and to many forms of engagement by the United Sates in Asian and world politics. (Nakanishi 2009, p. ix)

Emerging transnational identities and voices were amplified in two of the book's case studies: the California textbook controversies (Chapter 8) and the WWII Korean comfort women memorials (Chapter 9). In each of these case studies, the transnational politics of homeland emerged in complexly unique and fascinating ways during connective action that challenged ethno-racial solidarities. In the California textbook controversy, the intersection of transnational identities and homeland politics was at the heart of the mobilization led by Asian Indian organizations like the Vedic Foundation (VF), the Hindu Education Foundation USA (HEF-USA), and the Hindu American Foundation (HAF). These organizations are ideologically linked with the right wing of the Hindu Nationalist party led by Prime Minister Modi and seek to mirror similar efforts by Hindu Nationalist governments in India to rewrite textbooks, but in this case within a U.S. context. For the South Asian Faculty group and their South Asian American allies who supported the proposed textbook edits, their transnational identities were shaped by factors within the regional and transnational hegemonies of India and Hinduism, which they sought to challenge in 2016 and likely will again in future California textbook evaluation proceedings.

The transnational dimensions of identity and homeland politics were equally evident in the Korean comfort women memorial case study among Korean Americans and Japanese ultra-conservative nationalists. Similar to the 2016 California textbook controversy, homeland politics and special interests also found their way into U.S. politics with the comfort women memorial movement, in which Twitter was likely utilized by the Japanese ultra-conservative nationalists and those sympathetic to their political views to discredit efforts to create comfort women memorials in the United States through the creation of Twitter bots guised as individuals and former Korean comfort women who were outspoken against these memorials or who challenged the narrative that they were exploited. This online, transnational counter-narrative strategy failed because of the local multiracial political coalitions that Korean Americans nurtured to establish comfort women memorials in their respective cities.

Building Progressive Interracial Coalitions through Connective Action

With the ability to express and share one's thoughts with the push of a button on their smartphone or laptop computer, and the ability to frame/reframe the discussion around contentious public issues without repercussions, one can clearly see how in the multiracial society of the United States connective action can be a powerful tool that can help facilitate as well as hinder coalition building between minority groups. As discussed in Chapter 2, Asian Americans occupy a unique and paradoxical position in the traditional U.S. racial hierarchy as both the model minority and the forever foreigner, which coexist simultaneously, as captured by Claire Kim's racial triangulation model (see Figure 2.1). The result of this unique position in comparison to African Americans and Latinx in traditional collective action has been a silo effect where there have been lost opportunities to build viable interracial coalitions around public policies.

It has been argued that for any coalition to be constructed, three important components must be present: common interests, common ideology, and strong leadership (Sonenshein 1993). With the Goals dimension interacting with the two other dimensions (Site and Medium), which form the Asian American connective action model (see Figure 3.2), one can see how connective action, unlike collective action, may serve as an important vehicle for articulating and building common interests, common ideology, and strong leadership that will foster future interracial coalitions where Asian Americans find themselves as a key partner. The findings of the case studies, on one hand, clearly suggest that one of the virtues of Asian American connective action is its ability to connect and amplify Asian ethnic voices around a common interest and thereby create a consensus to take political action as the next step. On the other hand, the case studies also reveal that coalitions can be created through both crowd- and organization-led Asian American connective action efforts.

One vivid example of how connective action can facilitate multiracial coalitions is discussed in Chapter 7 with 18MR and their role during the December 17 week of action, which featured a biracial coalition (#BlackAA-PIAction) of one hundred African American and Asian American Pacific Islander immigrants who converged on the U.S. Congress in Washington, DC, to demand a clean DREAM Act and a permanent solution to TPS holders. In this instance, traditional racial fault-line politics, which have divided and hindered multiracial coalitions through their use of social media to articulate common interests and ideology, were transcended by bringing groups together and, finally, by creating strong leadership within both groups. This coalition was significant because of the historic tensions within inner cities that often involved black patrons and Asian immigrant small-business entrepreneurs that culminated in the NAACP boycotts and what was perceived as the impetus for the 1992 Los Angeles riots and the 2015 Baltimore riots. To witness both African American and Asian American immigrant activists working together for comprehensive immigration reform through social media platforms that culminated in political action is a significant development that portends well for the ability to form multiracial coalitions. Perhaps this is the endgame of Asian American connective action in its ability to transcend racial fault lines of the traditional U.S. racial hierarchy if the common interests can be articulated through personal action frames during connective action, which challenge the model minority and forever foreigner at the same time.

The Echo Chamber Effect and How to Mitigate It

While social media and politics have received a great deal of criticism from the public—including former president Barack Obama, who stated in an interview about social media's threat to democracy after the 2016 U.S. presidential election:

> One of the biggest challenges we have to our democracy is the degree to which we don't share a common baseline of facts. What the Russians exploited, but it was already here, is we are operating in [a] completely different information universe. At a certain point, you just live in a bubble. And that's part of why our politics is so polarized right now. I think it is a solvable problem but it's one we have to spend a lot of time thinking about. (Chandran 2018, pars. 3 and 4)

There is no doubt that President Obama's comments reflect a sobering reality about the perils of social media when it comes to echo chambers, the proverbial elephant in the room. Social media platforms and websites have focused on monetizing our interests, as captured in complex algorithms that explain why certain types of suggested articles automatically appear on our Twitter or Facebook newsfeed. As a result, one could argue that these filter bubbles are producing what the major software company engineers and boards of directors intended: social silos where news stories and information are shared among those with the same perspectives and interests.

The economics behind social media companies is that they want to keep bringing you back to their sites for a sustained period of time, which generates advertisement revenue and thus effects future valuation of companies' stock shares in a positive direction. It is well established that many people seek information that supports their current convictions—the phenomenon of confirmation bias can significantly affect decisions about whether to spread content and, as a result, create echo chambers within identifiable communities. In these circumstances, online behavior can promote group polarization, as was clearly evident in this book's case studies.

We have seen in the various case studies and public opinion polls throughout this book that social media and civic discourse can create group polarization around contentious political and social issues. This is expected given the contemporary toxic social media environment, where participants can remain anonymous in their opinions of bellwether topics. They may also purposely attempt to spread misinformation to benefit their positions and/or undermine others. However, connective action has greater salience for outsider groups like Asian Americans as these messages are instantaneously conveyed to local, state, national, and international Asian American audiences at the push of a button. Moreover, the messages can be shared in multilingual dialects that reflect a large foreign-born, LEP community, which has historically served as an impediment to Asian American political participation, as language materials remain one contemporary form of group voter suppression. As a result, connective action may provide new affordances to Asian American civic engagement, but they are not without potential costs or challenges.

One of the major concerns of connective action is the existence of echo chambers in online chat groups and message boards. The echo chamber effect is the byproduct of incivility and anonymity often found in online discussion forums on social media sites such as Facebook, WeChat, and Twitter. Scholars have long argued that this echo chamber effect has prevented individuals from having constructive dialogue with each other (Gillani et al. 2018; Polonski 2016; Sunstein 2004).

Given that social media platforms are not effective tools for persuasion of those who disagree with one's views, what should be done to facilitate dialogue between two sides? One argument is that we should log off social media and have in-person conversations. According to Emily Parker, author of the *Washington Post* editorial "In Praise of Echo Chambers":

> Nobody likes the idea of echo chambers. They amplify fake news. They serve as breeding grounds for terrorists and white supremacists. They also widen the political divide, which can have serious political consequences. Make no mistake; if you want to win a political election, you have to communicate with people on the other side. But maybe social media isn't the best place to do that. . . . What social media can do is to urge people to shut their laptops and go knock on doors to talk to voters. (Parker 2017, pars. 12 and 13)

Traditional methods of engaging from different perspectives on critical public policies through town hall meetings and political forums are one of the key ways to move beyond echo chambers in contemporary politics. Even when ideological groups do not agree, such meetings can help bridge both real and perceived ideological gaps. For example, after the Peter Liang trial, a town hall meeting was organized by both African American and Asian American community-based organizations and professionals who believed that only face-to-face dialogue from both sides was needed if there was going to be progress between both communities. The goal underlying this approach was to find common interests that exist between both minority groups in New York City on police reform and economic and political disenfranchisement rather than the mainstream media's emphasis on interracial conflict between these communities.

Alternative Approaches to Echo Chambers

Twitter town halls constitute an effective online strategy to address the effects of echo chambers by getting individuals off their insulated forums and interacting with others with divergent perspectives. Part of the challenge of echo chambers is that individuals who are members of forums on smartphone apps like WeChat and WhatsApp are often limited and/or biased in information that is shared among members. Twitter town halls are online events, promoted through social media channels, where organizations (via organization-led connective action) invite public engagement for a scheduled date and time period in which users can ask questions or find out more information about a topic. To promote greater discussion and dialogue with the audience, an organization may provide several questions ahead of time. Online questions are then tagged with a predesignated hashtag, and the host organization and participants respond using that hashtag. The format of Twitter town halls is that the host explains the purpose for the gathering as well as the ground rules, welcomes attendees, and thanks them for participating. In order to close the communication circle, a suggested best practice after the town hall is to follow up with a blog post on the organization's website and disseminated through its social media networks revisiting key points that were discussed.

Can there possibly be one smartphone app that brings all the different platforms together? Although the smartphone has become ubiquitous, one contributing factor to the echo chamber effect is that there are no smartphone apps that allow for competing online narratives and discourses to intersect on one platform. As a result, those who choose to share and communicate information through smartphone social media apps that are commonly used among Asian American immigrants, such as WhatsApp, Line, KakaoTalk, and WeChat, are confined to using only these apps, which prevents the ideal type of discourse that allows one to have alternative perspectives from taking shape. As previously discussed, there exist relative benefits to these smartphone apps, as through them information can be shared in various Asian ethnic languages, allowing the large LEP population to circumvent language barriers. Another benefit is that they also allow the largely national and transnational diffused Asian American communities to connect and share information with the push of a button, which can set political action into motion, as we have seen in each of this book's case studies.

Future Challenges to Asian American Connective Action

1. Net Neutrality and Online Asian American Activists

While connective action can allow Asian American activists to have amplified voices and hearts expressed through social media networks facilitated by smartphone apps like WeChat, WhatsApp, Line, KakaoTalk, Facebook, and Twitter, the future to continue doing so is still uncertain as a result of internet policies. A recent major policy is net neutrality, which is the common principle that internet service providers should enable access to all content and applications regardless of the source while not favoring or blocking particular products or websites. Internet service providers were offering tiered prices for faster internet speeds and, in some cases, practicing the concept of "throttling," in which they slowed internet speeds to specific users to coerce them into purchasing faster speeds. Under President Obama's administration, efforts were made to establish a common principle for internet service providers through government regulation. This issue is significant to both group- and organization-led Asian American connective action efforts because as these online organizers attempt to create personal and group action frames around issues by reaching out to Asian Americans at the local, state, and national levels, net neutrality may limit their ability to and/or effectively determine the extent to which they can reach out to other Asian Americans throughout various parts of the country.

In 2017, President Obama's net neutrality principles would be rolled back when President Trump appointed Ajit Pai, who has been an opponent of net neutrality, as chairperson of the Federal Communications Commission (FCC). Under Pai's leadership, the FCC has reversed previous net neutrality rulings and reclassified internet sites that have arguably harmed online organizations. In December 2017, the FCC voted along party lines to pass the Restore Internet Freedom Order, which contained three parts that the FCC argued were necessary to restoring internet freedom: consumer protection, transparency, and removing unnecessary regulations to promote broadband investment (Federal Communications Commission, 2018). Opponents of net neutrality have argued that regulating the internet will stall innovation and hamper competition. Pai wrote in a June 2018 opinion editorial:

> I support a free and open internet. The internet should be an open platform without having to ask for anyone's permission. . . . Our framework (Restore Internet Freedom Order) will protect consumers and promote better, faster internet access and more competition. (Pai 2018, par. 1)

One of the potential collateral effects of the Restore Internet Freedom Order is its impact on Asian American online activists and organizations. Laura Li, a campaigner for 18MR, raised the important issues of net neutrality and funding of activist websites, like 18MR, that specifically engage in organization-led connective action around progressive movements and policies:

> The future of Asian American online activism depends on the future of net neutrality and economic feasibility and funding for activists who are doing the work. We must think about how the repeal of net neutrality is going to affect how online organizers are able to reach community members and how the additional economic barriers such as throttling, censorship and paywalls will force us to innovate and use different tools. . . . Asian Americans and Pacific Islanders live in scattered communities across the U.S. and our communications face unique challenges in organizing. If there is to be an expansion to organizing on native apps, there would need to be added capacity and funding to support activists doing that work.[2]

The 18MR case study (Chapter 7) illustrated the potentials of Asian American activist websites, and those who are professional online activists, in politically mobilizing various segments of this large, diverse, and underrepresented community throughout the continental United States. If censorship or paywalls are created and/or if traffic to these websites is made slower by internet providers through throttling, this can have an adverse effect on the reach of online activist organizations to the websites' visitors. Access to websites is critical in the world of Asian American online organizations that rely heavily on site traffic as one measurement of their effectiveness. Without traffic, future funding will be limited, and thus such online organizations will cease to exist. Moreover, if internet prices and speeds change for the worse, this could potentially harm current online activism strategies by these organizations for mobilizing the Asian American community, as Li mentioned. Whether Asian American online activism organizations like 18MR will be able to operate under these conditions should they occur remains to be determined under the new FCC framework. If so, new strategies will likely be developed, as online activist organizations will need to adapt to increase online outreach and capacity building around social justice and political issues during connective action.

2. Fake News and the Issues of Scale and Virality

Fake news has also become an issue for Asian American connective action, just as it has become a larger societal issue related to social media and democracy. Echo chambers on social media apps such as WeChat facilitate the spread of fake news that creates emotional reactions in its users, as seen among the educated Chinese American community in the Peter Liang, SCA 5, and AB 1726 case studies. These WeChat echo chambers have resulted in what has been described as a "self-contained news eco-system" (Wong 2018, par. 16).

Given the ability of social media to manipulate reactions among its vast users, will there be future efforts by individuals, organizations, and/or foreign governments during crowd- and organization-led Asian American connective action to create and spread fake news in order to generate backlash against a particular issue? To address this question, one need only look to the past to determine how this might look. The digital world is becoming more complex and connected than ever before, as exemplified by the transnational identities among many Asian American immigrants. An example of this can be seen with the World War II comfort women memorials case study, in which the conservative wing of the Japanese government, which was adamantly opposed to the memorials, appeared to have influence on its Japanese citizens and supporters in and outside of the United States who used Twitter as a persuasive tool to obfuscate issues related to the historical accuracies of comfort women and attack the legitimacy of local U.S. movements among Asian Americans.

Scale represents a critical reason why fake news in the world of Asian American connective action will be a major concern in the future. WeChat and Line have over one billion and over six hundred million active users worldwide, respectively. Scale is significant because of how amplified these issues can become through a myriad of social networks. Intentional efforts to spread misinformation can be quickly thwarted by the opponents. For example, during the SCA 5 and AB 1726 cases, Asian American activists responded to tweets by the opponents with data and/or links to opinion essays, which limited the effect of the efforts to obfuscate facts about affirmative action and data disaggregation. However, the collateral effects can be damaging to the public perception of Asian Americans, particularly among progressives and other racial minorities.

Efforts to create heightened sensationalism against an issue through the spread of misinformation was seen in the SCA 5 case study, among the first-generation Chinese American users on WeChat. Chi Zhang, in her article "WeChatting American Politics: Misinformation, Polarization, and Immigrant Chinese Media," writes:

> Low barrier to entry on WeChat has generated a profusion of content publishers native to the platform and intense competition for attention. The abundance of revenue-driven content published, cou-

pled with partisan forces, makes WeChat especially vulnerable to political misinformation. Emotionally stirring, sensational stories become amplified through the replication and embellishment of a long tail of WeChat outlets, which creates repetition and familiarity. (Zhang 2018, par. 4)

The long tails of WeChat outlets include Twitter, as seen with #SCA5. The findings illustrate the efforts to delegitimize affirmative action through tweets using #SCA5 as unfair and biased, and to scare Chinese Americans not only in California but also throughout the entire United States. This would explain how the national Chinese American immigrant community has been able to link up and become one of the public faces that have been impetuses to the recent attack on affirmative action policies, as illustrated earlier with the federal lawsuit against Harvard University for discriminating against Asian American students.

In the aftermath of the SCA 5 debate, the same Chinese American immigrant opponents of AB 1726 attempted to portray the bill as an extension of SCA 5. Discussion forums on AB 1726 that were created on WeChat and Twitter were also mobilizing to remove higher education institutions as one of the state public institutions required to disaggregate data on Asian Americans from the original version of AB 1726, which they were successful in doing.

Social media giants have begun to design features into their interfaces to limit the spread and impact of fake news. For example, Facebook proposed, in the aftermath of the 2016 U.S. presidential election, to combat the spread of fake news by providing users with a context button that will be part of its news feed update, to provide users with more context around links that they see (Wagner 2017). On September 19, 2018, the context button feature was publicly released. Another example is WhatsApp, which has been progressively limiting its virality by changing the feature that allows users to forward a message to others on the app. Initially, WhatsApp users could forward a message to 256 different conversations at once with as many as 256 people in each conversation, for a potential 65,536 people with one click of a button. As of July 2018, a person could forward a message to 20 different conversations with 256 people in each, for a potential total of 5,120 people. Currently, a user can forward a message to 5 different conversations with 256 people in each, for a potential total of 1,280 people (Wagner and Molla 2019). This WhatsApp development is significant for Asian American connective action because Asia-based competitors such as WeChat, KakaoTalk, and Line may likely follow. Therefore, while it remains to be seen whether limiting virality among Asian American social media users can combat fake news, it might move the needle in the effort to combat its impact, though not necessarily prevent it.

Logging Off: Connective Action and the Future of Asian American Coalitions

Each of the book's case studies shed light on connective action and the future of Asian American politics in regard to what types of coalitions may materialize among progressive and conservative Asian American groups, by illustrating the confluence of class and ideological differences during digital organized action in Asian American communities. The question often posited about Asian Americans and panethnic coalitions is whether they will find common interests and ideology around progressive issues and candidates that bind them together as a racial group, or will each Asian ethnic group go it alone (Lai 2000; 2021). However, it is critical to examine the contemporary political contours that facilitate or inhibit panethnic identity, as discussed in Chapter 2, such as rising class disparities, emerging ideological movements on social media platforms, and persisting transnational identities.

Rather than framing the research question on whether Asian Americans can coalesce with other ethno-racial groups rather than going it alone, the case studies illustrate how these emerging political contours reflect the socioeconomic heterogeneity of the larger Asian American community. It is thus possible to foresee a future Asian American politics where there would not be ideological cohesion as one racial group but where there could be competing panethnic coalitions pursuing different political positions around contentious issues along the entire ideological spectrum, as illustrated in the case studies throughout this book.

Political communication beyond online echo chambers will therefore remain a critical component in the future of Asian American politics to allow for constructive and balanced dialogues around policy and social justice issues so that misinformation, prejudice, fear, and self-interest do not rule the day and possibly lead to interracial conflict and strife. Acknowledging the unique racial privileges that Asian Americans possess and African Americans and Latinx do not must be part of this equation as well. Claire Kim refers to this process as a new "sociometry" for understanding the differences of racial privileges between Asian Americans, African Americans, and Latinx so that more equitable and nuanced affirmative action policies can be created to address persisting racial inequalities (Kim 2018, p. 217). Online campaigns, crowd and organization led, will likely play a critical role in determining whether shared interests and ideology on contested policies between Asian Americans and other racial minorities can be articulated into offline political action. Indeed, connective action can hold great promise for Asian Americans by providing new affordances for playing visible and active roles in panethnic and multiracial coalitions while at the same time dispelling the mainstream stereotypes of them as a monolithic and civically disengaged racial group in American politics.

Notes

PREFACE

1. In 2019, *Forbes* found that 97 percent of Asian Americans own a smartphone, 99 percent have internet access in the home, and 89 percent own a computer (Davis 2019).

CHAPTER 1

1. The November 2016 CMPS was the first multiracial national survey of its kind that focused on the political attitudes and participation of White people, African Americans, Latinxs, and Asian Americans. A total of 10,145 completed interviews were collected online in a respondent self-administered format from December 3, 2016, to February 15, 2017. The survey (and invitation) was available to respondents in English, Spanish, Chinese (simplified), Chinese (traditional), Korean, and Vietnamese. Because of the primary interest in the 2016 election, the project started with a large sample of registered voters, to provide a greater pool for analysis. The data also included a sample of adult unregistered voters as well, including noncitizens.

The full data were weighted within each racial group to match the adult population in the 2015 U.S. Census Bureau's American Community Survey (ACS) one-year data file for age, gender, education, nativity, ancestry, and voter registration status. A poststratification raking algorithm was used to balance each category within +/− 1 percent of the ACS estimates. Data were not weighted to their national combined racial average. White people accounted for 10 percent of all cases and each racial group roughly 30 percent.

Several strengths and limitations resulted from this unprecedented survey, in particular for the study of social media and political participation. Among the strengths, the survey instrument is multiracial, which allows for comparisons on topics ranging from where different ethnicities get their political news to how often they use social media platforms. In addition, the survey provided the option among the large LEP Asian sample to respond either in English or in Chinese, Korean, or Vietnamese, three of the largest Asian national origin groups. Despite these strengths, because of the large number of collaborators, the survey ended up being longer than anticipated, taking nearly sixty minutes to complete, which resulted in a lower initial response rate and potentially shortened responses.

2. See Latino Decisions, Collaborative Multiracial Post-Election Survey (CMPS) 2016 Coding Sheet, Questions C56–69. The survey questions can be found here: https://latinodecisions.com/wp-content/uploads/2019/06/CMPS_MASTER_INSTRUMENT.pdf.

3. Requests to Twitter were made by this author to obtain geocode data for all tweets related to the hashtags examined in this book's case studies. Unfortunately, these requests were denied. The other option to obtain geocode is through the Twitter API, a public interface that allows for various searches. A user must voluntarily set their account preferences to allow for location, which only 1 to 2 percent of Twitter users do. Thus, a search for user location on the Twitter API would yield only those who are in this small percentage of users. In comparison, a larger percentage of users voluntarily provide their location in their user bios, which are visible on their tweets, in one of the following categories: country, state, or city. As a result, the user bios were also coded for location for each tweet. The user's state represented the level of analysis for location that was utilized in this study.

CHAPTER 2

1. The sixty-four AACE members who were part of its 2015 federal complaint included some of the following groups: Beijing Institute of Technology Alumni Association at Silicon Valley; BIT Sindri Alumni Association of North India; Bostonese.com (English-Chinese online journal); Chinese American Association of Orange County; Chinese American Equalization Association; Chinese American for Progress and Equality; Chinese School of Tomorrow (Orlando, Florida); Conejo Chinese Cultural Association; Dallas Fort Worth Chinese Alliance; Global Organization of People of Indian Origin–Los Angeles Chapter; Great Neck Chinese Association; Houston Chinese Alliance; Houston Chinese Civic Center; Houston Jiangsu Association; Houston Shanghai Association; Howard County Chinese Parents Group; Huazhong University of Science and Technology Alumni Association of Southern California; International Chinese Transportation Professionals Association–Texas Chapter; Korean Parents Organization of Millburn and Short Hills; Livingston Chinese Association; Livingston Huaxia Chinese School; Long Island Chinese American Association; Long Island School of Chinese; Millburn Short Hills Chinese Association; Northern California Chinese Athletic-Cultural Federation; Overseas Chinese Association of Miami; Pakistan Policy Institute; Peking University Alumni Association of Southern California (PUAASC); San Antonio Chinese Alliance; Shandong Fellowship Association of Southern USA; Silicon Valley Chinese Association Foundation; Texas Northeast Chinese Association; The Federation of Florida Chinese Association; Tsinghua University Alumni Association of Southern California; United Chinese Association of Utah; and the U.S. Shangdong Fellowship Association.

CHAPTER 3

1. Shannon Peng, phone interview by author, January 20, 2017, Edison, New Jersey.

CHAPTER 4

1. Because many first-generation Chinese Americans arrived in the United States well after the Asian American Movement of the 1960s and 1970s, many do not identify with the larger and more established Asian American community's progressive ideologies.

2. The Lin Sing Association is a Chinese American organization established in 1900 to improve the rights and welfare of its members.

3. The thirty-eight U.S. and three Canadian cities where Liang demonstrations were held were the following: New York City (NY); Boston (MA); Washington, DC; Orlando (FL); Miami (FL); Raleigh (NC); Charlotte (NC); Atlanta (GA); Philadelphia (PA); Pittsburgh (PA); Boise (ID); Princeton (NJ); Austin (TX); Houston (TX); San Antonio (TX); Dallas (TX); Los Angeles (CA); San Diego (CA); San Francisco (CA); Sacramento (CA); Irvine (CA); Seattle (WA); Bellingham (WA); Salt Lake City (UT); Las Vegas (NV); Denver (CO); Ann Arbor (MI); Columbus (OH); Saint Louis (MO); Kansas City (MO); Portland (OR); Phoenix (AZ); Omaha (NE); St. Paul (MN); Chicago (IL); Indianapolis (IN); Nashville (TN); Little Rock (AR); Montreal (CN); Toronto (CN); and Calgary (CN).

CHAPTER 5

1. In 2014, an Asian American student group called Students for Fair Admissions (SFFA) filed a lawsuit demanding that Harvard University turn over documents revealing their confidential selection process. It was the first lawsuit over race-conscious admissions in higher education that involved Asian Americans as the plaintiffs (Kim 2018). The complaint alleged that Asian American applicants are discriminated against by Harvard University's "holistic" practices. It further argued that Asian American applicants with perfect test scores, top 1 percent grade point averages, and academic awards are unjustifiably rejected (Coalition of Asian-American Associations 2015). In November 2018, a federal district court began hearing a federal lawsuit filed by a coalition of plaintiffs that included the Department of Justice under the Trump administration, Edward Blum, and AACE on the grounds that Harvard University is discriminating against Asian American applicants. In August of 2018, the Department of Justice forced Harvard University to oblige to SFFA's request (K. Xu 2018). The internal documents revealed that Harvard University allegedly determined student admissions through three criteria: academics, extracurriculars, and "personality" (K. Xu 2018, par. 3). Personality traits consisted of both observable (i.e., "courage," "leadership," "relational skills," and "personal attractiveness") and unobservable characteristics. It was found that Asian Americans typically scored lower than non-Asian student applicants on unobserved characteristics that might be related to racial stereotypes of Asian Americans as one-dimensional, robot test takers (K. Xu 2018). Arguments on both sides rested on November 2, 2018. On October 1, 2019, the final decision was issued by Judge Allison D. Burroughs, a federal judge in Massachusetts, who ruled that Harvard University does not discriminate against Asian American applicants by meeting the strict constitutional standard when using race in its admissions process (Hartocollis 2019).

2. Chris Zhang, personal interview by author, October 26, 2016, Cupertino, California.

3. Jason Xu, email interview by author, November 27, 2018, Santa Clara, California.

4. Paul Fong, personal interview by author, May 5, 2017, San Jose, California.

5. Zhang interview.

6. Gilbert Wong, personal interview by author, March 16, 2017, Cupertino, California.

7. Zhang interview.

8. Diane Wong, email interview by author, May 16, 2019, Santa Clara, California.

9. Asian Americans serving in the State Assembly during 2016–17 included Rob Bonta (D-District 18), Phil Ting (D-District 19), Evan Low (D-District 28), Ed Chau (D-District 49), David Chiu (D-District 17), Kansen Chu (D-District 25), Todd Gloria (D-District 78), Ash Kalra (D-District 27), Al Muratsuchi (D-District 66), and Adrin Nazarian (D-District 46). Those in the State Senate during 2016–17 included Richard Pan (D-District 6) and Kevin de Leon (D-District 24).

CHAPTER 6

1. Fong interview.

2. Evan Low, personal interview by author, May 12, 2017, Cupertino, California.

CHAPTER 7

1. Cayden Mak, personal interview by author, October 6, 2017, Santa Clara, California.

2. The National AAPI immigrant Rights Organizing Table is a coalition of eighteen Asian American and Pacific Islander undocumented youth groups that include 18MR, Asian Americans Advancing Justice, Asian American Legal Defense and Education Fund, Association of Asian Pacific Community Health Organizations, Asian Pacific American Labor Alliance, ASPIRE, HANA Center, Korean Resource Center, NAKASEC, National Asian Pacific American Women's Forum, National Council of Asian Pacific Americans, National Federation of Filipino American Associations, OCA-Asian Pacific American Advocates, OCA-Asian Pacific American Advocates Greater Seattle, Revolutionizing Asian American Immigrant Stories on the East Coast, South Asian Americans Leading Together, Southeast Asian Resource Action Center, Uplift, and the office of Philadelphia City Council Member Helen Gym.

3. Laura Li, email interview, January 4, 2018, Santa Clara, California.

4. Li interview.

5. Li interview.

CHAPTER 8

1. Samir Kalra, personal interview by author, April 4, 2019, San Jose, California.

2. Kalra interview.

3. Mat McDermott, personal interview by author, April 4, 2019, San Jose, California.

CHAPTER 10

1. Jason Xu, email interview by author, November 27, 2018, Santa Clara, California.

2. Li interview.

References

Abbas, Syed Akif (@akif_abbas). 2016. "I am Pakistani but I think [the] name India has strong roots to the history of that region so #donteraseindia." Twitter, May 5, 2016. Available at https://twitter.com/akif_abbas/status/728076301022597125.

Abe, Shinzo. 2015. "'Toward an Alliance of Hope'—Address to a Joint Meeting of the U.S. Congress by Prime Minister Shinzo Abe." Prime Minister of Japan and His Cabinet. Last modified April 29, 2015. Available at https://japan.kantei.go.jp/97_abe/statement/201504/uscongress.html.

Allcott, Hunt, and Matthew Gentzkow. 2017. "Social Media and Fake News in the 2016 Election." *Journal of Economic Perspectives* 31, no. 2 (Spring): 211–236. Available at http://web.stanford.edu/~gentzkow/research/fakenews.pdf.

Allyn, Bobby. 2021. "Biden Drops Trump's Ban on TikTok and WeChat—But Will Continue the Scrutiny." NPR. June 9, 2021. Available at https://www.npr.org/2021/06/09/1004750274/biden-replaces-trump-bans-on-tiktok-wechat-with-order-to-scrutinize-apps.

Anschuetz, Nika. 2015. "Is Hashtag-Based Activism All Talk, No Action?" *USA Today College*, October 26, 2015. Available at https://www.usatoday.com/story/college/2015/10/26/is-hashtag-based-activism-all-talk-no-action/37407851/.

APIAVote and Asian Americans Advancing Justice. 2014. "An Agenda for Justice: Contours of Public Opinion Among Asian Americans." Asian and Pacific Islander American Vote. Last modified November 7, 2014. Available at https://www.apiavote.org/sites/default/files/APV-AAJC-issues--nov7.pdf.

APIAVote, Asian Americans Advancing Justice, and AAPI Data. 2016. "Inclusion, Not Exclusion: Spring 2016 Asian American Voter Survey." Asian and Pacific Islander American Vote. Accessed June 3, 2017. Available at https://www.apiavote.org/sites/default/files/Inclusion-2016-AAVS-final.pdf.

Asian Pacific American Labor Alliance (@APALAnational). 2017. "Strength in unity at the #BlackAAPIAction!" Twitter, December 5, 2017. Available at https://twitter.com /APALAnational/status/938122656586653697.

Baldassare, Mark, Dean Bonner, Alyssa Dykman, and Rachel Lawler. 2020. "PPIC State-wide Survey: Californians & Their Government." Public Policy Institute of California. September 2020. Available at https://www.ppic.org/publication/ppic-statewide -survey-californians-and-their-government-september-2020/.

Basch, Linda, Nina Glick Schiller, and Cristina Blanc. 1993. *Nations Unbound: Trans-national Projects, Postcolonial Predicaments, and Deterritorialized Nation States*. New York: Routledge Press.

Belkin, Douglas. 2015. "Harvard Accused of Bias against Asian-Americans." *Wall Street Journal*, May 15, 2015. Available at http://www.wsj.com/articles/asian-american-orga nizations-seek-federal-probe-of-harvard-admission-policies-1431719348.

Benkler, Yochai. 2007. *The Wealth of Networks: How Social Production Transforms Mar-kets and Freedom*. New Haven, CT: Yale University Press.

Bennett, W. Lance, and Alexandra Segerberg. 2013. *The Logic of Connective Action: Digital Media and the Personalization of Contentious Politics*. Cambridge, UK: Cambridge University Press.

Berlatsky, Noah. 2015. "Hashtag Activism Isn't a Cop-Out." *The Atlantic*, January 7, 2015. Available at https://www.theatlantic.com/politics/archive/2015/01/not-just-hashtag -activism-why-social-media-matters-to-protestors/384215/.

Bimber, Bruce, Andrew J. Flanagin, and Cynthia Stohl. 2005. "Reconceptualizing Col-lective Action in the Contemporary Media Environment." *Communication Theory* 15 (4): 365–388.

———. 2012. *Collective Action in Organizations: Interaction and Engagement in an Era of Technological Change*. Cambridge, UK: Cambridge University Press.

Blitzer, Jonathan. 2017. "The Minnesota Eight Don't Want to Be Deported to a Country They've Never Lived In." *New Yorker*, April 5, 2017. Available at https://www.new yorker.com/news/news-desk/the-minnesota-eight-dont-want-to-be-deported-to-a -country-theyve-never-lived-in.

Bonta, Rob. 2016a. "Governor Signs Bonta Bill to Uncover Health Disparities in the API Community." Assemblyman Rob Bonta Press Release. Accessed September 25, 2016. Available at http://asmdc.org/members/a18/news-room/press-releases/governor-signs -bonta-bill-to-uncover-health-disparities-in-the-api-community.

———(@RobBonta). 2016b. "The path to good public policy is paved with accurate data! #AHEADAct #caleg #AB1726 #API." Twitter, March 28, 2016. Available at https:// twitter.com/RobBonta/status/714502529812271104?s=20.

Bose, Purnima. 2008. "Hindutva Abroad: The California Textbook Controversy." *Global South* 2 (1): 11–34.

Brady, Henry, Sidney Verba, and Kay Lehman Schlozman. 1995. "Beyond SES: A Resource Model of Political Participation." *American Political Science Review* 89 (2): 271–294.

Browning, Rufus P., Dale R. Marshall, and David H. Tabb. 2003. *Racial Politics in Amer-ican Cities*. Third Edition. New York: Longman Press.

Budiman, Abby. 2021a. "Indians in the U.S. Fact Sheet." Pew Research Center, April 29, 2021. Available at https://www.pewresearch.org/social-trends/fact-sheet/asian-amer icans-indians-in-the-u-s/.

———. 2021b. "Koreans in the U.S. Fact Sheet." Pew Research Center, April 29, 2021. Available at https://www.pewresearch.org/social-trends/fact-sheet/asian-americans -koreans-in-the-u-s/.

CAAAV. 2014. "#JusticeforAkaiGurley National Sign-On Letter." Accessed March 15, 2016. Available at http://caaav.org/justiceforakaigurley-national-sign-on-letter.

Cai, Weiyi, Audra D. S. Burch, and Jugal K. Patel. 2021. "Swelling Anti-Asian Violence: Who Is Being Attacked and Where." *New York Times*, April 3, 2021. Available at https://www.nytimes.com/interactive/2021/04/03/us/anti-asian-attacks.html.

California Board of Education. 2013. *Standards for Evaluating Instructional Materials for Social Content*. Last modified May 8, 2013. Available at https://www.cde.ca.gov/ci/cr/cf/documents/socialcontent2013.doc.

California Legislative Information. 2014. "SB-1057 Pupil Curriculum: History-Social Science Content Standards." 2013–2014. Available at https://leginfo.legislature.ca.gov/faces/billStatusClient.xhtml?bill_id=201320140SB1057.

Carapezza, Kirk. 2017. "DOJ Looks into Whether Harvard Discriminates against Asian-Americans." *All Things Considered*, National Public Radio. August 3, 2017. Available at http://www.npr.org/2017/08/03/541430130/trump-admin-looking-into-whether-harvard-discriminates-against-asian-americans.

Castells, Manuel. 2015. *Networks of Outrage and Hope: Social Movements in the Internet Age*. Malden, MA: Polity.

Chan, Nathan K. 2020. "Political Inequality in the Digital World: The Puzzle of Asian American Political Participation Online." *Political Research Quarterly*, August 10, 2020. Available at https://journals.sagepub.com/doi/10.1177/1065912920945391.

Chan, Sucheng. 1991. *Asian Americans: An Interpretive History*. Philadelphia, PA: Temple University Press.

Chandran, Nyshka. 2018. "Obama to David Letterman: Media Is Dividing Americans." CNBC. January 12, 2018. Available at https://www.cnbc.com/2018/01/12/former-president-barack-obama-warns-on-polarizing-media-us-electoral-system.html.

Chang, Jeff. 1993. "Race, Class, Conflict and Empowerment: On Ice Cube's 'Black Korea.'" *Amerasia Journal* 19 (2): 87–107.

Chang, Shenglin E., and Willow Lung Amam. 2010. "Born Glocal: Youth Identity and Suburban Spaces in the U.S. and Taiwan." *Amerasia Journal* 36 (3): 29–52.

Chau, Ed. 2014. "Assemblymember Ed Chau's Statement on SCA 5." Press Release. Last modified February 25, 2014. Available at http://www.chinesetoday.com/en/article/851270.

Chen, Christine, James S. Lai, Karthick Ramakrishnan, and Alton Wang. 2016. "From Citizens to Elected Representatives: The Political Trajectory of Asian American Pacific Islanders by 2040." *AAPI Nexus* 14, no. 1 (Spring): 162–180.

Chen, Fan. 2016. "Peter Liang National Parade Held Simultaneously 2/20." *Sing Tao Daily*. Accessed February 15, 2016. Available at http://ny.stgloballink.com/community/2016/0215/286560.shtml.

Chen, Fan, and Rong Xiaoqing. 2016. "Bring Peter Justice White House Website." *Sing Tao Daily*, February 15, 2016. Available at http://ny.stgloballink.com/community/2016/0215/286545.shtml.

Chen, Yujie, Zhifei Mao, and Jack Linchuan Qiu. 2018. *Super-Sticky WeChat and Chinese Society*. Bingley, UK: Emerald Publishing.

Cheng, Wendy. 2013. *The Changs Next Door to the Diazes: Remapping Race in Southern California*. St. Paul, MN: University of Minnesota Press.

Chew, Erin. 2017. "Japanese Government Files a Lawsuit in Support of Removing a 'Comfort Women' Statue in Glendale." *You Offend Me You Offend My Family* (*YOMYOMF*). Accessed March 18, 2017. Available at https://www.yomyomf.com/japanese-government-file-a-lawsuit-in-support-of-removing-a-comfort-women-statue-at-glendale/.

Chhuon, Vichet. 2017. "8 Cambodian Refugees in Minnesota Prove Why Deportations Must Be Stopped." *Huffington Post*, April 1, 2017. Available at https://www.huffing tonpost.com/entry/deporting-refugees-is-wrong-the-case-of-chamroeun_us_58df 0c7ce4b03c2b30f6a673.

China Xinhua News (@XHNews). 2016. "Legal experts voice serious concern, objections over conviction of former NY cop #PeterLiang." Twitter, February 21, 2016. Available at https://twitter.com/FactcheckChina/status/701588105002930176.

Chinese for Affirmative Action (CAA). 2016. Statement on Assembly Bill l726, Data Disaggregation Bill. March 24, 2016. Available at https://caasf.org/press-release/statement-on -ab-1726-data-disaggregation-bill/.

Choudhury, Sheli Roy. 2020. "Trump Issues Executive Orders Banning U.S. Transactions with WeChat and TikTok in 45 Days." CNBC. August 6, 2020. Available at https:// www.cnbc.com/2020/08/07/trump-issues-executive-orders-to-ban-us-transactions -with-wechat-tiktok.html.

Chung, Lori. 2015. "Sources: Officer Indicted on Manslaughter Charge in Akai Gurley Case." NY1. February 11, 2015. Available at http://www.ny1.com/nyc/all-boroughs /news/2015/02/10/officer-indicted-in-shooting-death-of-akai-gurley.html.

Coalition of Asian-American Associations. 2015. "Complaint against Harvard University and the President and the Fellows of Harvard College for Discriminating against Asian-American Applicants in the College Admissions Process." Last modified May 15, 2015. Available at https://web.archive.org/web/20150607120224/http://www.asian americancoalition.org/files/harvard/AisanComplaintHarvardDocumentFinal .pdf.

Cohen, Cathy J. 1999. *The Boundaries of Blackness: AIDS and the Breakdown of Black Politics*. Chicago, IL: University of Chicago Press.

Cohen, Cathy J., and Joseph Kahne. 2012. *Participatory Politics: New Media and Youth Political Action*. Oakland, CA: YPP Research Network. Accessed September 15, 2016. Available at https://ypp.dmlcentral.net/publications/107.html.

"Comfort Women" Justice Coalition. 2018. "About CWJC." Available at https://remem bercomfortwomen.org/about-cwjc/.

Constante, Agnes. 2017. "Supreme Court Declines Case over Lawsuit to Remove 'Comfort Women' Memorial." NBC News. March 31, 2017. Available at https://www.nbc news.com/news/asian-america/supreme-court-declines-case-over-lawsuit-remove -comfort-women-memorial-n740996.

Cui, Carolyn. 2017. "Chinese-Americans' Influence on New Jersey School Boards Grows." *Wall Street Journal*, January 24, 2017. Available at http://www.wsj.com/articles/chi nese-americans-influence-on-new-jersey-school-boards-grows-1485259208.

"Cyber Bullying Law and Legal Definition." 2019. USLegal.com. Available at https:// definitions.uslegal.com/c/cyber-bullying/.

Dalton, Russell J. 2017. *The Participation Gap: Social Status and Political Inequality*. Oxford, UK: Oxford University Press.

Dao, Loan Thi. 2017. "Out and Asian: How Undocu/DACAmented Asian Americans and Pacific Islander Youth Navigate Dual Liminality in the Immigrant Rights Movement." *Societies* 7 (3): 17. Available at https://doi.org/10.3390/soc7030017.

Davis, Krystle. 2019. "12 Facts You Need to Know When Marketing to Asian American Consumers." *Forbes*, July 18, 2019. Available at https://www.forbes.com/sites/forbes contentmarketing/2019/07/18/12-facts-you-need-to-know-when-marketing-to -asian-american-consumers/#734ef21b50d4.

Dawson, Michael C. 1994. "A Black Counterpublic? Economic Earthquakes, Racial Agenda(s), and Black Politics." *Public Culture* 7 (1): 195–223.

———. 2001. *Black Visions: The Roots of Contemporary African-American Political Ideologies.* Chicago, IL: University of Chicago Press.

De la Cruz-Viesca, Melany, Paul M. Ong, Andre Comandon, William A. Darity Jr., and Darrick Hamilton. 2018. "Fifty Years after the Kerner Commission Report: Place, Housing, and Racial Wealth Inequality in Los Angeles." *RSF: The Russell Sage Foundation Journal of the Social Sciences* 4, no. 6 (September): 160–184. Available at https://doi.org/10.7758/RSF.2018.4.6.08.

DiNapoli, Thomas P. 2016. "The Asian Community in New York State." New York State Comptroller's Office. Available at https://www.osc.state.ny.us/osdc/rpt9-2016_eng.pdf.

Do, Ahn. 2018. "In Fighting Homeless Camp, Irvine's Asians Win, but at a Cost." *Los Angeles Times*, April 1, 2018. Available at https://www.latimes.com/local/lanow/la-me-homeless-asians-20180401-story.html.

Dorell, Oren. 2015. "Japanese Prime Minister Stands by Apologies for Japan's WWII Abuses." *USA Today*, April 29, 2015. Available at https://www.usatoday.com/story/news/world/2015/04/29/japan-shinzo-abe-joint-session-of-congress-speech/26566135/.

Duke, Alan. 2013. "Jimmy Kimmel Apologizes for 'Killing Everyone in China' Skit." CNN. October 29, 2013. Available at http://www.cnn.com/2013/10/29/showbiz/jimmy-kimmel-china-apology/.

Earl, Jennifer, and Katrina Kimport. 2011. *Digitally Enabled Social Change: Activism in the Internet Age.* Cambridge, MA: MIT Press.

Eberlin, Xujun. 2016. "Tomorrow They Will Come Out Like Ants." *An Immigrant's Evolving Perspective* (blog). February 19, 2016. Available at https://insideoutchina.blogspot.com/2016/02/tomorrow-they-will-come-out-like-ants.html.

Edsall, Thomas B. 2017. "Democracy, Disrupted." *New York Times*, March 2, 2017. Available at https://www.nytimes.com/2017/03/02/opinion/how-the-internet-threatens-democracy.html.

18MillionRising.org. 2016a. "Governor Brown: Make All AAPI Communities Visible!" Available at https://action.18mr.org/AB1726/.

———. 2016b. "Stop the Unjust Deportations of the Minnesota 8 #ReleaseMN8." Available at https://action.18mr.org/releasemn8/.

——— (@18millionrising). 2017a. "#BlackAAPIaction is kicking off to a great start here at the @SEARAC offices in D.C.! #DreamActNow." Twitter, December 4, 2017. Available at https://twitter.com/18millionrising/status/937827128770486273.

——— (@18millionrising). 2017b. "Call, call, call your members of Congress (all 3 of them). Jam their phone lines to demand that they don't go home without a #cleanDreamAct. #BlackAAPIaction #DreamActNow." Twitter, December 4, 2017. Available at https://twitter.com/18millionrising/status/937755481396924422.

——— (@18millionrising). 2017c. "A #cleanDreamAct also does not further bolster law enforcement or grant additional powers to abuse our communities. #DreamActNow #BlackAAPIaction." Twitter, December 4, 2017. Available at https://twitter.com/18millionrising/status/937752273224110081.

——— (@18millionrising). 2017d. "While there is no singular, monolithic 'AAPI experience,' our communities interfaced immigration in all different ways. The first ever immigrant ban targeted the Chinese. First mass ethnic immigrant incarceration targeted the Japanese. Etc etc #BlackAAPIAction." Twitter, December 4, 2017. Available at https://twitter.com/18millionrising/status/937758012579766273.

Elliott, Thomas, and Jennifer Earl. 2018. "Organizing the Next Generation: Youth Engagement with Activism Inside and Outside of Organizations." *Social Movements and Media*, February 1, 2018, 1–20. Available at https://doi.org/10.1177/2056305117750722.

Empowering Pacific Islander Communities (@EmpoweredPI). 2016. "We need #AB1726 so we can give our families the very best that we can. Support#AB1726!" Twitter, September 8, 2016. Available at https://twitter.com/EmpoweredPI/status/76684780 8850780160?s=20.

English, Bella. 2015. "To Get into Elite Colleges, Some Advised to 'Appear Less Asian.'" *Boston Globe*, June 1, 2015. Available at https://www.bostonglobe.com/lifestyle/2015 /06/01/college-counselors-advise-some-asian-students-appear-less-asian/Ew7g4Ji QMiqYNQlIwqEIuO/story.html.

Espenshade, Thomas J., and Alexandria Walton Radford. 2015. *No Longer Separate, Not Yet Equal: Race and Class in Elite College Admission and Campus Life*. Princeton, NJ: Princeton University Press.

Extremely Concerned Californians. 2014. "Say No to SCA 5" Petition. Change.org. Available at https://www.change.org/p/california-state-assembly-vote-no-to-sca-5.

Fang, Jenn. 2014a. "The Effect of Prop 209 on UC Admissions and Campus Diversity." Reappropriate. Last modified March 15, 2014. Available at http://reappropriate.co /2014/03/the-effect-of-prop-209-on-uc-admissions-and-campus-diversity-edu4all -noliesnohate-sca5/.

———. 2014b. "Top 5 Anti-Affirmative Action Myths about SCA-5." Reappropriate. Last modified March 7, 2014. Available at http://reappropriate.co/2014/03/top-5-anti-af firmative-action-myths-about-sca5-noliesnohate/.

———. 2016. "California's Proposed Bill to Disaggregate AAPI Data Significantly Weakened in New Amendments." Reappropriate. Last modified August 21, 2016. Available at http://reappropriate.co/2016/08/californias-proposed-bill-to-disaggregate-aapi -data-significantly-weakened-in-new-amendments/.

Federal Communications Commission. 2018. "Restoring Internet Freedom." Last modified January 4, 2018. Available at https://docs.fcc.gov/public/attachments/DOC-351 481A1.pdf.

Field, Norma, and Tomomi Yamaguchi. 2015. "'Comfort Woman' Revisionism Comes to the U.S.: Symposium on The Revisionist Film Screening Event at Central Washington University." *Asian-Pacific Journal* 13, no. 22 (1): 1–4. Available at https://apjjf .org/-Norma-Field--Tomomi-Yamaguchi/4323/article.pdf.

Fisher v. University of Texas. 2016. Supreme Court of the United States. 579 U.S. ___ (2016). Available at https://supreme.justia.com/cases/federal/us/579/14-981/case.pdf.

Fong, Joe Chung. 1996. "Transnational Newspapers: The Making of the Post-1965 Globalized/Localized San Gabriel Valley Chinese Community." *Amerasia Journal* 22 (3): 65–77.

Fong, Timothy. 1994. *The First Suburban Chinatown: The Remaking of Monterey Park, California*. Philadelphia, PA: Temple University Press.

Frasure, Lorrie. 2007. "Beyond the Myth of the White Middle-Class: Immigrant and Ethnic Minority Settlement in Suburban America." *National Political Science Review* 11: 65–86.

Frey, William H. 2011. "Melting Pot Cities and Suburbs: Racial and Ethnic Change in Metro America in the 2000s." Brookings Institution. Last modified May 4, 2011.

Available at https://www.brookings.edu/research/melting-pot-cities-and-suburbs-ra
cial-and-ethnic-change-in-metro-america-in-the-2000s/.

Frier, Sarah. 2013. "With $200 Million in Revenue, South Korea's Top Messaging App Is
All Smiley Faces." Bloomberg News Online. Last modified December 23, 2013. Available at http://www.bloomberg.com/news/2013-12-22/with-200-million-in-revenue
-south-korea-s-top-messaging-app-is-all-smiley-faces.html.

Fuchs, Chris. 2016a. "Complaint Filed against Yale, Dartmouth, and Brown Alleging
Discrimination." NBC News. May 23, 2016. Available at http://www.nbcnews.com
/news/asian-america/groups-file-complaint-against-yale-dartmouth-brown-alleg
ing-discrimination-n578666.

———. 2016b. "California Data Disaggregation Bill Sparks Debate in Asian-American
Community." NBC News. August 26, 2016. Available at http://www.nbcnews.com
/news/asian-america/california-data-disaggregation-bill-sparks-debate-asian-amer
ican-community-n638286.

Garces, Liliana, and OiYan Poon. 2018. "Asian Americans and Race-Conscious Admissions: Understanding the Conservative Opposition's Strategy of Misinformation,
Intimidation & Racial Division." The Civil Rights Project. Last modified November
1, 2018. Available at https://www.civilrightsproject.ucla.edu/research/college-access
/affirmative-action/asian-americans-and-race-conscious-admissions-understand
ing-the-conservative-opposition2019s-strategy-of-misinformation-intimidation
-racial-division.

Garchik, Leah. 2017. "Retired Judges Take 'Comfort Women' Fight to UNESCO in Korea."
San Francisco Chronicle, November 27, 2017. Available at https://www.sfchronicle
.com/entertainment/garchik/article/SF-official-adopts-Comfort-Women-statue
-as-12382599.php.

Gillani, Nabeel, Ann Yuan, Martin Saveski, Soroush Vosoughi, and Deb Roy. 2018. "Me,
My Echo Chamber, and I: Introspection on Social Media Polarization." WWW '18:
Proceedings of the 2018 World Wide Web Conference. April 23, 2018. Available at
https://dl.acm.org/doi/10.1145/3178876.3186130.

Gottfried, Jeffrey, Michael Barthel, Elisa Shearer, and Amy Mitchell. 2016. "The 2016
Presidential Campaign—A News Event That's Hard to Miss." Pew Research Center:
Journalism and Media. February 4, 2016. Available at http://www.journalism.org
/2016/02/04/the-2016-presidential-campaign-a-news-event-thats-hard-to-miss/.

Gottfried, Jeffrey, and Elisa Shearer. 2016. "News Use Across Social Media Platforms
2016." Pew Research Center: Journalism and Media. May 26, 2016. Available at http://
www.journalism.org/2016/05/26/news-use-across-social-media-platforms-2016/.

Greenwood, Shannon, Andrew Perrin, and Maeve Duggan. 2016. "Social Media Update
2016." Pew Research Center: Internet, Science, and Tech. November 11, 2016. Available at http://www.pewinternet.org/2016/11/11/social-media-update-2016/.

Guichard, Sylvie. 2010. *The Construction of History and Nationalism in India*. New York:
Routledge.

Guillermo, Emil. 2015. "More Than a 160 Asian-American Groups File Briefs in Support
of Affirmative Action." NBC News. November 3, 2015. Available at http://www.nbc
news.com/news/asian-america/more-160-asian-american-groups-file-briefs-sup
port-affirmative-action-n456666.

Gulezian, Lisa Amin. 2016. "'Don't Erase India' Social Media Campaign to Launch."
ABC7News. April 6, 2016. Available at https://abc7news.com/education/dont-erase
-india-social-media-campaign-to-launch/1278428/.

Guo, Jeff. 2015. "What People Don't Get about 'Black Twitter.'" *Washington Post*, October 22, 2015. Available at https://www.washingtonpost.com/news/wonk/wp/2015/10/22/why-it-can-be-offensive-to-use-the-term-black-twitter/?utm_term=.eec0fa7e0c2f.

Han, Hahrie. 2009. *Moved to Action: Motivation, Participation & Inequality in American Politics*. Stanford, CA: Stanford University Press.

HANA Center (@HANACenter). 2017. "#BlackAAPIAction debriefing our action and legislative visits, speaking out about anti-blackness and police brutality and owning the beauty and power of our immigrant community." Twitter, December 5, 2017. Available at https://twitter.com/HANACenter/status/938219832507551745.

Harrington, Theresa. 2017. "Hindus Urge California State Board to Reject Textbooks Due to Negative Images." EdSource. Last modified August 8, 2017. Available at https://edsource.org/2017/hindus-urge-california-state-board-to-reject-textbooks-due-to-negative-images/589996.

Hartocollis, Anemona. 2019. "Harvard Does Not Discriminate Against Asian-Americans in Admissions, Judge Rules." *New York Times*, October 1, 2019. Available at https://www.nytimes.com/2019/10/01/us/harvard-admissions-lawsuit.html.

Higashi, Julie, Yoshikata Veki, Norma Field, and Tomomi Yamaguchi. 2015. "'Comfort Women' Denial and the Japanese Right." *Asia-Pacific Journal* 13, 30, no. 2 (July 27). Available at https://apjjf.org/-Yoshikata-Veki--Norma-Field--Tomomi-Yamaguchi/4350/article.pdf.

Hindu American Foundation. 2016. "#DontEraseIndia: HAF Launches Campaign to Keep India and Hinduism in CA Textbooks." Hindu American Foundation. May 19, 2016. Available at https://www.worldhindunews.com/donteraseindia-haf-launches-campaign-to-keep-india-and-hinduism-in-ca-textbooks/.

Hollander, Rayna. 2018. "WeChat Has Hit 1 Billion Monthly Active Users." *Business Insider*, March 6, 2018. Available at https://www.businessinsider.com/wechat-has-hit-1-billion-monthly-active-users-2018-3.

Honda, Michael. 2007. "House Resolution 121." GovTrack.us. Last modified July 30, 2007. Available at https://www.govtrack.us/congress/bills/110/hres121/text.

Howard, Philip Eugene, and Muzammil M. Hussain. 2013. *Democracy's Fourth Wave? Digital Media and the Arab Spring*. Cambridge, UK: Oxford University Press.

Hu, Elise. 2017. "'Comfort Woman' Memorial Statues, a Thorn in Japan's Side, Now Sit on Korean Buses." National Public Radio. Last modified November 13, 2017. Available at https://www.npr.org/sections/parallels/2017/11/13/563838610/comfort-woman-memorial-statues-a-thorn-in-japans-side-now-sit-on-korean-buses.

Hu, Winnie, and Al Baker. 2016. "Shooting in Public Housing Project Highlight Risks of Stairwell Patrols." *New York Times*, February 5, 2016. Available at https://www.nytimes.com/2016/02/06/nyregion/shootings-in-public-housing-project-highlight-risks-of-stairwell-patrols.html.

Huang, Josie. 2014. "SCA 5: A Political Coming-of-Age Story for Chinese-Americans." 89.3 KPCC. Last modified March 21, 2014. Available at http://www.scpr.org/blogs/multiamerican/2014/03/21/16152/sca-5-chinese-americans-immigrants-asian-americans/.

———. 2020. "In California, a Vocal Minority of Asian Parents Helped Defeat Affirmative Action Once Before. This Time It Could Be Harder." LAist. June 12, 2020. Available at https://laist.com/2020/06/12/affirmative_action_california_aca_5_sca_5_asian_americans_chinese_universities_education_black_lives.php.

Hum, Tarry. 2014. *Making a Global Immigrant Neighborhood: Brooklyn's Sunset Park*. Philadelphia, PA: Temple University Press.

Hwang, Suein. 2005. "The New White Flight." *Wall Street Journal*, November 19, 2005. Available at http://www.wsj.com/articles/SB113236377590902105.

IndiaWest. 2016. "'India' Will Not Be Replaced with 'South Asia' in California Textbooks: Commission." *IndiaWest*, May 20, 2016. Available at https://www.indiawest.com/news /global_indian/india-will-not-be-replaced-with-south-asia-in-california/article _a57ce7d0-1ec4-11e6-9a7b-7f9c0a5d7fda.html.

———. 2020. "Asian American Organizations Applaud Defeat of Proposition 16 Banning Affirmative Action." *IndiaWest*, November 9, 2020. Available at https://www.india west.com/news/global_indian/asian-american-organizations-applaud-defeat-of -proposition-16-banning-affirmative-action/article_603796c4-22b2-11eb-aedf-7f3 41eed046b.html.

Internetlivestats.com. 2017. "Twitter Usage Statistics." Available at http://www.internet livestats.com/twitter-statistics/.

Ito, Mizuko, Elisabeth Soep, Neta Kligler-Vilenchik, Sangita Shresthova, Liana Gamber-Thompson, and Arely Zimmerman. 2015. "Learning Connected Civics: Narratives, Practices, Infrastructures." *Curriculum Inquiry* 45 (1): 10–29. Available at http://www .tandfonline.com/doi/full/10.1080/03626784.2014.995063.

Jang, Seung-Jin. December 2009. "Get Out on Behalf of Your Group: Electoral Participation of Latinos and Asian Americans." *Political Behavior* 21 (4): 511–534.

Jaschik, Scott. 2020. "Why Did Prop 16 Fail?" *Inside Higher Ed*, November 9, 2020. Available at https://www.insidehighered.com/admissions/article/2020/11/09/experts-dis cuss-failure-californias-proposition-16.

Jenkins, Henry, Sangita Shresthova, Liana Gamber-Thompson, Neta Kligler-Vilenchik, and Arely Zimmerman. 2016. *By Any Media Necessary: The New Youth Activism*. New York: New York University Press.

Jha, Lalit K. 2009. "California Education Board to Compensate Hindu-American Parents." *Rediff India Abroad*, June 10, 2009. Available at http://www.rediff.com/news /report/california-education-board-to-compensate-hindu-parents/20090610.htm.

Jiménez, Tomás R., and Adam L. Horowitz. 2013. "When White Is Just Alright: How Immigrants Redefine Achievement and Reconfigure the Ethnoracial Hierarchy." *American Sociological Review* 78 (5): 849–871.

Jones-Correa, Michael. 2004. "Racial and Ethnic Diversity and the Politics of Education in Suburbia." Paper presented at the annual meeting of the American Political Science Association, September 2, 2004, Hilton Chicago and the Palmer House Hilton, Chicago, IL.

Jost, John T., Pablo Barbera, Melanie Lange, Megan Metzger, Jonathan Nagler, Joanna Sterling, and Joshua A. Tucker. 2018. "How Social Media Facilitates Political Protest: Information, Motivation, and Social Networks." *Advances in Political Psychology* 39, suppl. I (2018). Available at https://onlinelibrary.wiley.com/doi/pdf/10.1111/pops.12478.

Jung, Carrie. 2018. "Harvard Discrimination Trial Ends, but Lawsuit Is Far from Over." National Public Radio. November 2, 2018. Available at https://www.npr.org/2018/11 /02/660734399/harvard-discrimination-trial-is-ending-but-lawsuit-is-far-from-over.

Kahne, Joseph, and Benjamin Bowyer. 2016. "Revisiting the Measurement of Political Participation in the Digital Age." In *Civic Media, Technology, Design, Practice*, edited by Eric Gordon and Paul Milhailidis, 539–562. Cambridge, MA: MIT Press.

Kahne, Joseph, Nam-Jin Lee, and Jessica T. Feezell. 2012. "Digital Media Literacy Education and Online Civic and Political Participation." *Communication* 6: 1–24. Available at http://dmlhub.net/wp-content/uploads/files/International_Journal_Commu nication.pdf.

Kahne, Joseph, and Ellen Middaugh. 2012. "Digital Media Shapes Youth Participation in Politics." *Kappan Magazine*, Phi Delta Kappa International, November 2012. Available at http://ypp.dmlcentral.net/sites/default/files/publications/Digital_Media _Shapes_Participation.pdf.

Kang, Jay Caspian. 2016. "How Should Asian-Americans Feel about the Peter Liang Protests?" *New York Times Magazine*, February 23, 2016. Available at http://www .nytimes.com/2016/02/23/magazine/how-should-asian-americans-feel-about-the -peter-liang-protests.html.

Kaplan, Greg Jay. 2016. *Earning Admission: Real Strategies for Getting into Highly Se- lected Colleges*. Scotts Valley, CA: CreateSpace Independent Publishing Platform.

Kassie, Emily. 2018. "Sexual Assault Inside ICE Detention: 2 Survivors Tell Their Sto- ries." *New York Times*, July 17, 2018. Available at https://www.nytimes.com/2018/07/17 /us/sexual-assault-ice-detention-survivor-stories.html.

Kim, CeFaan. 2016. "Judge Says No Jail Time for Former NYPD Officer Peter Liang in Fatal Shooting of Akai Gurley." ABC7NY. April 19, 2016. Available at https://abc 7ny.com/news/no-jail-time-for-ex-nypd-officer-peter-liang-in-fatal-shooting/12 98037/.

Kim, Claire Jean. 1999. "The Racial Triangulation of Asian Americans." *Politics & So- ciety* 27, no. 1 (March): 105–138.

———. 2000. *Bitter Fruit: The Politics of Black-Korean Conflict in New York City*. New Haven, CT: Yale University Press.

———. 2017. "Opinion: The Trial of Peter Liang and Confronting the Reality of Asian American Privilege." *Los Angeles Times*, April 21, 2017. Available at https://www.la times.com/opinion/opinion-la/la-ol-peter-liang-asian-american-privilege-2016 0421-snap-story.html.

———. 2018. "Are Asians the New Blacks? Affirmative Action, Anti-Blackness, and the 'Sociometry' of Race." *Du Bois Review: Social Science Research on Race* 18 (2): 217–244.

Kishida, Fumio. 2015. "Announcement by Foreign Ministers of Japan and the Republic of Korea at the Joint Press Occasion." Ministry of Foreign Affairs of Japan. Decem- ber 28, 2015. Available at https://www.mofa.go.jp/a_o/na/kr/page4e_000364.html.

Kleinfeld, Zoe. 2014. "California Lawmakers Push Off College Affirmative Action Bill." *The Daily Californian*. Last modified March 20, 2014. Available at http://www.daily cal.org/2014/03/18/california-lawmakers-postpone-deliberation-bill-regarding-af firmative-action-college-admissions/.

Kono, Taro. 2017. "The Announcement of the Results of the Assessment by the Taskforce to Review the Agreement on Comfort Women Issue Reached between the Govern- ments of Japan and the ROK." Ministry of Foreign Affairs of Japan. December 27, 2017. Available at https://www.mofa.go.jp/press/release/press4e_001857.html.

Kono, Yohei. 1993. "Statement by the Chief Cabinet Secretary Yohei Kono on the Result of the Study on the Issue of 'Comfort Women.'" Ministry of Foreign Affairs of Japan. August 4, 1993. Available at https://www.awf.or.jp/e6/statement-02.html.

The Korean Council. 2011. "The Korean Council for the Women Drafted for Military Sex- ual Slavery by Japan." Last modified December 14, 2011. Available at https://www .koreaverband.de/wp-content/uploads/2011/07/ComfortWomen_1000Dem_PR -from-Korea_Dec2011.pdf.

Koseff, Alexei. 2020. "California's Affirmative Action Ban, Proposition 209, Targeted for Repeal." *San Francisco Chronicle*, March 10, 2020. Available at https://www.sfchron icle.com/politics/article/California-s-affirmative-action-ban-15121025.php.

Koyama, Emi. 2015. "The U.S. as 'Major Battleground' for 'Comfort Woman' Revisionism: The Screening of Scottsboro Girls at Central Washington University." *The Asian Pacific Journal* 13, 22, 2: 1–13. Available at https://apjjf.org/-Emi-Koyama/4324/article.pdf.

Krogstad, Jens Manuel. 2014. "Asian American Voter Turnout Lags behind Other Groups; Some Non-Voters Say They're 'Too Busy.'" Pew Research Center, April 9, 2014. Available at https://www.pewresearch.org/fact-tank/2014/04/09/asian-american-voter-turnout-lags-behind-other-groups-some-non-voters-say-theyre-too-busy/.

Kurien, Prema. 2006. "Multiculturalism and American Religion: The Case of Hindu Indian Americans." *Social Forces* 85 (2): 723–741.

Kwong, Peter. 1996. *The New Chinatown*. New York: Hill and Wang.

———. 2016. "Asian American and African American Communities after the Peter Liang Case." *CUNY FORUM* 4, no. 1 (fall/winter 2016–2017): 87–90.

Kyodo News. 2018. "New apology from Japan needed over 'comfort women:' S. Korea's Moon." *Kyodo News*. January 10, 2018. Available at https://english.kyodonews.net/news/2018/01/2c11442fe4bc-s-korea-leader-says-japan-needs-to-apologize-to-comfort-women.html.

Laguerre, Michel S. 2010. "A Cosmonational Theory of Global Neighborhoods." *Amerasia Journal* 36 (3): xv–xxxiii.

Lai, James S. 2000. "Asian Pacific Americans and the Pan-Ethnic Question." In *Minority Politics at the Millennium*, edited by Richard Keiser and Katherine Underwood, 203–226. New York: Garland.

———. 2011. *Asian American Political Action: Suburban Transformations*. Boulder, CO: Lynne Rienner.

———. 2015. "From Central Cities to Ethnoburbs: Asian American Political Incorporation in the San Francisco Bay Area." In *Minority Voting in the United States*, edited by Kyle L. Kreider and Thomas J. Baldino, 304–325. Santa Barbara, CA: ABC-CLIO.

———. 2021. "Revisiting Panethnicity: Emerging Political Contours in Asian Pacific American Politics." *PS: Political Science & Politics* 54, no. 2: 235–237. Available at https://www.cambridge.org/core/journals/ps-political-science-and-politics/article/revisiting-panethnicity-emerging-political-contours-in-asian-pacific-american-politics/F909E327A0712DE47A6B8ED9DB0F5A85.

Lai, James S., and Kim Geron. 2006. "When Asian Americans Run: The Suburban and Urban Dimensions of Asian American Candidates in California Local Politics." *California Politics & Policy* (June): 62–88.

Lang, Robert F., and Thomas W. Sanchez. 2006. "The New Metro Politics: Interpreting Recent Presidential Elections Using a County-Based Regional Typology." Metropolitan Institute 2006 Election Brief. Virginia Tech University.

Lartey, Jamiles. 2016. "NYPD Officer Breaks Down during Testimony about Akai Gurley Shooting." *The Guardian*, February 8, 2016. Available at https://www.theguardian.com/us-news/2016/feb/08/nypd-officer-peter-liang-testifies-akai-gurley.

Leonard, Paul. 2016. "Council Member Chin Calls for Leniency for Peter Liang." New York City Council, District 1, Margaret Chin. April 26, 2016. Available at http://council.nyc.gov/margaret-chin/2017/04/26/council-member-chin-calls-for-leniency-for-peter-liang/.

Levitt, Leonard. 2016. "Peter Liang: Guilty Verdict—But Maybe Not Guilty." NYPD Confidential: An Inside Look at the New York City Police Department. February 14, 2016. Available at http://nypd-confidential.com/columns/2016/160214.html.

Lewis, Paul, and Karthick Ramakrishnan. 2004. "Open Arms? The Receptivity of Cities and Local Officials to Immigrants and Their Concerns." Paper presented at the 100th Annual Meeting of the American Political Science Association, September 2004, Hilton Chicago and the Palmer House Hilton, Chicago, IL.

Li, Wei. 1998. "Anatomy of a New Ethnic Settlement: The Chinese Ethnoburb in Los Angeles." *Urban Studies* 75: 479–501.

Lien, Pei-te, Margaret Conway, and Janelle Wong. 2004. *The Politics of Asian Americans: Diversity & Community*. New York: Routledge.

Liu, Wen. 2018. "Complicity and Resistance: Asian American Body Politics in Black Lives Matter." *Journal of Asian American Studies* 21 (3): 421–451.

Lorin, Janet. 2015. "Harvard Faces Admissions Bias Complaint from Asian-Americans." Bloomberg News. May 15, 2015. Available at http://www.bloomberg.com/news/ar ticles/2015-05-15/harvard-faces-admissions-bias-complaint-from-asian-americans.

Louie, Steven G. 2001. "When We Wanted It Done, We Did It Ourselves." In *Asian Americans: The Movement and the Moment*, edited by Steven G. Louie and Glenn K. Omatsu, xxiv–xxv. Los Angeles: UCLA Asian American Studies Center Press.

Louie, Steven G., and Glenn K. Omatsu, eds. 2001. *Asian Americans: The Movement and the Moment*. Los Angeles: UCLA Asian American Studies Center Press.

Lung-Amam, Willow. 2017. *Trespassers? Asian Americans and the Battle for Suburbia*. Berkeley: University of California Press.

Luntao, Lange Parks (@langeluntao). 2016. "#AB1726 gives ALL API communities visibility. Visibility = equity = opportunity . . . Support #AllCACounts." Twitter, August 10, 2016. Available at https://twitter.com/langeluntao/status/763424475400384513 ?s=20.

Luttig, Matthew D., and Cathy J. Cohen. 2016. "How Social Media Helps Young People— Especially Minorities and the Poor—Get Politically Engaged." *Washington Post*, September 9, 2016. Available at https://www.washingtonpost.com/news/monkey-cage/wp /2016/09/09/how-social-media-helps-young-people-especially-minorities-and-the -poor-get-politically-engaged/.

Maira, Sunaina. 2008. "Flexible Citizenship/Flexible Empire: South Asian Muslim Youth in Post-9/11 America." *American Quarterly* 60 (3): 697–720.

Makinen, Julie. 2016. "Chinese Social Media Platform Plays a Role in U.S. Rallies for NYPD Officer." *Los Angeles Times*, February 24, 2016. Available at http://www.la times.com/world/asia/la-fg-china-liang-protests-20160224-story.html.

Mallein, Jet (@KLAITB). 2018. "#Comfortwomen were recruited by private #sexbrokers NOT coerced by #Japanese government. #Fairfax #VA #Virginia #Glendale." Twitter, November 27, 2018. Available at https://twitter.com/KLAITB/status/10705373834 25171456.

Margetts, Helen, Peter John, Scott Hale, and Taha Yasseri. 2015. *Political Turbulence: How Social Media Shape Collective Action*. Princeton, NJ: Princeton University Press.

Masuoka, Natalie, and Jane Junn. 2013. *The Politics of Belonging: Race, Public Opinion, and Immigration*. Chicago, IL: University of Chicago Press.

McCarthy, Mary M., and Linda C. Hasunuma. 2018. "Coalition Building and Mobilization: Case Studies of the Comfort Women Memorials in the United States." *Politics, Groups, and Identities* 6 (3): 411–434.

McCurry, Justin. 2018. "Osaka Drops San Francisco as Sister City over 'Comfort Women' Statue." *The Guardian*, October 4, 2018. Available at https://www.theguardian.com /world/2018/oct/04/osaka-drops-san-francisco-as-sister-city-over-comfort-women -statue.

McGrane, Sally. 2017. "An Important Statue for 'Comfort Women' in San Francisco." *New Yorker*, October 12, 2017. Available at https://www.newyorker.com/culture/culture-desk/an-important-statue-for-comfort-women-in-san-francisco.

Medina, Jennifer. 2016. "Debate Erupts in California over Curriculum on India's History." *New York Times*, May 4, 2016. Available at https://www.nytimes.com/2016/05/06/us/debate-erupts-over-californias-india-history-curriculum.html.

Merl, Jean. 2014. "Affirmative Action Controversy Costs Sen. Ted Lieu Six Endorsements." *Los Angeles Times*, April 3, 2014. Available at http://articles.latimes.com/2014/apr/03/local/la-me-pc-lieu-dropped-endorsements-20140403.

Merriam-Webster. 2017. "Social Media." Available at https://www.merriam-webster.com/dictionary/social%20media.

Miller, Vincent. 2004. "Mobile Chinatowns: The Future of Community in a Global Space of Flows." *The Journal of Social Issues* 2: 1. Available at http://www.whb.co.uk/social issues/vol2vm.htm.

Ministry of Foreign Affairs of Japan. 1993. "Statement by the Chief Cabinet Secretary Yohei Kono on the Result of the Study on the Issue of 'Comfort Women.'" Documents of Japanese Government and the Asian Women's Fund. August 4, 1993. Available at https://www.awf.or.jp/e6/statement-02.html.

———. 1995. "Statement by Prime Minister Tomiichi Murayama 'On the Occasion of the 50th Anniversary of the War's End.'" August 15, 1995. Available at https://www.mofa.go.jp/announce/press/pm/murayama/9508.html#:~:text=Minister%20Tomiichi%20Murayama-,%22On%20the%20occasion%20of%20the%2050th%20anniversary%20of%20the%20war's,(15%20August%201995)&text=The%20world%20has%20seen%20fifty,by%20a%20flood%20of%20emotions.

Mishra, Sangay K. 2016. *Desis Divided: The Political Lives of South Asian Americans*. Twin Cities: University of Minnesota Press.

Mitchell, Amy, Tom Rosenstiel, Laura Houston Santhanam, and Leah Christian. 2012. "Future of Mobile News." Pew Research Center, Journalism and Media. October 1, 2012. Available at http://www.journalism.org/2012/10/01/future-mobile-news/.

Molla, Rani. 2017. "Workers from India and China Received 82 Percent of U.S. H-1B Visas Last Year." *Recode*. April 13, 2017. Available at https://www.recode.net/2017/4/13/15281170/china-india-tech-h1b-visas.

Morris, Ruth. 2000. *Stories for Transformative Justice*. Toronto: Canadian Scholars' Press and Women's Press.

Mozumder, Suman Guha. 2006. "Hindu Groups Sue California Board of Education." *Rediff India Abroad*. March 19, 2006. Available at http://ia.rediff.com/news/2006/mar/19edu.htm.

Murthy, Dhiraj, Alexander Gross, and Alexander Pensavalle. 2016. "Urban Social Media Demographics: An Exploration of Twitter Use in Major American Cities." *Journal of Computer-Mediated Communication* 21 (1): 33–49. Available at http://onlinelibrary.wiley.com/doi/10.1111/jcc4.12144/full.

Murthy, Dhiraj, Sawyer Bowman, Alexander J. Gross, and Marisa McGarry. 2015. "Do We Tweet Differently from Our Mobile Devices? A Study of Language Differences on Mobile and Web-Based Twitter Platforms." *Journal of Communication* 65 (5): 816–837. Available at http://onlinelibrary.wiley.com/wol1/doi/10.1111/jcom.12176/full.

Nakanishi, Don T. 2009. "Foreword." In *The Transnational Politics of Asian Americans*, edited by Christian Collet and Pei-te Lien, ix–xiv. Philadelphia, PA: Temple University Press.

Ngai, Mae. 2004. *Impossible Subjects: Illegal Aliens and the Making of Modern America.* Princeton, NJ: Princeton University Press.

Nguyen, Tung (@ARCHDrNguyen). 2016. "Our @UCSFCancer @UCD_Cancer study showing lay health care workers increase colon cancer screening in Hmong." Twitter, August 26, 2016. Available at https://twitter.com/ARCHDrNguyen/status/769241098346573824.

Nielsen. 2017. "How Asian-American Media Consumption Could Be a Glimpse into the Future." May 24, 2017. Available at http://www.nielsen.com/us/en/insights/news/2017/how-asian-american-media-consumption-could-be-glimpse-into-future.html.

Nir, Sarah Maslin. 2016a. "Officer Liang's Partner Testifies He Got Little CPR Training." *New York Times,* February 4, 2016. Available at https://www.nytimes.com/2016/02/05/nyregion/officer-liangs-partner-testifies-he-got-little-cpr-training.html.

———. 2016b. "Officer Peter Liang Convicted in the Fatal Shooting of Akai Gurley in Brooklyn." *New York Times,* February 11, 2016. Available at https://www.nytimes.com/2016/02/12/nyregion/officer-peter-liang-convicted-in-fatal-shooting-of-akai-gurley-in-brooklyn.html.

NJTV News. 2012. "Comfort Women Memorial States in Palisades Park, Despite Objection from Japanese Government." *NJTV News.* July 23, 2012. Available at https://www.njtvonline.org/news/video/comfort-women-memorial-stays-in-palisades-park-despite-objection-from-japanese-government/.

Noguchi, Sharon. 2014. "Chinese-Americans Wooed by the GOP over Anti-affirmative Action in Public Universities." *San Jose Mercury News,* March 16, 2014. Available at http://www.mercurynews.com/2014/03/16/chinese-americans-wooed-by-the-gop-over-anti-affirmative-action-in-public-universities/.

Office of the Governor. 2015. "Letter to the Members of the California State Assembly." Last modified October 7, 2015. Available at https://www.gov.ca.gov/docs/AB_176_Veto_Message.pdf.

Oliver, J. Eric, and Shang E. Ha. 2007. "Vote Choice in Suburban Elections Vote Choice in Suburban Elections." *American Political Science Review* 101 (3): 373–391.

Olson, Mancur. 1965. *The Logic of Collective Action: Public Goods and the Theory of Groups.* Cambridge, MA: Harvard University Press.

Oluo, Ijeoma. 2016. "Jenny Yang and Ijeoma Oluo talk about Peter Liang and Racial Justice." *The Seattle Globalist,* February 25, 2016. Available at http://www.seattleglobalist.com/2016/02/25/ijeoma-oluo-jenny-yang-peter-liang-akai-gurley/47865.

Omatsu, Glenn. 1993. "The 'Four Prisons' and the Movements of Liberation: Asian American Activism from the 1960s to the 1990s." In *The State of Asian America: Activism and Resistance in the 1990s,* edited by Karin Aguilar-San Juan, 19–70. Boston, MA: South End.

Omi, Michael, and Howard Winant. 2014. *Racial Formation in the United States.* Third Edition. New York: Routledge.

Ong, Paul, and Elena Ong. 2015. "The Future of Asian America in 2040: Asian American Electorate to Double." UCLA Center for the Study of Inequality and Asian Pacific American Institute for Congressional Studies. May 7, 2015. Available at http://luskin.ucla.edu/sites/default/files/AA2040_report.pdf.

Oxford Dictionary. 2018a. "Dalit." Available at https://en.oxforddictionaries.com/definition/us/dalit.

———. 2018b. "Desi." Available at https://en.oxforddictionaries.com/definition/desi.

Pai, Ajit. 2018. "FCC Chairman: Our Job Is to Protect a Free and Open Internet." Cnet. June 10, 2018. Available at https://www.cnet.com/news/fcc-chairman-our-job-is-to-protect-a-free-and-open-internet/.

Papacharissi, Zizi. 2015. *Affective Publics: Sentiment, Technology, and Politics.* Oxford, UK: Oxford University Press.

Parker, Emily. 2017. "Opinion: In Praise of Echo Chambers." *Washington Post*, May 22, 2017. Available at https://www.washingtonpost.com/news/democracy-post/wp/2017/05/22/in-praise-of-echo-chambers/.

PeaceWithFairnessBack (@FairnessBack). 2020. "You should know what #ComfortWomen issue is. It's not about stories of pitiful women but fictions created by pro-Pyongyang activists based on forgeries and propaganda." Twitter, December 1, 2020. Available at https://twitter.com/FairnessBack/status/1333794075103772676.

Perrin, Andrew. 2016. "English-Speaking Asian Americans Stand Out for Their Technology Use." Pew Research Center Fact Tank: News in the Numbers. Last modified February 18, 2016. Available at http://www.pewresearch.org/fact-tank/2016/02/18/english-speaking-asian-americans-stand-out-for-their-technology-use/.

Pettersen, William. 1966. "Success Story, Japanese-American Style." *New York Times*, January 9, 1966. Available at http://inside.sfuhs.org/dept/history/US_History_reader/Chapter14/modelminority.pdf.

Pew Research Center. 2013. "The Rise of Asian Americans" Report. Last modified April 4, 2013. Available at http://www.pewsocialtrends.org/2012/06/19/the-rise-of-asian-americans/.

———. 2016. "In Presidential Contest, Voters Say 'Basic Facts,' Not Just Policies, Are in Dispute." Last modified October 14, 2016. Available at http://www.people-press.org/2016/10/14/in-presidential-contest-voters-say-basic-facts-not-just-policies-are-in-dispute/.

Polonski, Slava. 2016. "The Biggest Threat to Democracy? Echo chambers in your social media feed." *Medium*, August 7, 2016. Available at https://medium.com/@drpolonski/the-biggest-threat-to-democracy-echo-chambers-in-your-social-media-feeds-cd2c3049f7.

Pomfret, John. 2017. "The Split at the Heart of Chinese America." *SupChina*. June 14, 2017. Available at https://supchina.com/2017/06/14/split-heart-chinese-america/.

Poon, OiYan. 2014. "Hate, Fear, and Lies: How Anti-Affirmative Action Haters Are Shoveling Bullsh*t about SCA 5." *Angry Asian Man* (blog), March 10, 2014. Available at http://blog.angryasianman.com/2014/03/hate-fear-and-lies-how-anti-affirmative.html.

———. 2018. "Reconnecting Heart and Head: Racism, Immigration Policy, WeChat, and Chinese Americans." Reappropriate. May 24, 2018. Available at http://reappropriate.co/2018/05/reconnecting-heart-and-head-racism-immigration-policy-wechat-and-chinese-americans/.

Potter, Chanida Phaengdara. 2017. "Worth Fighting For." Available at https://www.pollenmidwest.org/stories/worth-fighting-for/.

Prior, Markus. 2005. "News vs. Entertainment: How Increasing Media Choice Widens Gaps in Political Knowledge and Turnout." *American Journal of Political Science* 49 (3): 577–592. Available at https://scholar.princeton.edu/sites/default/files/mprior/files/prior2005.news_v_entertainment.ajps-3.pdf.

Purkayastha, Bandana. 2005. *Negotiating Ethnicity: Second Generation South Asian Americans Traverse a Transnational World.* New Brunswick, NJ: Rutgers University Press.

Ramakrishnan, Karthick. 2005. *Democracy in Immigrant America: Changing Demographics and Political Participation.* Palo Alto, CA: Stanford University Press.

Ramakrishnan, Karthick, and Farah Z. Ahmad. 2014. "Language Diversity and English Proficiency." Part of the *State of Asian Americans and Pacific Islanders Series,* May 27, 2014. Center for American Progress.

Ramakrishnan, Karthick, and Taeku Lee. 2014. "Views of a Diverse Electorate: Opinions of California Registered Voters in 2014." National Asian American Survey. Available at http://naasurvey.com/wp-content/uploads/2016/10/NAAS-Field-2014-final.pdf.

Ramakrishnan, Karthick, and Sono Shah. 2017. "One Out of Every 7 Asian Immigrants Is Undocumented." *Data Bits,* a blog for AAPI Data, September 8, 2017. Available at https://aapidata.com/blog/asian-undoc-1in7/.

Ramakrishnan, Karthick, Janelle Wong, Taeku Lee, and Jennifer Lee. 2016. "Asian American Voices in the 2016 Election: Report of Registered Voters in the Fall 2016 National Asian American Survey." 2016 National Asian American Survey. October 5, 2016. Available at http://naasurvey.com/wp-content/uploads/2016/10/NAAS2016 -Oct5-report.pdf.

Rankin, Kenrya. 2016. "NYC to Pay Family of Akai Gurley $4 Million+ for Shooting Death." Colorlines. August 16, 2016. Available at http://www.colorlines.com/articles /nyc-pay-family-akai-gurley-4-million-shooting-death.

Rauhala, Emily. 2016. "Peter Liang Case Echoes All the Way to China." *Washington Post,* February 25, 2016. Available at https://www.washingtonpost.com/news/worldviews /wp/2016/02/25/peter-liang-case-echoes-all-the-way-to-china/.

Reappropriate. 2016. "All Californians Deserve to Be Counted: Why Data Disaggregation Matters for AAPIs (#AllCACounts)." Reappropriate. April 28, 2016. Available at http://reappropriate.co/2016/04/all-californians-deserve-to-be-counted-why-data -disaggregation-matters-for-aapis-allcacounts/.

Roberts, Sam. 2007. "In Shift, 40% of Immigrants Move Directly to Suburbs." *New York Times,* October 17, 2007. Available at http://www.nytimes.com/2007/10/17/us/17cen sus.html.

Rodriguez, Joe, and Lisa Fernandez. 2011. "Indian Population Diversifying Bay Area's Asian Population." *San Jose Mercury News,* May 11, 2016, updated August 13, 2016. Available at https://www.mercurynews.com/2011/05/11/indian-population-diversi fying-bay-areas-asian-population/.

Ruggles, Steven, Sara Flood, Sophia Foster, Ronald Goeken, Jose Pacas, Megan Schouweiler, and Matthew Sobek. 2021. IPUMS USA: Version 11.0 [dataset]. Minneapolis, MN: IPUMS. https://doi.org/10.18128/D010.V11.0.

Ryu, David E (@davideryu). 2016. "It's crucial for policymakers to have more info re: the communities they serve. Proud to support #AB1726 . . . #AllCACounts." Twitter, August 23, 2016. Available at https://twitter.com/davideryu/status/768242649287446529?s=20.

Sarwari, Khalida. 2018. "Group Says It Has Enough Signatures for Referendum to Block Vallco Development." *San Jose Mercury News,* October 30, 2018. Available at https:// www.mercurynews.com/2018/10/30/anti-vallco-development-group-says-it-has -enough-signatures-to-stop-project/.

Savidge, Nico. 2020. "Proposition 16: Why Some Asian Americans Are on the Front Lines against Affirmative Action." *San Jose Mercury News,* September 17, 2020. Available at https://www.mercurynews.com/2020/09/17/proposition-16-why-some-asian-ameri cans-are-on-the-front-lines-of-the-campaign-against-affirmative-action/.

Scholars for People. 2016. "Don't Replace 'India' with 'South Asia' in California History Social Sciences Frameworks." Change.org. Last modified April 4, 2016. Available at

https://www.change.org/p/academia-don-t-replace-india-with-south-asia-in-cali
fornia-history-textbooks.

Semotiuk, Andy J. 2019. "Recent Changes to the H1B Visa Program and What Is Coming in 2019." *Forbes*, January 2, 2019. Available at https://www.forbes.com/sites/andy jsemotiuk/2019/01/02/recent-changes-to-the-h1b-visa-program-and-what-is-com ing-in-2019/#22cba06c4a81.

Sepia Mutiny (@sepiamutiny). 2016. "#DontEraseIndia is nothing but Hindu Nationalist propaganda infecting America. I hope CA schools don't succumb to their campaign." Twitter, May 5, 2016. Available at https://twitter.com/sepiamutiny/status /728210931348475906.

Shi, Yu. 2005. "Identity Construction of the Chinese Diaspora, Ethnic Media Use, Community Formation, and the Possibility of Social Activism." *Continuum: Journal of Media & Cultural Studies* 19, no. 1 (March): 55–72.

Shimura, Tomoya. 2016. "Online Service WeIrvine Helps New Immigrants While Attracting More of Them to the City." *Orange County Register*, December 15, 2016. Available at https://www.ocregister.com/2016/12/15/online-service-weirvine-helps-new -immigrants-while-attracting-more-of-them-to-the-city/.

———. 2018. "About 250 Irvine Residents Convene to Oppose Proposed Homeless Camp Next to Great Park." *Orange County Register*, March 23, 2018. Available at https:// www.ocregister.com/2018/03/23/about-250-irvine-residents-convene-to-oppose -proposed-homeless-camp-next-to-great-park/.

Shyong, Frank. 2016. "Why This Cop's Conviction Brought Thousands of Asian Americans into New York's Streets." *Chicago Tribune*, April 13, 2016. Available at https:// www.chicagotribune.com/la-na-liang-brooklyn-shooting-20160413-story.html.

SimilarWeb. 2017. Overview of HindustanTimes.com. Available at https://www.similar web.com/website/hindustantimes.com.

Skop, Emily, and Wei Li. 2005. "Asians in America's Suburbs: Patterns and Consequences of Settlement." *Geographical Review* 95, no. 2: 167–188.

Smith, Aaron. 2013. "Civic Engagement in the Digital Age." Pew Research Center: Internet, Science and Tech. April 25, 2013. Available at http://www.pewinternet.org/2013 /04/25/civic-engagement-in-the-digital-age/.

———. 2015. "U.S. Smartphone Use in 2015." Pew Research Center: Internet, Science and Tech. April 1, 2015. Available at http://www.pewinternet.org/2015/04/01/us-smart phone-use-in-2015/.

Smith, Aaron, Kay Lehman Schlozman, Sidney Verba, and Henry Brady. 2009. "The Internet and Civic Engagement." Pew Internet and American Life Project. September 1, 2009. Available at https://www.pewresearch.org/internet/2009/09/01/the-internet-and -civic-engagement/.

Son, Elizabeth. 2018. *Embodied Reckonings: "Comfort Women," Performance, and Transpacific Redress.* Ann Arbor: University of Michigan Press.

Sonenshein, Raphael. 1993. *Politics in Black and White: Race and Power in Los Angeles.* Princeton, NJ: Princeton University Press.

Southeast Asian Resource Action Center. 2017. "Breaking: Chamroeun Phan of #ReleaseMN8 Finally Released to His Family." September 22, 2017. Available at https:// www.searac.org/immigration/breaking-chamroeun-phan-releasemn8-finally-re leased-family/.

Sriram, Shyam. 2016a. "Review: Mishra's *Desis Divided* Looks at South Asian American Politics through An Intersectional Lens." *The Aerogram.* April 29, 2016. Available at http://theaerogram.com/book-review-desis-divided/.

———. 2016b. "A Tulsi by Another Name: An Analysis of South Asian American Support for a Hindu Congressional Candidate." In *Distinct Identities: Minority Women in U.S. Politics*, edited by Nadia E. Brown and Sarah Allen Gershon, 116–133. New York: Routledge.

"Success Story of One Minority Group in the U.S." 1966. *U.S. News and World Report*. December 26, 1966. Available at https://www.dartmouth.edu/~hist32/Hist33/US%20 News%20&%20World%20Report.pdf.

Sunstein, Cass R. 2004. "Democracy and Filtering." *Communications of the ACM 47*, no. 12 (December): 57–59.

Swift, Mike. 2007. "Other Tongues Overtaking English as Language Spoken in Majority of Santa Clara County Homes." *San Jose Mercury News*, March 3, 2007. Available at http://www.mercurynews.com/valley/ci_7666999.

Tan, Annie. 2016. "Peter Liang Was Justly Convicted. He's Not a Victim." *Huffington Post*. Last modified February 23, 2016. Available at http://www.huffingtonpost.com /annie-tan/peter-liang-was-justly-convicted_b_9299860.html.

Tasaki, Aya (@asiannomad). 2018. "When Japan refuses and continues to deny that sex slavery—cloaked under terms like 'war time' and 'comfort women'—was and is our history and reality, it continues to perpetrate violence and trauma." Twitter, November 29, 2018. Available at https://twitter.com/asiannomad/status/106840901198753 7920.

Tatsumi, Yuki. 2018. "The Japan-South Korea 'Comfort Women' Agreement Survives (Barely)." *The Diplomat*, January 11, 2018. Available at https://thediplomat.com/2018 /01/the-japan-south-korea-comfort-women-agreement-survives-barely.

Teixeira, Ruy. 2006. *The New Frontier: A New Study of Exurbia*. Washington, DC: The New Politics Institute.

Ten, Soksreinith. 2017. "Cambodians Face Deportations to Homelands They've Never Known." *VOA News*, February 10, 2017. Available at https://www.voanews.com/a /cambodians-face-deportations-to-homeland-they-never-knew/3718283.html.

Thaker, Aria. 2018. "The Latest Skirmish in California's Textbooks War Reveals the Mounting Influence of Hindutva in the United States." *The Caravan*, February 6, 2018. Available at https://caravanmagazine.in/vantage/californias-textbooks-war-reveals -mounting-influence-hindutva-united-states.

Tufekci, Zeynep. 2018. *Twitter and Tear Gas: The Power and Fragility of Networked Protests*. New Haven, CT: Yale University Press.

Turque, Bill. 2017. "These First-Generation Chinese Americans Are Vigorously Opposing Sanctuary Laws." *Washington Post*, March 20, 2017. Available at https://www .washingtonpost.com/local/md-politics/these-first-generation-chinese-americans -are-loudly-opposing-sanctuary-laws/2017/03/17/92728e94-09db-11e7-93dc-00f9 bdd74ed1_story.html.

UndocuBlack Network (@UndocuBlack). 2017a. "Join our #BlackAAPIAction day to demand a #ACleanDreamAct & to #SaveTPS With the full understanding that our communities are often invisibilized in the immigration debate, we believe it's time to fight back! Follow the link to stand with us!" Twitter, December 5, 2017. Available at https://twitter.com/UndocuBlack/status/936271345893171205.

———. 2017b. "#RP @krclaorg Drumming, chanting, and marching in solidarity with @undocublack, @nakasec, @unitedwedream, and so many other organizations and allies for a #cleanDREAMact out here at the Capitol. We're not gonna stop until we get it. #blackAAPIaction #AAPIs4dream #DREAMactNOW." Twitter, December 6, 2017. Available at https://twitter.com/UndocuBlack/status/938510136422948864.

————. 2017c. "Yesterday, over 120 Black & AAPI Immigrants came to DC for our joint action day. We struggled, we learned, we demanded, we laughed and we sang. Deep in our hearts, we do believe we shall overcome. #BlackAAPIAction." Twitter, December 6, 2017. Available at https://twitter.com/UndocuBlack/status/93840405158 2177280.

United Californians. 2016. "Vote No on AB-1726." Change.org. Available at https://www .change.org/p/california-governor-veto-ab-1726.

Van de Donk, Wim, Brian D. Loder, Paul G. Nixon, and Dieter Rucht, eds. 2004. *Cyberprotest: New Media, Citizens and Social Movements.* New York: Routledge.

Vashisht, Kanupriya. 2006. "The Hindutva Deluge in California." *Hindustan Times.* Last modified January 25, 2006. Available at https://www.hindustantimes.com/india /the-hindutva-deluge-in-california/story-InH6qvgTnMguTjttCFJ9CP.html.

Vincent (@Vincent_usa22). 2016. "#AB1726 collect the type of racial profiling data used by Congress in the passage of the Chinese Exclusion Act of 1882." Twitter, September 23, 2016. Available at https://twitter.com/Vincent_usa22/status/779423971246825472?s=20.

Vuong, Zen. 2014. "Asians Rally against SCA 5, Call It Revival of Affirmative Action." *Pasadena Star-News*, March 8, 2014. Available at http://www.pasadenastarnews.com /social-affairs/20140308/asians-rally-against-sca-5-call-it-revival-of-affirmative -action.

Wagner, Kurt. 2017. "Facebook's Latest Idea to Combat Fake News Is a 'More Info' Button." *Recode.* Last modified October 5, 2017. Available at https://www.recode.net /2017/10/5/16429786/facebook-fake-news-articles-news-feed-context.

Wagner, Kurt, and Rani Molla. 2019. "WhatsApp Is Fighting Fake News by Limiting Its Virality. Could Facebook and Twitter Do the Same?" *Recode.* Last modified January 25, 2019. Available at https://www.recode.net/2019/1/25/18197002/whatsapp-message -limit-fake-news-facebook-twitter.

Wang, Frances Kai-Hwa. 2016. "California Passes Textbook Standards Including 'Comfort Women,' Sikhs." NBC News. Last modified July 18, 2016. Available at https:// www.nbcnews.com/news/asian-america/california-passes-textbook-standards-in cluding-comfort-women-sikhs-n611501.

————. 2017. "Deportation to Cambodia Halted for 'Minnesota 8' Refugee." NBC News. Last modified March 9, 2017. Available at https://www.nbcnews.com/news/asian -america/deportation-cambodia-halted-minnesota-8-refugee-n731451.

Weisman, Jonathan. 2012. "After an Online Firestorm, Congress Shelves Antipiracy Bills." *New York Times*, January 20, 2012. Available at https://www.nytimes.com/2012 /01/21/technology/senate postpones-piracy-vote.html.

Wheeler, Ian. 2016. "Why Asians Have Become the Dominant Group in Irvine, and What That Means for the City." *Orange County Register*, September 21, 2016. Available at https://www.ocregister.com/2016/09/21/why-asians-have-become-the-dom inant-group-in-irvine-and-what-that-means-for-the-city/.

White, Jeremy B. 2014. "Capitol Report: In Sign of Affirmative-Action Backlash, Democrats Help Stall Al Muratsuchi Bill." *Sacramento Bee*, April 8, 2014. Available at http://blogs.sacbee.com/capitolalertlatest/2014/04/in-sign-of-backlash-democrats -help-stall-al-muratsuchi-bill.html.

The White House, Office of the Vice President. 1998. "Remarks by Vice President Al Gore at Digital Divide Event." April 28, 1998. Available at https://clintonwhitehouse2 .archives.gov/WH/EOP/OVP/speeches/edtech.html.

Wilkinson, James. 2016. "Nearly 15,000 People Protest in New York over Asian-American Cop's Manslaughter Conviction for Shooting an Unarmed Black Man." *Daily*

Mail, February 21, 2016. Available at http://www.dailymail.co.uk/news/article-345 6387/Thousands-rally-NYC-US-officers-conviction.html.

Wilson, Michael. 2014. "Officer's Errant Shot Kills Unarmed Brooklyn Man." *New York Times*, November 21, 2014. Available at https://www.nytimes.com/2014/11/22/nyre gion/new-york-police-officer-fatally-shoots-brooklyn-man.html.

Wineburg, Sam, and Sarah McGrew. 2016. "Why Students Can't Google Their Way to the Truth." *Education Week*. Last modified November 1, 2016. Available at http://www.edweek.org/ew/articles/2016/11/02/why-students-cant-google-their-way-to .html.

Witzel, Michael. 2005. Correspondence Letter to the California Board of Education. November 8, 2005. Available at http://www.people.fas.harvard.edu/~witzel/witzel letter.pdf.

Wolf, Jessica, and Melissa Abraham. 2020. "Prop. 16 Failed in California. Why? And What's Next?" UCLA Newsroom. November 18, 2020. Available at https://news room.ucla.edu/stories/rop-16-failed-in-california.

Wong, Alia. 2018. "The App at the Heart of the Movement to End Affirmative Action." *The Atlantic*, November 20, 2018. Available at https://www.theatlantic.com/educa tion/archive/2018/11/asian-americans-wechat-war-affirmative-action/576328/.

Wong, Janelle, S. Karthick Ramakrishnan, Taeku Lee, and Jane Junn. 2011. *Asian American Political Participation: Emerging Constituents and Their Political Identities*. New York: Russell Sage Foundation.

Wong, Tom K. 2015. "Reaching Undocumented Asian Americans and Pacific Islanders in the United States." Center for Migration Studies. Available at http://cmsny.org /publications/reaching-undocumented-asian-americans-and-pacific-islanders-in -the-united-states/.

Wortham, Jenna. 2012. "Public Outcry over Antipiracy Bills Began as Grass-Roots Grumblings." *New York Times*, January 19, 2012. Available at https://www.nytimes.com /2012/01/20/technology/public-outcry-over-antipiracy-bills-began-as-grass-roots -grumbling.html?pagewanted=1&ref=technology.

Xiaoqing, Rong. 2019. "The Rise of the Chinese-American Right." *National Review*, July 17, 2019. Available at https://www.nationalreview.com/2019/07/chinese-american -right-new-generations-immigrants/.

Xinhua. 2017. "Feature: 'Comfort Women' Memorial Unveiled in San Francisco." New China, Xinhuanet.com. September 24, 2017. Available at http://www.xinhuanet.com// english/2017-09/24/c_136632768.htm.

Xu, Kenny. 2018. "Harvard Gives Asian-Americans Low 'Personality' Ratings to Justify Discrimination." *Daily Signal*. Last modified November 30, 2018. Available at https:// www.dailysignal.com/2018/11/30/harvard-gives-asian-americans-low-personality -ratings-to-justify-discrimination/.

Yamaguchi, Tomomi. 2017. "What Is the Aim on Nippon Kaigi, the Ultra-Right Organization That Supports Japan's Abe Administration?" *Asia-Pacific Journal* 15, 21, no. 1 (November). Available at https://apjjf.org/2017/21/Tawara.html.

Yang-Stevens, Kat. 2016. "Reframing the Conversation." Accessed July 12, 2017. Available at http://www.katyangstevens.com/reframingtheconversation.

Yap, Audrey Cleo. 2016. "South Asian Community Debates 'South Asia,' 'India' Ahead of Textbook Updates." NBC News. Last modified May 16, 2016. Available at https:// www.nbcnews.com/news/asian-america/south-asian-community-debates-south -asia-india-ahead-textbook-updates-n570671.

Yee, Amy. 2016. "In 179 NYPD-Related Deaths, Only 3 Indicted." Last modified February 19, 2016. Available at https://www.linkedin.com/pulse/179-nypd-involved-deaths-only-3-indicted-amy-yee.

Yin, Steph. 2016. "Why Asian-Americans Who Defend Peter Liang Are Enabling Police Brutality." Last modified February 25, 2016. Available at http://www.complex.com/life/2016/02/peter-liang-akai-gurley.

Yoshimura, Hirofumi. 2018. "Termination of Sister City Relationship." Osaka City. Last modified October 2, 2018. Available at http://www.city.osaka.lg.jp/hodoshiryo/cms files/contents/0000448/448185/letter.pdf.

You, Roy (@RoyYou5). 2016. "No matter how you spin it, #AB1726 is a racist bill. It either try [*sic*] to 'benefit' Asians ONLY or try to divide Asians. Shame on its supporters." Twitter, August 24, 2016. Available at https://twitter.com/RoyYou5/status/76840114 0669042688.

Zhang, Chi. 2018. "WeChatting American Politics: Misinformation, Polarization, and Immigrant Chinese Media." Tow Center for Digital Journalism, *Columbia Journalism Review*. Last modified April 19, 2018. Available at https://www.cjr.org/tow_cen ter_reports/wechatting-american-politics-misinformation-polarization-and-immi grant-chinese-media.php.

Zhu, Lia. 2016. "Chinese Community Mixed on Data Bill." *ChinaDaily USA*. Last modified March 28, 2016. Available at http://usa.chinadaily.com.cn/epaper/2016-03/28/con tent_24132927.htm.

———. 2017. "Japan Condemned for Interference with 'Comfort Women' Memorial Lawsuit." *ChinaDaily USA*. Last modified March 2, 2017. Available at http://www .chinadaily.com.cn/world/2017-03/02/content_28404395.htm.

Zimmerman, Arely. 2012. "Documenting Dreams: New Media, Undocumented Youth and the Immigrant Rights Movement." University of Southern California, Annenberg School for Communication and Journalism. Available at https://www.academia .edu/21700497/Documenting_DREAMs_New_Media_Undocumented_Youth _and_the_Immigrant_Rights_Movement_A_Case_Study_Report_Working _Paper_Media_Activism_and_Participatory_Politics_Project_Civic_Paths _Annenberg_School_For_Communication_and_Journalism.

Index

Page numbers with *t* refer to tables. Page numbers with *f* refer to figures.

James S. Lai is a Professor in the Ethnic Studies Department at Santa Clara University with a courtesy appointment in the Department of Political Science. He is the author of *Asian American Political Action: Suburban Transformations* and coeditor of *Asian American Politics: Law, Participation, and Policy.*

www.ingramcontent.com/pod-product-compliance
Lightning Source LLC
Chambersburg PA
CBHW022355280326
41935CB00007B/198